BALLADS AND POEMS

RELATING TO THE

BURGOYNE CAMPAIGN

THE OLD CATAMONT TAVERN, BENNINGTON.

BALLADS AND POEMS

RELATING TO THE

BURGOYNE CAMPAIGN

ANNOTATED BY

WILLIAM L. STONE

KENNIKAT PRESS
Port Washington, N. Y./London

KENNIKAT AMERICAN BICENTENNIAL SERIES
Under the General Editorial Supervision of
Dr. Ralph Adams Brown
Professor of History, State University of New York

BALLADS AND POEMS RELATING TO
THE BURGOYNE CAMPAIGN

First published in 1893
Reissued in 1970 by Kennikat Press
Library of Congress Catalog Card No: 71-120891
ISBN 0-8046-1284-6

Manufactured by Taylor Publishing Company   Dallas, Texas

KENNIKAT AMERICAN BICENTENNIAL SERIES

TABLE OF CONTENTS.

APPENDICES.

PREFACE.

In giving to the public, and especially to those who have my " Burgoyne's Campaign and St. Leger's Expedition," a few words are, perhaps, necessary to explain the purpose of the present work.

During my researches while engaged upon that particular episode of our Revolutionary history, I came across a number of quaint ballads relating to that campaign *par excellence*,* and it occurred to me that my subscribers to " Burgoyne's Campaign" would gladly welcome an *addenda*, so to speak, of that work.

Hoping, therefore, that those of my friends who have so kindly aided me in my former publications will appreciate the spirit in which this volume has been prepared, I have published it, though at a pecuniary sacrifice to myself.

My thanks are due for help in this compilation to Gen-

---

* I use this phrase advisedly, since all historical students know that Frank Moore has given us a little volume on " Revolutionary Poems." This collection, however, though admirable, does not include, save in a very few instances, those which particularly relate to the campaign of Burgoyne.

Preface.

eral John Meredith Read, Consul-General to France at Paris during the Franco-German War, the siege of that city and the Commune, and for many years United States Minister to Greece; Mr. James A. Holden, of Glens Falls, N. Y.; Mr. Charles M. Bliss, of Bennington, Vt.; Mrs. Charles Stone, of Sandy Hill, N. Y.; Mr. Franklin Burdge, of New York City; Mr. Jared C. Markham, the architect of the Saratoga Monument, of Jersey City, N. J.; Mr. Theodore F. Dwight, of the Boston Public Library; Mr. William T. Peoples, of the New York Mercantile Library; Mr. George Watson Cole, of the Jersey City Free Library; Mr. Frederick Saunders, of the Astor Library; Dr. Smith Ely, of Newburgh, N. Y.; Mr. John W. Jordan, of Philadelphia, Pa.; Mr. Bauman L. Belden, of Elizabeth, N. J.; Hon. Charles S. Lester and Hon. Winsor B. French, of Saratoga Springs, N. Y., and Mr. August Hund, of Hoboken, N. J.—to all of whom I here return my hearty thanks.*

---

* Mrs. Julia C. Dorr, of Rutland, Vt., the deservedly celebrated poetess, contributed to the Bennington Centennial an exquisitely beautiful poem entitled "Vermont." As, however, it contains only one or two incidental allusions to the battle of Bennington, and does not, therefore, come within the scope of this work, it is not given in this collection.

WILLIAM L. STONE.

MT. VERNON, N. Y., October 1, 1893.

THE BURGOYNE BALLADS.

SKETCH OF GENERAL BURGOYNE.

IT seems eminently proper for a just appreciation of the circumstances under which the following ballads were written, that the reader should have a sketch of the personage who called them forth.

JOHN BURGOYNE, a British soldier, was born on February 24th, 1723. He was the eldest son of John Burgoyne and Anna Maria, daughter of Charles Burneston of Hackney, in Middlesex. The popular belief that he was a natural son of Lord Bingley is pure fiction, and had its rise in the malicious gossip of that prince of gossips—Horace Walpole. Burgoyne was educated at Westminster, and entered the army at an early age. While at Preston with his regiment he eloped with Lady Charlotte Stanley, daughter of the eleventh Earl of Derby; and the earl, becoming reconciled to the marriage, obtained for him a captaincy in the Eleventh Dragoons, June 14th, 1756. He was in the attack on Cherbourg in 1758, and also in the abortive attempt on St. Malo the same year; was appointed, May 10th, 1758, captain-lieutenant in the Coldstream Guards, and the following year was promoted to the command of the Sixteenth Dragoons, called subsequently "Burgoyne's Light-horse." He was elected to Parliament in 1762, held his seat in that

body continuously until his death, and took an active
part in matters relating to India, hence incurring the
displeasure of "Junius," by whom he was severely
criticised.   He was made major-general, May 25th,
1772. Appointed to a command in America, he arrived
in Boston, May 25th, 1775, and witnessed the battle
of Bunker Hill, of which he gave a graphic descrip-
tion in a letter to his brother-in-law, Lord Stanley. He
was commissioned, January 1st, 1776, lieutenant-gen-
eral in America only, and took part in the opera-
tions of that year for expelling the Americans from
Canada ; but in November, dissatisfied with his sub-
ordinate position under Carleton, he returned to Eng-
land.   In December of that same year he concerted
with the British ministry a plan for the campaign of
1777.   A large force under his command was to go to
Albany by way of Lakes Champlain and George, while
another body, under Sir Henry Clinton, advanced
up the Hudson. Simultaneously, Colonel Barry St.
Leger was to make a diversion, by way of Oswego, on
the Mohawk River.

In pursuance of this plan, Burgoyne, in June, began
his advance with one of the best-equipped armies that
had ever left the shores of England.   Proceeding up
Lake Champlain, he easily forced the evacuation of
Crown Point, Ticonderoga and Fort Anne.   But in-
stead of availing himself of the water-carriage of Lake
George, at the head of which there was a direct road
to Fort Edward, he advanced upon that work by land,
consuming three weeks in cutting a road through the
woods and building bridges over swamps.   This gave
time for Schuyler to gather the yeomanry together, and
for Washington to re-enforce that general with troops,
under Morgan, from the Southern Department.   Bur-
goyne, also, lost valuable time and received a fatal

check by his disastrous attack on Bennington. At length, finding his progress stopped by the entrenchments of Gates at Bemus Heights, nine miles south of Saratoga (Schuylerville, N. Y.), he endeavored to extricate himself from his perilous position by fighting. Two battles were fought on nearly the same ground on September 19th and October 7th, 1777. The first was indecisive: the second resulted in so complete a rout for the British, that, leaving his sick and wounded to the compassion of Gates, Burgoyne retreated to Saratoga. Here, finding that his provisions were giving out, Stark in his rear, and that there was no chance of escape, he capitulated with his entire army, October 17th, 1777. This event was the turning-point in the American Revolution. It secured the French alliance, and lifted the clouds of moral and financial gloom that had settled upon the leaders, even the hopeful Washington.

Burgoyne, until his unfortunate campaign, stood very high in his profession. He had made a most brilliant record on the banks of the Tagus for dash under that master in the art of war, the famous Count Schaumberg-Lippe. He also added to a prepossessing exterior the polished manners and keen sagacity of a courtier. He was likewise witty and brave, but he was also hasty and self-willed. Desirous of doing everything himself, he rarely consulted with others ; yet he never knew how to keep a plan secret. While in a subordinate position he was continually carping at his military superiors; yet when given a separate command, he was guilty of the same faults that he had reprehended in others. His boastful ways—as will be seen in some of the following ballads—drew upon him the nicknames of "Sir Jack Brag" and "Chrononnotonthologos," a character in a burlesque

play by Henry Carey. Being a sybarite, he often
neglected the duties of a general ; and while he was
enjoying his wines and choice food, his army suffered
the keenest want.   Early in 1778 he returned to Eng-
land, and justly threw the failure of the expedition
upon the Ministry, since, in arranging the campaign,
he had most strenuously insisted that success depended
upon Howe's co-operation.   Had he been properly
supported, he would, despite mistakes, have unques-
tionably reached Albany, as Gates would not have
been at Bemus Heights to oppose him.   On his
arrival in England he was received very coldly by the
court and people, the king, indeed, refusing to see
him.*   Having in vain demanded a court-martial, he
finally succeeded in obtaining a hearing on the floor
of Parliament ; and in 1780 he published a narrative
of the campaign and a vindication of himself in a
work entitled "A State of the Expedition."   Joining
the opposition, he resigned, in 1779, all his offices.
Upon a change in the ministry, he regained somewhat
of his popularity, and in 1782 was restored to his
rank in the army, and appointed prize-councillor and
commander-in-chief in Ireland.   In 1784 he retired
from public life, and, possessing considerable literary
ability, amused himself in writing numerous comedies
and poems, which were published in two volumes in
1808.   He had already, while in America, written two
farces, entitled respectively " The Siege of Boston" and
" The Maid of the Oaks," both of which were performed
with great *éclat*.   Two other dramas, both of which

---

* Indeed, had the king granted him an audience, it
would have been tantamount to acknowledging that
he, George III., had erred—and when was a king,
especially this one, ever known to admit a mistake !

were equally successful, were " The Lord of the Manor"
and " Richard Cœur de Lion." He was also the
author of a comedy entitled " The Heiress," which had a
great run, and has been pronounced by competent
critics "one of the best productions of the modern
British drama."

The tale of " The Lord of the Manor" seems, in some
degree, to have been disguised in the modification
of the character and circumstances by the incident
of his own matrimonial connection ; for, as above
stated, his was a clandestine and unauthorized mar-
riage, at a time when he held only a subaltern's com-
mission in the army, and is said to have excited at
first the resentment of the lady's father to such a
degree that he declared his resolution never to admit
the offenders into his presence. As we have seen, a
reconciliation was effected, and was succeeded by a
warm and lasting attachment. It is probable, also,
that the memory of his wife, who died in 1776, at
Kensington Palace, during his absence in America, is
embalmed by the affectionate regrets of Burgoyne in
that beautiful air of his composition :

" Encompassed in an angel's frame,
    An angel's virtues lay ;
Too soon did heaven assert the claim,
    And call its own away.

" My Anna's worth, my Anna's charms,
    Must never more return !
What now shall fill these widow'd arms,
    Ah me ! my Anna's urn !"*

---

* One would suppose from this affectionate effusion
that his devoted attachment to his wife—and of that
fact there seems to be no doubt—would have pre-

Burgoyne, also, was one of the managers of the
trial for the impeachment of Lord Hastings, but he
did not live to see the result of that famous trial, his
death occurring in London, on August 4th, 1792,
caused by gout in the stomach. There were, how-
ever, not a few of his enemies who did not scruple to
say that he was a suicide, one American Loyalist,
who was in England at the time, and resided within a
few doors of his (Burgoyne's) dwelling, writing home
as follows : " He fell by his own hand, a prey to dis-
appointment and neglect."   There seems, however, to
be no real foundation for this statement.

By his wife, Burgoyne had but one daughter, who
died in childhood ; but by Miss Susan Caulfield, after
his wife's death, he had four children, of whom the

---

vented the licentious conduct of Burgoyne during his
American campaign (see the account of his revelling
in the arms of his mistress during the sufferings of his
army, just before his surrender, as given by Mrs. Gen-
eral von Riedesel, " Letters of Madame von Riedesel,"
Munsell & Son, Albany, N. Y.) ; but these inconsis-
tencies are hard to account for.   Indeed, public men
of that time seem to have thought that the breaking
of their marriage vows was but a venial offence.   On
this subject see Alexander Hamilton's account of his
liaison with a woman, given unblushingly to the public
as a defence against the charge of his having, while
Secretary of the Treasury, been careless in money
affairs.   This pamphlet, in which Hamilton gave this
statement to the public, is now extremely rare, the
only two copies of it in existence, as we are aware,
being one in the library of the New York Historical
Society, and the other in the possession of Mr. B. L.
Belden, of Elizabeth, N. J.

late Sir John Burgoyne, of Crimean fame, was the eldest. His descendants have filled many honorable positions in the British army and navy, and several of them are still (1893) living. For an exhaustive sketch of Burgoyne and an analysis of his campaigns, See " Hadden's Journal," edited by that indefatigable and authoritative writer, General Horatio Rogers, of Providence, R. I.*

BURGOYNE'S PROCLAMATION.†

[A burlesque ballad by Governor William Livingston, of New Jersey. First published in the *New York Journal*, September 8th, 1777.]

By John Burgoyne and Burgoyne John, sir,
And grac'd with titles still more higher,

---

* As there are a number of allusions in the following ballads to the forces of the two contending armies, and as scarcely any writer, either contemporary or otherwise, agrees in the number, it is thought entirely germane to the present work to give in Appendix No. I. a correct authorized statement both of the beleaguering army, under Gates, and of those who surrendered to it, under Burgoyne.

† As a prelude to his operations, Burgoyne issued from Crown Point, on Lake Champlain, a pompous, grandiloquent, and haughty-minded proclamation, in which, after reciting a number of his own titles, eked out with a string of *et cæteras*, to indicate the rest, he made a magnificent parade of the number and strength of his army, and displayed in formidable view the body of savages by which he announced he was going to accomplish great things; at the same time commanding the Americans to lay down their arms

For I'm lieutenant-general too,
Of Georgie's troops both red and blue,

---

and return to their duty, and promising them mercy
upon their speedy submission, but threatening them
with the most terrible vengeance if they persisted
in their rebellion. The effects of this proclama-
tion, however, were entirely different from what its
author surmised would be the case. Instead of the
terror which he thought it would excite, it produced
throughout the colonies only indignation and con-
tempt. Governor Livingston, of New Jersey (and
not Francis Hopkinson, as some have supposed), by
turning it ingeniously into Hudibrastic verse, made
the proclamation an object both of general derision and
of diversion. John Holt, of New York City, an old
and highly respectable editor, published it in his
newspaper, the *Gazette*, in Poughkeepsie, heading it
with " Pride Goeth before Destruction, and a Haughty
Spirit before a Fall." " It is," says Dr. Dwight, in his
" Travels," "remarkable that the four most haughty
proclamations issued by military commanders in mod-
ern times have prefaced their ruin—this of General
Burgoyne, that of the Duke of Brunswick, when he
was entering France, that of Bonaparte in Egypt,
and that of General Le Clerc, on his arrival at St.
Domingo." To this list might also be added that of
General Lee of the Confederate Army in our late Civil
War, just previous to his surrender.

Governor William Livingston, the author of this
poem and the Governor of New Jersey, was born in
Albany, N. Y., November 30th, 1723, and died in
Elizabethtown, N. J. (now Elizabeth), July 25th,
1790. He was graduated at Yale in 1741, at the head
of his class, and then began the study of law under

On this extensive continent,
And of Queen Charlotte's regiment
Of eight dragoons the colonel,
And governor eke of Castle Will,
And furthermore when I am there,
In house of commons there appear,
(Hoping ere long to be a peer)
Being a member of that virtuous band
Who always vote at North's command,
Directing too the fleets and troops
From Canada as thick as hops ;
And all my titles to display,
I'll end with thrice et cetera.

The troops consign'd to my command,
Like Hercules to purge the land,
Intend to act in combination
With th' other forces of the nation,

James Alexander, completing his course under
William Smith. He served with distinction in many
civic and State offices, and in 1787 was a delegate to
the convention that framed the United States Consti-
tution. He was also one of the original trustees of the
New York Society Library, and in 1751 was made
one of the trustees of King's (now Columbia) College,
but declined to qualify when he found that the Presi-
dent must be a clergyman of the Church of England.
He was the author of various works of distinction
in their day. As President Dwight says, " His imag-
ination was brilliant, his wit sprightly and pungent, his
understanding powerful, his taste refined and his con-
ceptions bold and masterly. His views of political
subjects were expansive, clear and just. Of freedom,
both civil and religious, he was a distinguished cham-
pion."

Displaying wide thro' every quarter
What Britain's justice would be after.
It is not difficult to show it,
And every mother's son must know it,
That what at first she meant to gain
By requisitions and chicane,
She's now determined to acquire
By kingly reason ; sword and fire.
I can appeal to all your senses,
Your judgments, feelings, tastes and fancies ;
Your ears and eyes have heard and seen,
How causeless this revolt has been ;
And what a dust your leaders kick up,
In this rebellious civil hickup,
And how upon this curs'd foundation,
Was rear'd the system of vexation,
Over a stubborn generation.

But now inspired with patriot love
I come th' oppression to remove ;
To free you from the heavy clog
Of every tyrant demagogue,
Who for the most romantic story,
Claps into limbo loyal Tory,
All hurly burly, hot and hasty,
Without a writ to hold him fast by ;
Nor suffers any living creature
(Led by the dictates of his nature),
To fight in green for Britain's cause,
Or aid us to restore her laws ;
In short the vilest generation
Which in vindictive indignation,
Almighty vengeance ever hurl'd
From this to the infernal world.
A Tory cannot move his tongue,
But whip, in prison he is flung,

His goods and chattels made a prey
By those vile mushrooms of a day,
He's tortur'd too, and scratch'd and bit
And plung'd into a dreary pit;
Where he must suffer sharper doom,
Than ere was hatched by church of Rome.

These things are done by rogues, who dare
Profess to breathe in freedom's air.
To petticoats alike and breeches
Their cruel domination stretches,
For the sole crime, or sole suspicion,
(What worse is done by th' inquisition?)
Of still adhering to the crown,
Their tyrants striving to kick down,
Who by perverting law and reason,
Allegiance construe into treason.
Religion too is often made
A stalking horse to drive the trade,
And warring churches dare implore
Protection from th' Almighty Pow'r;
They fast and pray, in Providence
Profess to place their confidence;
And vainly think the Lord of all
Regards our squabbles on this ball;
Which would appear as droll in Britain
As any whims that one could hit on;
Men's consciences are set at naught
Nor reason valued at a groat;
And they that will not swear and fight
Must sell their all, and say good-night.

By such important views they're pres't to,
I issue this, my manifesto.
I, the great knight of de la Mancha,
Without Squire Carleton my sancho,

Will tear you limb from limb asunder,
With cannon, blunderbuss and thunder ;
And spoil your feathering and your tarring ;
And cagg you up for pickled herring
In front of troops as spruce as beaux,*
And ready to lay on their blows,
I'll spread destruction far and near :
And when I cannot kill I'll spare,
Inviting by these presents all,
Both young and old and great and small,
And rich and poor and Whig and Tory,
In cellar deep or lofty story ;
Where'er my troops at my command
Shall swarm like locusts o'er the land.
(And they shall march from the North Pole,
As far at least as Pensacole,)
To break off their communications,
That I can save their habitations ;
For finding that Sir William's plunders†
Prove in the event apparent blunders,

---

* "Spruce as beaux," in allusion to the fact that during the entire march of the British troops under Burgoyne, the officers seemed to look upon the expedition as a kind of gala day, and, clothed in their best regimentals in most dandified fashion, they escorted the ladies of the party through the forest in the most gallant style. This march through the wilderness is graphically illustrated in one of the bronze tablets in the Saratoga Monument at Schuylerville, N. Y., built by Booth Brothers, of New York City, and by whom its corner-stone was presented to the Saratoga Monument Association.

† Sir William Howe is here alluded to. He was, as is well known, depended on both by the British min-

It is my full determination
To check all kinds of depredation ;
But when I've got you in my pow'r,
Favor'd is he I last devour.

From him who loves a quiet life,
And keeps at home to kiss his wife,
And drink success to King Pygmalion,
And calls all congresses rebscallion,
With neutral stomach eats his supper,
Nor deems the contest worth a copper,
I will not defalcate a groat,
Nor force his wife to cut his throat ;
But with his doxy he may stay,
And live to fight another day ;
Drink all the cider he has made
And have to boot a green cockade.
But as I like a good Sir Loin,
And mutton chop when e'er I dine,
And my poor troops have long kept Lent,
Not for religion but for want,
Who e'er secretes cow, bull, or ox,
Or shall presume to hide his flocks,
Or with felonious hand eloign
Pig, duck, or gosling from Burgoyne,

---

istry and by Burgoyne to effect a diversion in the latter's
favor by advancing up the Hudson, toward Albany,
thus directing the forces under Gates. Why he did
not do so is now plain—his special instructions to that
effect having been by accident pigeoned-holed, and
never having reached him. See Stone's " Burgoyne"
and Rogers's " Hadden."

Or dare to pull the bridges down,
My boys to puzzle or to drown ;
Or smuggle hay, or plough, or harrow,
Cart, horses, wagons, or wheelbarrow ;
Or 'thwart the path lay straw or switch,
As folks are wont to stop a witch,
I'll hang him as the Jews did Haman ;
And smoke his carcass for a gammon.
I'll pay in coin for what I eat,
Or continental counterfeit ;
But what's more likely still, I shall
(So fare my troops) not pay at all.
With the most Christian spirit fir'd,
And by true soldiership inspir'd,
I speak as men do in a passion
To give my speech the more impression,
If any should so harden'd be
As to expect immunity,
Because *procul a fulmine*,
I will let loose the dogs of Hell,
Ten thousand Indians, who shall yell,
And foam, and tear, and grin, and roar,
And drench their moccasins in gore ;
To these I'll give full scope and play
From Ticonderog to Florida ;
They'll scalp your heads, and kick your shins,
And rip your guts, and flay your skins,
And of your ears be nimble croppers,
And make your thumbs tobacco-stoppers.
If after all these lovely warnings,
My wishes' and my bowels' yearnings,
You shall remain as deaf as adder,
Or grow with hostile rage the madder,
I swear by George and by St. Paul
I will exterminate you all.

Subscrib'd with my manual sign
To test these presents, JOHN BURGOYNE.*

A VISION OF JUDGMENT.

BY JOHN TRUMBULL.†

I SAW along the prostrate strand
Our baffled gen'rals quit the land,

---

* Two burlesque proclamations, written in a similar caustic vein as this one, were published by the wags of the day while Gage was in command at Boston, in 1775, and Lord Rawdon was in command of the South, in 1781. The first was entitled "Tom Gage's Proclamation," and the second "Lord Rawdon's Proclamation." As these do not come within the scope of this work, they are not given. The curious reader, however, will find them in Moore's "Diary of the American Revolution," Vol. I., page 93. The proclamation of Burgoyne, however, will be found in Appendix No. III.

† John Trumbull, poet, born in Westbury (now Watertown), Conn., April 24th, 1750; died in Detroit, Mich., May 10th, 1831. He graduated from Yale in 1767, and with his friend, Timothy Dwight, wrote papers in the style of the *Spectator*, which were published in the Boston and New Haven journals in 1769. He wrote many works, the chief of which and on which rests his principal reputation, was "McFingal" (Hartford, 1782). Its popularity was great—so much so that there were more than thirty pirated impressions of the poem in pamphlet and other forms. This poem was one of the keenest satires of the Revo-

And swift as frighted mermaids flee*
T' our boasted element, the sea !
Resign that long contested shore,
Again the prize of rebel power,
And tow'rd their town of refuge fly,
Like convict Jews condemn'd to die.†
Then tow'rd the north I turned my eyes,
Where Saratoga's heights arise,
And saw our chosen vet'ran band
Descend like terror o'er the land ; ‡

---

lutionary period; and despite of its doggerel rhymes and Hudibrastic measure, it is a profoundly scholarly production. The above lines are from the fourth canto of this poem.

* Alluding to the hasty departure of the British from Boston, when Howe perceived that he could no longer keep it. Although Washington had tacitly consented, on the application of Howe, to allow him to depart unmolested, yet great terror pervaded the ranks of the enemy and the households of the Tories. They all went aboard the ships on Sunday morning, March 17th; and on the same day the deserted city was taken possession of by General Putnam in the name of the *Thirteen United Colonies.*

† This is an allusion to the cities among the Jews, in which, if a murderer or other criminal could reach before arrest, he was safe from punishment. The city of refuge here alluded to was Halifax, in Nova Scotia, to which the British army fled.

‡ This was, up to that time, the victorious army of Burgoyne, which after capturing Ticonderoga and Mount Independence gained a victory at Hubbardton, and destroyed the American stores at Skenesborough (now Whitehall, N. Y.), at the head of Lake

T' oppose this fury of alarms,
Saw all New England wake to arms,
And ev'ry Yankey full of mettle
Swarm forth like bees at sound of kettle.*
Not Rome, when Tarquin raped Lucretia,†
Saw wilder must'ring of militia.
Thro' all the woods and plains of fight,
What mortal battles fill'd my sight,
While British corses strew'd the shore,
And Hudson ting'd his streams with gore!
What tongue can tell the dismal day,
Or paint the parti-color'd fray ;

Champlain.   Then, flushed with these successes, Burgoyne marched slowly (being greatly impeded by the action of General Schuyler in felling trees across his path) through the wilderness toward Fort Edward— his objective point on the Hudson River.   The farmers along this route fled in terror, dreading the savages who accompanied the invaders.

* When bees are swarming, loud beating upon sonorous metal, such as tin pans, kettles, etc., causes them to alight, or "settle," when they are without difficulty placed in a newly prepared hive.

† The rape of Lucretia, by Sextus Tarquinius, is given in the old legends as the proximate cause of kingly power in Rome.   The tragic result of the outrage caused Brutus to swear, by the pure blood which incarnadined a dagger with which Lucretia had stabbed herself, that he would pursue to the uttermost Tarquinius and all his race, and thenceforward suffer no man to be king at Rome.   The aroused people gathered together, and passed a decree to the same effect, and Tarquin the Superb was banished.

When yeomen left their fields afar
To plough the crimson plains of war ;
When zeal to swords transformed their shares,
And turned their pruning-hooks to spears,
Changed tailor's geese to guns and ball,
And stretch'd to pikes the cobbler's awl ; *
While hunters fierce like mighty Nimrod,
Made on our troops a daring inroad ;
And levelling squint on barrel round,
Brought our beau-officers to ground ;†

---

* The Loyalists often taunted the Whigs because some of their leaders were mechanics and tradesmen (Greene was a blacksmith and Knox a bookseller). In the temporary theatres established by the British in Boston, New York, Philadelphia and Charlottesville, Va., during the war, these taunts formed a staple of the amusements. It was so even after the war. Thus, on one occasion, a play was in course of performance in a London theatre, in which American officers were represented as mechanics of every kind. In the midst of the hilarity which the play occasioned on that account, an American sailor in the gallery shouted, " Hurrah! England whipped by cobblers and tailors !" Thus, the tables were turned upon John Bull.

† This has reference to the death of General Fraser during the second battle of Saratoga, on October 7th, 1777. Dressed in full uniform, he made a conspicuous mark. Colonel Daniel Morgan, the commander of the Rifle Brigade, and who had been sent on by Washington from the Southern department to aid General Gates, perceiving that the fate of the day rested upon that officer (Fraser), took twelve of his sharpshooters aside, among whom was the celebrated marks-

While rifle-frocks sent gen'rals cap'ring,
And redcoats shrunk from leather apron,
And epaulette and gorget run
From whinyard brown and rusty gun ;
While sunburnt wigs in high command
Rush furious on our frighted band,
And ancient beards and hoary hair
Like meteors stream in troubled air.*
With locks unshorn not Samson more
Made useless all the show of war,
Nor fought with asses' jaw for rarity,
With more success or singularity.†
I saw our vet'ran thousands yield
And pile their muskets on the field,
And peasant guards in rueful plight
March off our captured bands from sight ;

---

man, "Tim" Murphy—men on whose precision of aim
he could rely—and said to them : " That gallant officer
yonder is General Fraser.   I admire and respect him,
but it is necessary for our good that he should die.
Take your station and do your duty.   Within a few
moments a rifle-ball cut the crupper of Fraser's horse,
and another, a moment after, passed through his horse's
mane.   Calling his attention to this, Fraser's aide said :
" It is evident that you are marked out for particular
aim ; would it not be prudent for you to retire from
this place ?"   Fraser replied: " My duty forbids me to
fly from danger."   The next moment he fell mortally
wounded by a ball from the rifle of Murphy, and was
carried off the field by two grenadiers.

  * " Loose his beard and troubled hair
    Streamed like a meteor to the troubled air."
                        —GRAY.

† Judges 15 : 15.

While ev'ry rebel fife in play
To yankey-doodle tun'd its lay,
And like the music of the spheres,
Mellifluous sooth'd their vanquish'd ears.*
" Alas !" said I, " what baleful star
Sheds fatal influence on the war,
And who that chosen chief of fame,
That heads this grand parade of shame ?"

There, see how fate, great Malcolm cried,
Strikes with its bolts the tow'rs of pride.
Behold that martial macaroni,†

---

* After Burgoyne had surrendered, the prisoners started under guard across the country to Cambridge, Mass. They began their march to the tune of " Yankee Doodle," which they had so often heard in derision in the British camp. Indeed, the pride of Burgoyne was dreadfully humbled by the whole affair. He had but a short time previous declared that he would eat his Christmas dinner in Albany as a victor. He did, indeed, dine there earlier than Christmas, but as a prisoner, although a guest at the table of his magnanimous foe, General Schuyler, whom he had greatly injured by having burned his house, mills, and other property at Saratoga.

† This allusion to Burgoyne's foppery is a very happy one, as the young men of fashion, who composed the Macaroni Club, had very recently produced a great sensation in England. They were young men who had travelled in Italy, and had returned, bringing with them all the vices and follies which they had picked up abroad. Their club was formed in London in 1772, and it was particularly distinguished for the extravagance of its members in dress. The members wore

Compound of Phœbus and Bellona,*
With warlike sword and singsong lay,
Equipp'd alike for feast or fray,
Where equal wit and valour join ;
This, this is he, the famed Burgoyne ;
Who pawn'd his honor and commission
To coax the patriots to submission,
By songs and balls secure obedience,
And dance the ladies to allegiance.†

---

enormous knots of hair behind, an exceedingly small cocked hat, an enormous walking-stick with long tassels, jacket, waistcoat and breeches, cut very close. Soon everything that was fashionable was *à la macaroni.* Macaroni articles everywhere abounded, and macaroni songs were set to music. One song closed with this stanza :

> " Five pounds of hair they wear behind,
>   The ladies to delight, O !
> Their senses give unto the mind,
>   To make themselves a fright, O !
> The fashion who does e'er pursue,
>   I think a simple-toney ;
> For he's a fool, say what you will,
>   Who is a macaroni !"

Indeed, the word " macaroni" took the place of "beau" and " fribble," which had previously been given to men of fashion, in the same way that " dude," at the present day, has succeeded the word "dandy."

* Phœbus was another name for Apollo, or the sun. Bellona was the accomplished Goddess of War.

† When setting out for America, Burgoyne playfully remarked that he meant to dance the Whig ladies to obedience, when their husbands would soon follow. In

Oft his camp muses he'll parade
At Boston in the grand blockade,
And well invoked with punch of arrack,
Hold converse sweet in tent or barrack,
Inspired in more heroic fashion,
Both by his theme and situation ;
While force and proclamation grand,
Rise fair beneath his plastic hand.*

this, as in many other things, he, as well as the British officers, was grievously disappointed. Howe and Clinton and some of their subordinates expected to crush the rebellion in a week almost ; and it is said that they actually brought fishing-tackle with them to have some fine sport after the smoke of gunpowder had cleared away.

* Burgoyne's proclamations, like those of Gage, were, as before stated, very pompous, and caused the wits of the day to publish in a burlesque vein counter-proclamations, as the ballads in this volume show. He was evidently very fond of making them, for he always delighted in the use of his pen. While in Boston, for instance, during the siege, he wrote a farce called "Boston Blockaded," in which the person designed to represent Washington enters with uncouth gait, wearing a large wig, a long, rusty sword, and attended by a servant armed with a dilapidated and rusty gun. Other American officers in this same play were similarly burlesqued. While this farce was in course of performance in the temporary theatre in Boston, on the night of January 8th, 1776, a sergeant suddenly entered and exclaimed : "The Yankees are attacking our works on Bunker Hill!" The audience at first thought this was a part of the performance, and laughed immoderately at the idea,

For genius swells more strong and clear
When close confined, like bottled beer;
So Prior's wit gained greater pow'r,
By inspiration of the Tow'r;*
And Raleigh fast in prison hurl'd
Wrote all the history of the world;†
So Wilkes grew, while in gaol he lay,
More patriotic ev'ry day,
But found his zeal, when not confined,
Soon sink below the freezing point,
And public spirit once so fair,
Evaporate in open air.‡

---

but they were soon undeceived by the burly voice of
Howe shouting: "Officers, to your alarm posts!" The
people, it is needless to say, dispersed in the greatest
confusion. The fact was, that majors Knowlton,
Carey and Henley, three gallant American officers, had
crossed the mill-dam from Cobble Hill, and had set
fire to some houses in Charlestown, at the foot of Bun-
ker Hill, occupied by some British soldiers. They
burned eight houses, killed one man and carried off
five prisoners.

   * Matthew Prior wrote his " Alma," the best of his
works, while in confinement in the Tower of London.

   † Sir Walter Raleigh wrote his famous "History of
the World" while confined in the Tower of London on
a charge of treason. The first volume appeared in
1614.

   ‡ John Wilkes was a fearless political writer dur-
ing the early years of the reign of George III., in
whose flesh he was a constant thorn, and was for a
long time editor of the *North Britain.* In the forty-
fifth number of that newspaper, published in 1763, he
uttered sentiments considered libellous, and was sent

But thou, great favorite of Venus,*
By no such luck shalt cramp thy genius;

---

to the Tower. His arrest was proved to be illegal, and he was released. For several years subsequent, as editor, as alderman in London and as a member of the House of Commons, he was considered a very dangerous enemy to the Crown. Wilkes was a licentious, un-principled man; and because he wrote an indecent "Essay on Woman" he was arraigned before the King's Bench, and, upon conviction, was expelled from Parliament. He afterward obtained a verdict against Wood, the under-secretary of State, with $5000 damages, and soon went to Paris. He afterward returned to England, and was again elected to the House of Commons, in 1768, but was deprived of his seat. He became Lord Mayor of London in 1774, when he took his seat in the House of Commons, becoming a stanch friend of the Americans in their contest with Great Britain. He was subsequently Chamberlain of London. Wilkes flourished but in the midst of agitation. When out of the troubled sea of politics, he sunk into obscurity, and died in the Isle of Wight, in 1797, at the age of seventy years. For a detailed account of the political career of Wilkes, the reader is referred to "The Journals of Horace Walpole, during the Reign of George III."

* In allusion to the well-known licentious propensities of Burgoyne. It was at this time a well-known fact—since confirmed by the letters of Mrs. General von Riedesel—that during the retreat of his army after the disastrous defeat of October 7th, he thought much more of enjoying the charms of his mistress than of how to administer to the comfort of his forlorn troops. "Burgoyne, however," says Mrs. General von Riedesel, in her

Thy friendly stars till wars shall cease,
Shall ward th' ill fortune of release,
And hold them fast in bonds not feeble,
In good condition still to scribble.
Such merit fate shall shield from firing,
Bomb, carcass, langridge and cold iron,
Nor trusts thy doubly laurel'd head
To rude assaults of flying lead.
Hence in this Saratogue retreat,
For pure good fortune thou'lt be beat;
Nor taken oft, released or rescued,
Pass for small change, like simple Prescott;*

Journal, "would not, though urged by his generals, think of a farther advance that night; and while his army were suffering from cold and hunger, and every one was looking forward to the immediate future with apprehension, the illuminated mansion of General Schuyler [of which he had taken possession] rang with singing, laughter and the jingling of glasses. There Burgoyne was sitting with some merry companions, at a dainty supper, while the champagne was flowing. Near him sat the beautiful wife of an English commissary, his mistress. Great as the calamity was, the frivolous general still kept up his orgies. Indeed, some were of the opinion that he had merely made that inexcusable stand for the sake of passing a merry night." See Stone's " Burgoyne's Campaign," pp. 87, 88.

* General Prescott was twice taken prisoner during the Revolution. The first time he was captured at Montreal by Montgomery, near the close of 1775; and the second time he was seized in his rooms, while in command of the British forces in Rhode Island, in July, 1777. He was taken to the headquarters of the American army, and afterward exchanged for

But captured then, as fates befall,
Shalt stand thy hand for't, once for all.
Then raise thy daring thoughts sublime,
And dip thy conq'ring pen in rhyme,
And changing war for puns and jokes,
Write new blockades and maids of oaks.*

that traitor, General Charles Lee, who had been cap-
tured in New Jersey in the December previous.   The
circumstances of his last capture were these: Colonel
William Barton, with a few men in whale-boats,
crossed Narragansett Bay in the night, for the purpose
of seizing Prescott, who was a most despicable, petty
tyrant of, as Lossing well says, "the meanest stamp."
He was, like Lee—for whom, as has been said, he was
afterward exchanged—taken from his bed, conveyed
across to Warwick, and thence to Providence, and
afterward to headquarters.   A full account of the
affair, with a portrait of Barton and a picture of the
house from which Prescott was taken, may be found
in Lossing's "Pictorial Field-Book of the Revolution."

* This is another allusion to Burgoyne's farce of "The
Siege of Boston." "The Maid of the Oaks" was another
farce from his fertile and versatile pen—for that he had
extraordinary literary ability no one can doubt—a play
which was much thought of, and was often performed
in the English theatres.   He also wrote a comedy, as
mentioned in the introduction to the "Burgoyne
Ballads" (see *ante*), entitled "The Heiress," which had
a great reputation.

For many of the above notes I am indebted to my
old friend, the late Mr. Benson J. Lossing, who first
published them in an annotated edition of "McFingal."

THE PROGRESS OF SIR JACK BRAG.*

SAID Burgoyne to his men, as they pass'd in review,
　　Tullalo, tullalo, tullalo, boys!
These rebels their course very quickly will rue,
And fly as the leaves 'fore the autumn tempest flew,
　　When *him who is your leader* they know, boys!
　　They with *men* have now to deal,
　　And we soon will make them feel,
　　Tullalo, tullalo, tullalo, boys!
That a loyal Briton's arm and a loyal Briton's steel
　　Can put to flight a rebel as quick as other foe,
　　　boys!
　　Tullalo, tullalo, tullalo—
　　Tullalo, tullalo, tullalo-o-o-o, boys!

---

*" Burgoyne, more frequently than any other British officer, was the butt of the Continental wits. His verses were parodied, his amours celebrated in the songs of the mess-table, and his boasts and the weaker points in his nature caricatured in ballads and *petite* comedies. We obtained a manuscript copy of the song from which the above verses are quoted from an octogenarian Vermonter, who, with feeble frame, shrill voice and silvered locks of eighty-seven, would give the echoing chorus with as much enthusiasm as when he joined in it with his camp companions more than half a century ago. The only clue to its authorship with which we are acquainted is the signature, ' G. of H.' It was probably written soon after its hero's defeat at Saratoga."—*Rufus W. Griswold, in the American Supplement to Disraeli's " Curiosities of Literature."*

As to Sa-ra-tog'* he came, thinking how to *jo* the
          game,
     Tullalo, tullalo, tullalo, boys!
He began to fear the grubs, in the branches of his fame,
He began to have the *trembles* lest a flash should be
          the flame,
     For which he had agreed his perfume to forego,
          boys!
     No lack of skill, but fates,
     Shall make us yield to Gates,
     Tullalo, tullalo, tullalo, boys!
The devil may have leagued, as you know, with the
          States!
     But we never will be beat by any mortal foe, boys!
     Tullalo, tullalo, tullalo—
     Tullalo, tullalo, tullalo-o-o-o, boys!

---

* The present word " Saratoga," the world's famous
watering-place, has had many different spellings. Dr.
Steel says, in his work, that it is a corruption of the
Indian word Sah-rah-ka, meaning " the side hill," and
"was applied by the natives more particularly to that
part of the country which lies between Saratoga Lake
and the Hudson, where the application of the term is
amply justified by the appearance of the country."
This explanation, however plausible, I believe is not
correct. Saratoga is an Indian word of the Iroquois
language, derived from " Saragh-aga" or "oga," and, ac-
cording to Sir William Johnson, means " the place of
the herrings," from the fact that, in early colonial times,
before the mills were built at Troy. Schuylersville, etc.,
herrings used to run up in large shoals into Saratoga
Lake by way of Fish Creek and the Hudson. The
inflections " oga" and "aga" are local phrases, and sig-
nify "place" or "inhabitants of." In the same sense

BURGOYNE'S DEFEAT.

(From an old pamphlet.)

YE powers above, look down and pity our case,
For the once great Burgoyne is now in distress;
For I am surrounded with a numerous foe,
Which I fear my whole army will soon overthrow.

O curs'd be the men that did us deceive,*
And curs'd be old Schuyler, that made us believe

---

the inflection "aga" is used in the words On-ond-aga,
Sac-and-aga, Ti-con-der-aga, Ca-nand-aga, etc. See
Stone's "Life of Sir William Johnson;" also Henry
Schoolcraft's letter to the author.

* Alluding to Philip Skene (after whom Skenesbor-
ough, now Whitehall, N.Y., was named), who continual-
ly advised Burgoyne to pursue Schuyler and to under-
take the expedition against Bennington, telling him
most positively that all he (Burgoyne) had to do was
to leave some plunder in his track, when all the Am-
ericans would be so engaged in gathering it up, that
he could easily overcome them. Skene, also, was
responsible for the fatal mistake Burgoyne made of
taking the route from Whitehall to Fort Edward by
way of Wood Creek, instead of at once proceeding by
way of Lake George by water-carriage—a course which
gave Schuyler ample opportunity of obstructing his
path by felling trees, etc., thus giving time for the
yeomanry to rally and for Washington to send Mor-
gan to the help of Gates. This advice was given
to Burgoyne by Skene solely to enable him, at the
army's expense, to have a good road cut for him from
Skenesborough (Whitehall, N. Y.) to the lower set-

30   *The Burgoyne Ballads.*

That he would retreat before us and make no alarm
'Till we'd landed in Albany free from all harm.

O, I am surrounded with sorrow and grief,
Ye Goddess Diana, O! send some relief,
Or send me some comfort my mind for to feed,
Or send me a cordial, for I ne'er had more need.

And now fellow-soldiers, what to advise to do,
Go forward we cannot—nor back we can't go,
And if we stay here we surely must die;
My heart is overwhelmed, O! where shall I fly?

What say you, my lads, must we yield unto men
That we've so long held in so great disdain,
And called them rebels and despised Yankees too,
And looked upon them as a cowardly crew?

O, safety says yes, but honor says no—
Our case is deplorable, what shall we do?
Our honor is sweet, but our lives are more dear,
My eyes do break forth in a fountain of tears.

O curs'd be the day that I e'er came here,
And crossed the Atlantic to buy wit so dear;
And curs'd be the villains that did so much hurt
By carrying to England so false a report.

For it is commonly reported in fair England
That the sight of one Briton will make ten Yankees
    run—
The report of a cannon will make Yankees fly,*
E'en were they as numerous as stars in the sky.

---

tlements. See Ramsey's "American Revolution," than
which there is no better authority.

 * Burgoyne is said to have stated to his king that

But alas! by experience I find it is false;
For of the two, Yankees are better than us;
They will fight with great valor in the open field—
Take them in the forest, then Britons must yield.

They'll shut up one eye and squint on their gun,
We're certainly dead boys as soon as that's done;
We can stand no more chance among Yankee boys
Than to throw an old cat into Bedlam without claws.

Then what shall we do?   Diana don't hear,
To our supplications she turns a deaf ear;
We'll complain to our gods of our sorrow and woe,
Our good old friend Jupiter will hear us, I know.

We'll complain to Mars, and Saturn also,
And likewise mild Venus shall hear of our woe;
And if they'll not regard us, will make our complaint
To the lady Mary and the good old saint.

You gentlemen all think on't as you will,
The Britons have used the Americans ill;
And for that same reason we are brought into stall.
We never shall prosper in this war at all.

For our gods will not hear us, though we cry and
        weep,
They have gone a long journey or fallen asleep;
They are regardless of our requests,
As the British Court is of the American Congress.

Thus I think it in vain on our gods for to call,
For they are not able to help us at all;
We'll go to brave Gates—that's complete,
He'll give us an answer in hopes that is sweet.

"with one regiment he could march triumphantly
through all the American colonies."

He'll grant us the privilege for to march out
In the honor of war though in the worst route;
And if he'll do so we'll bless his name,
And let him be crowned with honor and fame.

We are all 'greed to do as you have said,
We'll go very humble with hopes on our head,
Acknowledge before him we all deserve death,
If he saves us we'll praise him whilst we have breath.

We sent to his honor, our request he did grant;
His bountiful hands did supply all our wants;
He opened his stores, our wants did supply,
Let brave Gates' enemy before him all fly.

Ye Heavens, send down your blessings amain
On the head of brave Gates, let his foes be slain,
Or otherwise bow to that brave general,
Let Britons and foreigners before him all fall.

For his honour is great and his valour unknown,
He scorns in his heart the thoughts of a clown;
He's gallant and brave and generous too,
Right worthy gen'ral, I bid you adieu.

THE FATE OF JOHN BURGOYNE.

When Jack, the king's commander,
　　Was going to his duty,
Through all the crowd he smiled and bow'd
　　To every blooming beauty.

The city rung with feats he'd done
　　In Portugal and Flanders,
And all the town thought he'd be crown'd
　　The first of Alexanders.*

---

* See sketch of General Burgoyne, *ante.*

To Hampton Court he first repairs
  To kiss great George's hand, sirs ;
Then to harangue on state affairs
  Before he left the land, sirs.

The Lower House sat mute as mouse
  To hear his grand oration ;
And all the peers, with loudest cheers,
  Proclaimed him to the nation.

Then off he went to Canada,
  Next to Ticonderoga,
And quitting those away he goes
  Straightway to Saratoga.

With great parade his march he made
  To gain his wished for station,
While far and wide his minions hied
  To spread his Proclamation.

To such as staid he offers made
  Of "*pardon* on *submission ;*
But savage bands should waste the lands
  Of all in opposition."

But ah, the cruel fates of war !
  This boasted son of Britain,
When mounting his triumphal car
  With sudden fear was smitten.

The sons of Freedom gathered round,
  His hostile bands confounded,
And when they'd fain have turned their back
  They found themselves surrounded !

In vain they fought, in vain they fled,
  Their chief, humane and tender,
To save the rest soon thought it best
  His forces to surrender.

Brave St. Clair,* when he first retired
Knew what the fates portended ;

---

* The troops with which General St. Clair had garrisoned Ticonderoga, in view of a possible attack by Burgoyne, were ill equipped, badly armed, and amounted, including nine hundred militia, to about three thousand men. As General Philips, with the right wing of Burgoyne's army, approached Ticonderoga, the Americans abandoned their outworks, and the British, without hindrance, immediately took possession of and fortified Mount Defiance, a mountain completely overlooking Ticonderoga, and the possibility of which event had been suggested by Governor Trumbull, but which hint, on account of lack of men, was not acted upon. Under these circumstances St. Clair had no alternative but to evacuate the fort during the night and retreat into Vermont, sending his stores and sick on bateaux up Lake Champlain to Skenesborough.

No event during the Revolutionary War, as it has been justly said, produced such consternation throughout the colonies as the evacuation of Ticonderoga —a fortress which, even by Washington himself, had been regarded as a tower of strength, and one, too, before which, as a matter of course, Burgoyne would be stopped on his march southward to Albany. Indeed, nothing could have been more unexpected than this event. " It was," says Dr. Dwight, who lived as a contemporary with the actors in these scenes, " the bursting of a meteor, which, by its awful peal, shook every habitation from Maine to Georgia." That there was a fault somewhere admits of no doubt. But whatever was the cause—whether the officers and their subordinates overrated the strength of the enemy, or what—the excessive disappointment of the

And Arnold and heroic Gates*
His conduct have defended.

Thus may America's brave sons
With honor be rewarded,
*And the fate of all her foes
The same as here recorded.*

---

people was most terrible, and greatly increased the astonishment and dismay.   General St. Clair was afterward tried by a court-martial for the loss of this fort, but was acquitted of all blame.   The consequence, however, of this terrible misfortune has received no mitigation by his acquittal.

This much, however, must be said—viz., that though St. Clair failed in being a great genius, he was a noble man in his feelings and sympathies, and was not unsuccessful, as Headley has justly said, " from want of patriotism or willingness to sacrifice himself."   Washington knew this, and hence never withdrew his confidence.   He had him by his side at Brandywine, though holding no commission, and as soon as the court-martial pronounced his acquittal, again intrusted him with the highest responsibilities.   This is saying a great deal in his praise ; and finally, in 1788, when the Northwestern Territory was erected into a government, St. Clair, doubtless with the concurrence of Washington, was appointed governor of that territory, which office he held until 1802.

* For a short sketch of General Gates, see Appendix No. II.

THE CAPTURE AT SARATOGA.*

HERE followeth the direful fate
Of Burgoyne and his army great,
Who so proudly did display
The terrors of despotic sway.
His power and pride and many threats
Have been brought low by fort'nate Gates,
To bend to the United States.

British prisoners by convention, - -	2442
Foreigners by contravention, - - -	2198
Tories sent across the lake, - - -	1100
Burgoyne and his suite in state, - - -	12
Sick and wounded, bruised and pounded, ⎱ Ne'er so much before confounded, ⎰ -	528
Prisoners of war before convention, - -	400
Deserters come with kind intention, - -	300
They lost at Bennington's great battle, ⎱ Where Stark's glorious arms did rattle, ⎰ -	1220
Killed in September and October, - -	600
Ta'en by brave Brown,† some drunk, some sober,	413
Slain by high-famed Herkerman,‡ ⎱ On both flanks, on rear and van, ⎰ - -	300
Indians, settlers, butchers, drovers, ⎫ Enough to crowd large plains all over ⎪ And those whom grim Death did prevent ⎬ From fighting against our continent; ⎪ And also those who stole away, ⎪ Lest they down their arms should lay, ⎭	4413

* From a contemporary magazine, though copied extensively in the newspapers of the day.

† Colonel John Brown, of Massachusetts. See note under "The North Campaign."

‡ General Herkimer, of New York.

Abhorring that obnoxious day;
The whole make fourteen thousand men, ⎱   ————
Who may not with us fight again, ⎰   14000

    This is a pretty just account
    Of Burgoyne's legions' whole amount,
    Who came across the northern lakes
    To desolate our happy States.
    Their brass cannon we have got all,
    Fifty-six—both great and small:
    And ten thousand stand of arms,
    To prevent all future harms:
    Stores and implements complete,
    Of workmanship exceeding neat;
    Covered wagons in great plenty,
    And proper harness, no ways scanty.
    Among our prisoners there are
    Six generals of fame most rare ;
    Six members of their parliament
    Reluctantly they seem content:
    Three British lords, and Lord Balcarras*
    Who came our country free to harass.

---

* Balcarras, Alexander Lindsay, earl of, British soldier, born in 1752; died in London, March 27th, 1825. He was the eldest son of the fifth earl of Balcarras, whom he succeeded in 1767. He became an ensign in the Fifty-third foot, and was made major December 9th, 1775. In this country he saw three years of service under Carleton and Burgoyne. He was present at the defeat of the Americans, under General Thompson, at Three Rivers, June 1st, 1776, and commanded the light infantry at Ticonderoga and at Hubbardton, Vt., July 7th, 1777. In the latter action he was wounded—thirteen balls passing through his clothes. In the battle of September 19th he com-

Two baronets of high extraction
Were sorely wounded in the action.

BURGOYNE'S ADVANCE AND FALL.

(An extract from *America Independent*.)

BY PHILIP FRENEAU.*

LED on by lust of lucre and renown,
Burgoyne came marching with his thousands down ;

---

manded the advanced corps of the army at Free-
man's Farm ; and in the action of October 7th, 1777,
on the death of General Fraser, October 8th, 1777, he
was made lieutenant-colonel of the Twenty-fourth
foot.   He became major-general in 1793, commander
in Jamaica ; lieutenant-governor of that island in 1794 ;
lieutenant-general in 1798, and general in 1803.   His
bravery and prominence in both of the battles of Sar-
atoga have always received particular mention.

* Philip Freneau, poet, born in New York City,
January 2d, 1752 ; died near Freehold, N. J., December
18th, 1832.   Some of his published poems were written
before he left college (Princeton).   On a voyage to
the West Indies, in 1780, he was captured by an
English cruiser, and his experiences as a prisoner are
recorded in bitter terms in his " British Prison-Ship."
On regaining his liberty, the following year, he wrote
frequently, both in prose and verse, for the *Freeman's
Journal*.   After the close of the war he became
editor of the New York *Daily Advertiser*.   The
violence of this paper's attacks on the Federalists
aroused Hamilton's anger, who accused him of being

High were his thoughts, and furious his career,
Puff'd with self-confidence, and pride severe,
Swoln with the idea of his future deeds,
On to ruin each advantage leads.
Before his hosts his heaviest curses flew,
And conquer'd worlds rose hourly to his view :
His wrath, like Jove's, could bear with no control,
His words bespoke the mischief in his soul ;
To fight was not this miscreant's only trade,
He shin'd in writing, and his wit display'd.
To awe the more with titles of command
He told of *forts he rul'd* in Scottish land ;
Queen's *colonel* as he was he did not know
That thorns and *thistles*, mix'd with honors, grow ;
In Britain's senate though he held a place,
All did not save him from one long disgrace.
One stroke of fortune that convinc'd them all
That we could conquer, and *lieutenants* fall.
Foe to the rights of man, proud plunderer, say
Had conquest crown'd thee on that mighty day
When you to GATES, with sorrow, rage and shame
Resign'd your conquests, honors, arms, and fame,
When at his feet Britannia's wreaths you threw,
And the sun sicken'd at a sight so new ;
Had you been victor—what a waste of woe !
What souls had vanish'd to where souls do go !

---

the "tool of Jefferson," which forced the latter to write
an explanatory letter to Washington. He afterward
was connected with several newspapers. He is the
author of many works, both of prose and verse. A
volume of his poems, published in Philadelphia in
1786, abounds in patriotic sentiments and allusions
to the various events of the war. Indeed, he has been
not unaptly styled " the poet of the Revolution."

What dire distress had mark'd your fatal way,
What deaths on deaths disgrace that dismal day!
Can laurels flourish in a soil of blood,
Or on those laurels can fair honors bud?
Curs'd be that wretch who murder makes his trade,
Curs'd be all arms that e'er ambition made!
What murdering tory now relieves your grief
Or plans new conquests for his favorite chief;
Designs still dark employ that ruffian race,
Beasts of your choosing, and our own disgrace.
So vile a crew the world ne'er saw before,
And grant, ye pitying heavens, it may no more.
If ghosts from hell infest our poison'd air,
Those ghosts have enter'd these base bodies here,
Murder and blood is still their dear delight—
Scream round their roots, ye ravens of the night!
Whene'er they wed, may demons, and despair,
And grief, and woe, and blackest night be there;
Fiends leagu'd from hell, the nuptial lamp display,
Swift to perdition light them on their way.
Round the wide world their devilish squadrons chase,
To find no realm that grants one resting place.
Far to the north, on Scotland's utmost end,
An isle there lies, the haunt of every fiend,
There screeching owls, and screaming vultures rest,
And not a tree adorns its barren breast!
No shepherds there attend their bleating flocks,
But wither'd witches rove among the rocks:
Shrouded in ice, the blasted mountains show
Their cloven heads, to fright the seas below;
The lamp of heaven in his diurnal race
Here scarcely deigns to unveil his radiant face;
Or if one day he circling treads the sky
He views this island with an angry eye;
Or ambient fogs their broad, moist wings expand,
Damp his bright ray, and cloud the infernal land;

The blackening wind incessant storms prolong,
Dull as their night, and dreary as my song;
When stormy winds with rain refuse to blow,
Then from the dark sky drives the unpitying snow;
When drifting snow from iron clouds forbear,
Then down the hailstones rattle through the air.
No peace, no rest, the elements bestow,
But seas forever rage, and storms forever blow.
Here, miscreants, here with loyal hearts retire,
Here pitch your tents, and kindle *here* your fire;
Here desert Nature will her stings display,
And fiercest hunger on your vitals prey.
And with themselves let *John Burgoyne* retire
To reign the monarch, whom your hearts admire.

ST. CLAIR'S RETREAT, AND BURGOYNE'S DEFEAT.

By Rev. Wheeler Case.*

St. Clair is stationed in our Northern fort,
T' oppose *Burgoyne*, sent from the *British* coast.

---

* Rev. Wheeler Case was born at Southold, Long Island, in 1732. He died in 1788, at Pleasant Valley, Dutchess County, N. Y., where his tombstone is yet (1893) still to be seen. The poems were first published anonymously in 1778, and have since been reproduced by Dodd in 1852. Rev. Mr. Case was the pastor for many years of the Presbyterian Church of Pleasant Valley, N. Y. In his preface to his pamphlet he states that the poems were first composed for his own amusement, without any idea of printing them; but afterward, thinking they might contribute a little toward

The fortress all complete in every part,
Well fortified by nature and by art ;
How firm the walls! the lines completely mann'd,
Huge cannon planted round, all parts well scann'd.
The gen'ral now his soldiers all address'd,
And like a hero thus himself express'd:
"Let martial courage in your bosoms glow,
Nor fear to face a proud invading foe;
You know our cause is just; we need not fear,
The *God* of armies will for us appear.
Fair Liberty commands; here make the stand,
Here we will die, or save our injur'd land.
You all detest the shameful name of *slave ;*
Then play the man, and rank among the brave.
My orders you will all as one obey,
Our foes, all panic-struck, will sneak away.
Then we————————————————————
But who—what troops are these just here in sight,
All clad in arms complete, prepar'd to fight?

———————————————————————

promoting the noble cause of liberty, he consented to
their publication. "If the friends of liberty," he adds
in his preface, "should be of the same mind with him,
he hopes they will be good enough to excuse practical
errors, as he had never made the art of poetry his
study. As for others, he is not concerned about them,
being persuaded the time is drawing nigh when they
will be fully convinced that liberty is better than
slavery, and independence is much better than being
dependent upon a prince who chooses that they should
live no longer than during his pleasure, or submit to
abject slavery." I am indebted for the above facts to
his great-grandson, Walter C. Anthony, of New-
burgh, N. Y.

They are Great Britain's troops—a rising storm—
They all appear of a gigantic form!
These sons of *Anak* spread all o'er the land,
Before this mighty host we cannot stand.
Should we foolhardy with them now engage,
We fall at once sure victims to their rage ;
With sword unsheath'd they're all advancing nigh.
Let ev'ry man prepare himself to fly.
I now *command* you all with speed to run,
Leave all your baggage, and not fire a gun."
The soldiers with reluctance now obey,
They all retreat, and *St. Clair* leads the way.
Whether with panic struck he took the flight,
Or to ensnare *Burgoyne* in dismal plight,
The muse must leave till she has further light.
Perhaps by impulse he foreknew the fates,
And fled to save the whole United States.
Whether fear or impulse govern'd in his breast,
Kind Providence o'erruled it for the best.[*]
Burgoyne, elated, now pursues the chase,
And threatens vengeance to the rebel race ;

---

[*] Here the author, writing at the time that the evacuation of Ticonderoga was fresh in the public mind, and with every patriot smarting under what was then considered a needless surrender of that fort, does St. Clair *great injustice.* St. Clair could not have done otherwise, and if Colonel Trumbull's advice had been followed in regard to fortifying Sugar-Loaf Hill (see Stone's " Burgoyne's Campaign"), the fort need not have been given up. St. Clair, however, did as a true patriot what was the best, and thus saved his army, which eventually captured all of Burgoyne's army. The subsequent court-martial of St. Clair, undertaken at the demand of public opinion, fully vindicated his conduct.

He boasts aloud, his threat'nings round he hurl'd,
As tho' assur'd of conquering all the world.
With hellish pride he triumphs o'er the north,
Enumerates his titles and his worth,
And sends his thund'ring proclamation forth.*
Persuasive arguments at first he us'd,
Then blood and slaughter, if they him refus'd.
He dipp'd his pen in oil to soothe and please,
Then his address began in words like these :
" Why will you thus desert my master's cause,
And trample underfoot his righteous laws ?
Cease to rebel, repent, return and live,
I've sealed pardons in my hand to give.
Remain upon your farms, there safely stay,
With all your horses, cattle, and your hay ;
Nor hide your oats, your barley, or your wheat,
Then you from me shall safe protection meet ;
You need not fear, no one shall you annoy,
Come and submit, I'll find you full employ ;
I'll bore your ear unto my master's door,
'Tis all he has in view, he wants no more.
Submit your necks to his most easy yoke,
So that you may avert the dreadful stroke.
As mediator, I do you entreat
With all submission fall at *George's* feet.
My royal master's pleasure and your good
Is my design, could it be understood.
Oh ! for the eloquence of a Demosthenes,
Could I your mind impress, or could I please,

---

* The writer here refers to the bombastic proclama-
tion of Burgoyne, sent out from his camp at the river
Bouquet, June 23d, 1777. To show the burlesque more
understandingly, the proclamation, as previously stated,
is given under Appendix No. III.

Could I but melt your stubborn temper down
To due submission to the *British* crown.
When I have done my work I am content
With what I'm to receive from Government.
But if my royal master you despise,
And 'gainst the clearest light you shut your eyes,
If you are still determined to rebel
And counteract his laws, all plann'd so well,
Then I'm in duty bound to let you know
What I have full authority to do:
I come commissioned from great *George's* throne,
To vindicate his honor and my own.
A great and potent army I command,
With floods of rebel blood to drench the land;
Thousands of *Indians* I've supplied with knives
To scalp your dearest children and your wives.
If I but nod the savage army flies,
And naught is heard but shrieks and female cries.
Believe my word, this sure will be your fate,*
You soon must feel the vengeance of *the State.*
Let not your *Hezekiahs* you deceive,
None of your pulpit *orators* believe.
In whom do you confide? Come tell,
That ye against my master dare rebel.
Is it on *Gallic* bands,† or is it *Spain?*
They'll disappoint your trust, your hope is vain.

---

* This, again, is an unjust imputation against
Burgoyne, who, notwithstanding the threats in his
proclamation, did all he could to restrain Indian
atrocities. Indeed, it was to this fact, that before the
battles of Saratoga nearly all his savage allies deserted
him.

† Referring to rumors, even then prevalent, that

Were they with you combined, they'd with you fall,
Just like a tottering fence or bowing wall.
What *Britain* did last war you know full well,
Her banners wav'd, united powers fell.
What armies ever could her force withstand?
Hath she not conquered both the sea and land?
What madness then to oppose a power so great,
While weak and feeble in. your infant state!"
Reply : Britain, 'tis true, her conquests far hath spread,
Nations to her have bow'd and tribute paid,
Her vict'ries she hath spread o'er sea and land,
Before her potent armies none could stand.
Horror and darkness now are spread around,
Our woes increase, and no deliverer's found.
Great *desolation* in the north is made,
Our strongest fort resigned, *St. Clair* is fled;
The poor distressed inhabitants now fly,
And on the Providence of GOD rely.
The baser sort are flocking to *Burgoyne*,
Others now tremble, lest they must resign.
Why these despairing tho'ts? Why all this fear?
Who knows but GOD will soon for us appear?
The night's the darkest, best observers say,
E'en just before the dawning of the day ;·
Who knows but these our groans and female cries,
Which sound thro' all the woods, may reach the skies?
Our cause is just, we dare appeal to heaven ;
We fight for what our gracious GOD has given.
You threaten vengeance with your dreadful rod,
As if you fill'd the seat and throne of GOD.
But hark ! the sov'reign speaks, Vengeance is mine,
And now I will repay it on *Burgoyne*.

France would soon take part with the colonies in their
struggle with the Mother country.

The horrors which you have denounced of late
Shall fall upon your own devoted pate.
Burgoyne is rushing on in quest of blood,
And *Indians* shout for victory thro' the wood.
He solemnly declares, unless we yield
Horror and death await us in the field.
He sends his bloody flag from house to house;
The mountains travail, and bring forth a mouse.
While thus he threatens ruin to these States,
Behold! here comes the brave heroic GATES.
The gloom dispell'd, the light doth now appear,
And shines thro' all the Northern Hemisphere;
Our troops collect and marshal in array,
Complete in arms, their banners they display.
Burgoyne now views them all in arms complete,
Struck with a panic, orders a retreat.
The soldiers trembling, his commands obey,
And he, the most intrepid, leads the way.
Our brave commander then pursues with speed,
Soon overtakes, and numbers lie and bleed;
Our valiant troops enclose *Burgoyne* around,
And take the best advantage of the ground.
The *British* hero that appear'd so prompt
Is now enclos'd by *Yankees* in a swamp.
The great *Burgoyne* is now overwhelm'd with grief,
Nor has he any hope to obtain relief.
The rebel army he with scorn defied
Have him encompass'd round on ev'ry side.
Alas! how great his grief, how 'cute *his* pain!
How great is his reproach, how great the stain!
Surprising strange! how singular his case!
By rebels close confined in such a place.
One thing especially that makes him mourn,
Great generals and lords that strut and spurn
Are fond of having room enough to turn.

What seiz'd his soul with horror and surprise,
He expects now soon to fall a sacrifice—
A sacrifice to Liberty's brave sons.
For blood of innocence and dying groans
His sorrows rise; an overwhelming flood,
Conscience accus'd, and justice cried for blood.
Whole rivers of such blood could ne'er atone
For all the horrid murders he had done.
Now, thunderstruck, with these ill-boding fates,
Resigns himself and army up to *Gates.*

THE FALL OF BURGOYNE.

By Rev. Wheeler Case.

Is this *Burgoyne, Burgoyne* the great,
  Who fill'd our land with woe,
And threaten'd vengeance from the State,
  Is he now fell so low?

Is't he that made the earth to tremble,
  That was so great a curse,
That doth great Babel's king resemble,
  Is he now weak like us?

To *Indians* he gives stretch no more,
  Nor them supplies with knives
To stain our land with crimson gore,
  With them to scalp our wives.

His threat'ning proclamation's stopped,
  He's now o'erspread with gloom,
The wings with which he flew are cropp'd,
  He has no *elbow room.*

His titles he proclaims no more,
   No more his triumphs spread,
His thund'ring cannon cease to roar,
   And all his joys are fled.

Where is his great and mighty host,
   That huge *gigantic* race,
The sons of *Anak*, Britain's boast?
   They're pris'ners in disgrace.

Pris'ners to rebels, *Yankees* too,
   O mortifying stroke!
They caught *Burgoyne* with all his crew,
   Britons now wear the yoke.

Great *Washington*, that man of might,
   Hath laid a snare for *Howe ;*
Unless with speed he takes his flight,
   He to the yoke must bow.

AN ANSWER FOR THE MESSENGERS OF THE NATION.

(Is. 14 : 32.)

By Rev. Wheeler Case.

When messengers come from a foreign land,
With peaceful branch of olive in their hand,
If hand and heart unite, if both agree,
From ill designs and all suspicion free,
We'll then receive them in the arms of love ;
They are not *men*, but *angels* from above.*

   *   *   *   *   *

Now let us view the Northern Hemisphere,
And see the footsteps of *Jehovah* there.

---

* The part omitted, marked by stars, refers entirely

We'll first survey the dark side of the cloud,
Where scenes of woe in dark succession crowd;
The cruel savage tribes in union join,
And with the *British* army all combine ;
They soon are in possession of Fort " Ti ;"
Our troops retreat, and with the country fly.
An heart of stone must bleed to hear the cries,
While numbers fall a bloody sacrifice
To *Britain's* cruel sons and savage rage.
As naught but blood their fury would assuage,
A dark and dismal gloom around us spread,
And joy and gladness from our souls were fled ;
We thought our country lost, our freedom gone,
And these United States were all undone.
The great BURGOYNE's most formidable host
Now march along, and as they march they boast.
They boldly rush along, they rage and roar,
Like swelling waves that dash against the shore.
Now is the time for *Zion's* God t' appear,
His people's groans and cries have reached his ear.
The Lord for them hath laid a secret snare ;
They'll not escape, but be entangl'd there.
Great Gen'ral *Gates* appears, inspir'd from heaven,
Wisdom and fortitude to him are given.
Our soldiers all collect from East to West,
With martial ardor glowing in their breast ;
They stop the great *Burgoyne* in his career,
Him they surround, his feet are in the snare ;
With forc'd submission now he bows to Gates,
He and his hosts made pris'ners to these States.

---

to Washington and the battles of Trenton and Prince-
ton. As this is not germane to the object of this
work, it is here omitted.

Thick clouds of darkness that our heads hung o'er
Have vanish'd suddenly, and seen no more;
The rays of light break forth, how clear the skies,
Our gloom is scatter'd, and our hopes arise.
May love and gratitude inspire our breast,
Praise God for these, and trust him for the rest.
These gracious smiles are to prepare the way
For greater things, for a more glorious day.
This horrid, bloody scene erelong will end,
And richer blessings from on high descend.
What's been a snare to us, what's prov'd our fate,
We've been too long corrupted with the great.
The *British* king and his most vicious court
Practise all kinds of vice, and them support.
Most nat'rally these painted vices flow
From higher ranks to those that are below;*
How rapidly they've flown down from the great,
In silver streams, and poison'd every State.
Jehovah reigns above, and rules below,
He dries our tears, and they shall cease to flow;
And blessings pour on those where virtue reigns,
The yoke of tyrants broke, and all their chains;
Vice, put to flight, hides its malignant head,
And plotting foes no more in corners hid;
Peace, like a river, flows thro' all the land,
No tyrant moves his tongue or lifts his hand;
Our liberty extends both far and wide,
Our borders lengthen out on every side;
States in successive growing numbers rise,
The greatest empire this below the skies.

---

* Those vices to which the writer alludes have been most admirably brought out by Mr. J. C. Markham in his *alto rilievos* which adorn the Saratoga Monument.

In gloomy deserts, our most distant land,
Large cities shall be built and churches stand;
There Zion's sons, commission'd from above,
Shall spread the news of their Redeemer's love.
Where wolves now range, and other beasts of prey;
Where Indian tribes more savage are than they;
Where now the war-whoop sounds they bow prostrate,
Shall worship at the King of Zion's gate;
Where stand the oak, the beech and the tall pine,
There shall be corn-fields and the fruitful vine;
Where marshes abound and the wild flag grows,
There shall be the lily and the blushing rose;
The most delicious fruits shall ripen there,
The peach, the plum, the apple and the pear.
Trade unconfined extensively shall grow,
And riches here from every nation flow.
Our naval force how great! our fleets abound,
Our flocks and herds spread o'er the land around:
Here every sort of fruit springs up and grows,
And all the *land with milk and honey flows.*

THE FIRST CHAPTER OF THE LAMENTA-
TIONS OF GENERAL BURGOYNE.

(Written in 1778.)

By Rev. Wheeler Case.*

Good heavens! how deep I'm plung'd in woe!
None knows what I now undergo.
Britain assum'd a sovereign power,
To crush her sons while in their flower.

---

* See previous poem for sketch of Rev. Mr. Case's life.

One now was wanting bold and brave
T' enforce her laws, the sons to enslave.
To get a name, to gain applause,
I readily espous'd her cause.
I undertook amidst the throng
To head her army, right or wrong.
Britain I left, and cross'd the seas,
His Majesty and *North* to please.
I landed on Canadia's shore,
The land and lakes I then pass'd o'er;
I march'd along, my banners spread,
And struck the rebels all with dread.
I soon was master of Fort "Ti;"*
Like sheep they all before me fly;
My *Indians* shout, my cannon roar,
The land is stained with crimson gore.
All things are pleasing, all things bright,
The rebel army dare not 'fight.
The sun in its meridian shone,
I thought the day was now my own.
To *Britain* I dispatch'd a post,
And joy was spread thro' all their coast,
But oh, the change, the sudden change!
Affairs now took a turn most strange.
The hero, *Gates*, appears in sight,
His troops all cloth'd with armor bright;
They all as one their banners spread,
With " *Death or Victory*" on their head.†

---

* Ticonderoga.   In the common conversation of the
day, this fort was called Fort " Ti," for short.
    † General Gates's soldiers wore this badge in capitals
on their hats, " *Death or Victory.*"   Note to the original
poem.

A sudden panic seiz'd my breast;
Now, to retreat I thought was best.
I gave the word and led the way,
My orders all as one obey.
In this precipitate retreat,
Our whole dependence was our feet.
Like *Tories*, they have thus deceiv'd,
Oh! that we'd never them believ'd.
While running thro' a swampy ground,
The rebel army us surround;
O horrid place! O dreadful gloom!
I mourn for want of *elbow room.*
My tawny soldiers, from me fled,
Have now return'd to scalp my head.
I hear them whoop, I hear them yell,
I'm at the very gates of *hell.*
O horror this! unhappy wretch!
They've took an unexpected *stretch;*
I'm here confin'd, and naught to eat,
They've robb'd me of my bread and meat.
Water, I thought, was always free,
But that is now denied to me.
O that my royal master knew
How I am treated by this crew!
He, lion-like, of whelps bereav'd,
Would see us instantly reliev'd—
No, the attempt would all be vain,
They fight like devils, not like men.
But who would ever have believ'd
That I could thus have been deceiv'd?
I thought five thousand men, or less,
Thro' all these States might safely pass,
March boldly on one steady course,
The States all trembling at our force.*

---

* In allusion to the remark of General Burgoyne to

My error now I see too late,
Here I'm confin'd within this State.*
Yes, in this little spot of ground,
Enclos'd by *Yankees* all around.
With this five thousand—yes with ten,
And these *Great Britain's* chosen men.
In *Europe* let it ne'er be known,
Nor publish it in *Askelon*,
Lest the uncircumcised rejoice,
And distant nations join their voice.†
What will my friends in *Britain* say?
I wrote them I had gained the day,
I made them both rejoice and sing,‡
But now they'll strike a mournful string.
Three things now strike me with surprise:
First, I believ'd the Tories' lies;
What also brought me to this plight,
I thought the *Yankees* would not fight.§

George IV., when contemplating his expedition—viz., that "with five thousand men he could easily march through the entire American colonies."

* Rhode Island, where Burgoyne was kept until his exchange.

† Burgoyne, as mentioned in the preliminary sketch of that general, before coming to America had served with great distinction in Europe—a fact which caused him to be selected to command this expedition. No wonder, then, that he should have felt terribly mortified at the unlucky result of his campaign in America.

‡ Burgoyne's despatches to England previous to his surrender had been of the most encouraging description.

§ Probably in allusion to the fact that Governor Skene had told Burgoyne, before the latter sent out his

Thirdly, I'm most asham'd to say,
I fled so fast I missed my way.
How strange that I should take this route,
When I'm so swamp'd and hemm'd about,
The de'il himself could ne'er get out.
Alas! I'm overborne with grief!
There's none appears for my relief!
Where are my titles and my fame?
I've lost my honor and my name.
At *Bennington*, *Stark* gave the wound
Which, like a gangrene, spread around
O'er Saratoga's cursed ground.
Heart-sickness seiz'd the camp so fast,
All courage fail'd; and there at last
Arnold and *Lincoln* gave the blow
That proved our final overthrow.
Arnold with wings our lines flew o'er,
The like I never saw before;

---

expedition to Bennington, that the inhabitants would
make no resistance—in fact, said Skene, "all you have
to do is to scatter plunder on your march, and then
the rebels will be so busily engaged in collecting it,
that you need have no fear of any attack." Skene, in
fact, in more senses than one, was Burgoyne's evil
genius; for it was through his advice that Burgoyne
advanced by land in pursuit of Schuyler, instead of tak-
ing Lake George, by which means so much time was
lost that Schuyler had ample time to gather his forces
to make his successful stand at Saratoga. Ramsey,
in his "History of the American Revolution," states
that Skene gave this advice, so that, at the expense
of Great Britain, he could have a road cut through
from Skenesborough (Whitehall, N. Y.) to benefit
himself.

He threaten'd death to every one
That dar'd to fire another gun.
The *Hessians,* thunderstruck, turn pale,*
The stupid asses' hearts now fail ;
Thus seiz'd with trembling and dismay,
Their new commander they obey ;
The panic spread from breast to breast,
And I was struck among the rest.
Language now fails—it can't express
Th' amazing horror and distress.
Cannon-like claps of thunder roar,
Their balls like hail upon us pour ;
Flashes of fire around us blaze :
The sun now lost his feebler rays :
Volumes of smoke o'ercloud the skies,
And scenes of blood salute our eyes.
The gloom of death around us waits,
And all the vengeance of the States.
I must submit or die—but how
To these despised *Yankees* bow ?
I wish I never had been born.
If I submit, I'm laugh'd to scorn ;

---

* *Brunswickers,* not *Hessians,* who were chiefly in
the Southern Department. The Brunswickers, at the
second battle of Saratoga, manned the Brunswick re-
doubt captured by Arnold in his impetuous charge at
the close of the battle. Through the patriotic efforts of
Mrs. E. H. Walworth, that most energetic trustee of
the Saratoga Monument Association, General de Pey-
ster has placed a beautiful tablet marking the site of
Arnold's charge. Hon. James M. Marvin, George M.
Pullman and others have also erected tablets on
different points of the battle-ground.

If I refuse, I know my doom—
Among the living I've no room.
The blood of innocence I've shed—
This fills my guilty soul with dread.
My brethren's blood against me cries,
And calls for vengeance from the skies.
Cain's crime was great, but not so bad,
The blood of only *one* he shed ;
But I have laid a country waste,
And human nature have disgrac'd ;
I've slain each sex of ev'ry age,
And slaughter'd victims to my rage.*
One demon only tempted Cain,
Legion, and more within me reign.
Horror and death do me surprise,
A shower of lead around me flies.
In *Saul*, when guilt and fear arise,
Away to *Endor* straight he goes ;
He prays the witch, tho' most unjust,
To raise up *Samuel*† from the dust,
That he might tell what would be best
For him to do while thus distress'd.
But I'm confined, and cannot go
To *Endor*, there to tell my woe ;
I'm here pent up to grieve and mourn,
I scarce have room enough to turn.

---

* As stated *ante*, this imputation on Burgoyne is most
unjust.   Still, allowance must be made for the bitter
partisan feeling of the day.

† The fact of the writer emphasizing *Samuel* would
seem to show he had some one particularly in his
mind—an allusion which, at the time this was written,
was probably understood, but which is lost to us
readers of the present day.

O that that prophet would arise,
My priests have told me naught but lies.
What shall I say?—what shall I do?
" My council, now I turn to you."
A council now of war is held ;
They all as one agree to yield;
Their colors strike, to *Gates* they bow,
Lay down their arms, and off they go.*

*   *   *   *   *

As they begin to march, as soon
  The conquerors all agree
To sound the " Yankee Doodle" tune
  Upon the highest key.†

---

* This, again, is in allusion to the fact that Burgoyne, against the advice of Riedesel and all the officers whom he had summoned into council, was at first determined not to surrender, but to try and reach Fort Edward, and thence, *via* Lakes George and Champlain, to Canada. And it was only after the most strenuous exertions on the part of his generals that he finally yielded. Had he not done so, his entire army would have been compelled to surrender most ignominiously, and without any *conditions* whatever.

† " The origin of this air," says Lossing, " is involved in obscurity. It seems to be older than the United States. It is also said to be the tune of an old English nursery song called ' Lucy Locket,' which was current in the time of Charles II. In New England Colonial times it was known as ' Lydia Fisher's Jig.' A song composed in derision of Cromwell began with

" ' Yankee Doodle came in town,
    Riding on a pony,
  With a feather in his hat,
    Upon a macaroni.' "

Musicians all of various kinds
With utmost skill now play,
To raise the pris'ners' drooping minds,
And *demons* drive away.

Such charms of music ne'er before
Were heard within our land,
But all their skill they now give o'er
For want of David's hand.*

A DIALOGUE BETWEEN COLONEL PAINE
AND MISS CLORINDA FAIRCHILD,
WHEN TAKING LEAVE OF HER TO
GO ON THE NORTHERN EXPEDITION
AGAINST BURGOYNE.

Col. Paine.—I'm come to let my dear Clorinda know
My bleeding country calls, and I must go.

---

* A surgeon who was with Sir William Johnson in
1755, at Lake George, composed a song to the air which
he called "Yankee," as a take-off of the uncouth appear-
ance of the Provincial troops. Contrary, however, to
his design, it was considered good martial music, and
became very popular. While the British were in
Boston some poet wrote a piece in derision of the New
England troops, which Mr. Lossing gives in full in his
"Cyclopædia of United States History" (Harper &
Bros.). This is the original "Yankee Doodle" song.
"The tune," says Lossing, "is so associated with the
patriotic deeds of Americans, that it always inspires a
love of country in the heart of any good citizen." It
is now accepted as our national air, and is in positive
contrast in spirit to the stately "God Save the King"
of Old England.

Distress'd it calls aloud, To arms! to arms!
The trumpet sounds, I now must leave your charms.
I've drawn my sword, I'll go forth with the brave,
And die a freeman, ere I live a slave.

    Clo.—Good Heavens! can this be true—can it be
        so?
You pierce my heart, I'm overwhelmed with woe.
Is this your love—is this the kind return,
To win my heart, and leave me thus to mourn?
Oh, should you fall a victim there to death,
I can't survive, I must resign my breath!

    Paine.—My dear *Clorain*, forbear to weep—forbear!
I trust my life to God's paternal care;
He will protect the men whose cause is just
And in the God of armies put their trust.
We'll boldly go and smite those rebels dead
Who dare oppose our *Continental Head;*
Then I'll return and my *Clorinda* wed.

    Clo.—If naught your mind will change, then take
        the field,
Go play the man, and *Heaven* be your shield.
Go forth and act the hero, crush our foes,
Who slav'ry love and liberty oppose.
May Liberty's brave sons the triumph spread,
Put all their foes to flight, or view them dead.
Should Heaven, propitious, our good cause maintain,
And our brave troops with you victorious reign,
Then cheerfully with them we'll victory sing,
And join with them in praise of Zion's King.
With what transporting joy I'd then receive
That dearest man with whom I wish to live.
But oh! the cruel fate of war—

    Paine.—My dear *Clorain*, forbear; we now must
        part.
Adieu, my love—but oh! my bleeding heart.

This said, the tears flow'd from her eyes,
    Her cheeks all pale spread o'er ;
Each other they embrace with sighs,
    'Till they could weep no more.

*   *   *   *   *

Clo.—Farewell, my dear, farewell, dear *Colonel Paine*
Heaven be your guard, while foes around are slain,
Return you safe, where love and freedom reign.
    Paine.—Farewell, my dear *Clorain*, my only fair,
May angels keep you safe from ev'ry snare,
Adieu, my dear, I leave you in their care.

A SHORT REVIEW OF BURGOYNE'S EXPEDITION.

BY ROBERT DINSMORE.*

My faithful friend and uncle, kind,
    I would bring some things to your mind,

---

* Robert Dinsmore, poet, born in Windham, N. H.,
October 7th, 1757; died there March 16th, 1836.
He was of Scotch-Irish descent. At the age of eigh-
teen he enlisted in the Revolutionary Army, and served
at the battle of Saratoga. He became a farmer at
Windham, was a zealous Presbyterian, and used to
make verses on topics arising from personal incidents.
He called himself the "Rustic Bard," and published, in
1828, a volume entitled "Incidental Poems." In his
"Old Portraits and Modern Sketches" Whittier says :
"He lived to a good old age, a home-loving, unpre-
tending farmer, cultivating his acres with his own
horny hands, and cheering the long rainy days and
winter evenings with homely rhyme. He wrote some-
times to amuse his neighbors, often to soothe their sor-

Which still impress'd on mine I find,
  By recollection ;
That seems my heart with yours to bind
  In strong affection.

From my first dawn of life you've known me ;
When Nature on the world had thrown me,
You did a first-born nephew own me,
  Or younger brother ;
And friendship ever since have shown me,
  Kind like my mother.

Childhood and youth, manhood and age,
You've been my friend in every stage ;
Sometimes in sport we would engage,
  Our nerves to try ;
Sometimes t' explore the music page,
  The genius ply.

When British laws would us enthrall,
Our country for defence did call ;
Then martial fire inspir'd us all,
  To arms we flew ;
And as a soldier, stand or fall,
  I went with you !

O'er western hills we travell'd far,
Pass'd Saratoga, the site of war,

---

row under domestic calamity, or to give expression to his own."

The poem here given was written to Deacon Isaac Cochran, of Antrim, N. H., his mother's brother, who was a lieutenant at the taking of General Burgoyne, October 17th, 1777.

Where Burgoyne roll'd his feudal car
    Down Hudson's strand : `
And Gates, our glorious western* star,
    Held high command.

From the green ridge† we glanced our eyes,
Where village flames illum'd the skies.
Destruction there was no surprise,
    On Hudson's shore!
Though smoke in burning pillars rise,
    And cannons roar!

But to Fort Edward we were sent,
Through icy Bartenskiln‡ we went,
And on that plain we pitch'd our tent,
    'Gainst rain and snow ;
Our orders there, was [*sic*] to prevent
    The flying foe.

By counter orders, back we came,
And cross'd the Hudson's rapid stream,
At Schuyler's Mills,§ of no small fame,
    Thence took our post,
Near Burgoyne's line, with fixèd aim
    To take his host!

---

*Gates's home was then in Pennsylvania, at that time considered West.

†Now, the road leading from the village of Quaker Springs to Schuylersville, N. Y. This road was first cut through by Burgoyne to make a path for General Fraser, who led the right wing in its advance south.

‡The Battenkill, which, rising in Vermont, empties into the Hudson, between Fort Miller and Schuylersville.

§The present village of Schuylersville, N. Y.

With courage bold, we took the field,
Our foes no more their swords could wield,
God was our strength, and He our shield,
    A present aid.
Proud Burgoyne's army there did yield,
    All captive made!

Great Britain's honor there was stain'd,
We sang a glorious victory gain'd!
From hence our States a rank obtain'd,
    'Mongst nations great;
Our future glory was ordain'd,
    As sure as fate!

To Windham, back with joy we turn'd,
Where parents dear our absence mourn'd;
And our fair friends in rapture burn'd
    To see our faces!
Sweet pearly drops their cheeks adorn'd
    In our embraces!

When all our vanquish'd foes were fled,
Love, peace and harmony were shed,
Like oil descending on the head,
    Or milk or wine;
Williams,* the man of God, us fed
    With food divine.

O! let not you and I [*sic*] forget
How often we've together met,
Like Heman and Jeduthon,† set
    In God's own house;
And solemnly his table at
    Renew'd our vows!

---

* Rev. Simon Williams.
† The two principal leaders of the singing in the congregation at Windham.

And when the sacred scene was past,
We sang Doxology at last,
To Father, Son, and Holy Ghost,
    United Three!
One God, our souls redeemed last,
    So let it be.

While Reason in her seat remains,
And blood runs streaming in my veins,
Or Memory her power retains,
    I shall review,
And think upon the various scenes
    I've past with you.

FOUR BURGOYNE EPIGRAMS.

I.*

In seventeen hundred and seventy-seven,
General Burgoyne set out for Heaven;
But, as the Yankees would rebel,
He missed his route and went to Hell.

II.

Burgoyne, alas! unknowing future fates,
Could force his way through *woods*, but not through
    Gates.†

---

* My friend, Dr. James D. Butler, formerly of Vermont, but now (1893) of Madison, Wis., sends me the above, which, he writes, was current in Vermont for a long time after the Revolution.

† The author of the above epigram, which was published in 1777, shortly after the battles of Saratoga, was David Edwards. He was born in the city of New York in the spring of 1747, of English parents. His

III.

A CABINET REPARTEE.*

To North the *Lean* said George the Wise,
Here's with *one* Arnold much ado ;

---

father, John Edwards, was a well-known character in
town, where he followed the profession of a "tea-water
man." At the early age of twelve years, David was
apprenticed to Garret Noel, at the Meal Market
Noel was the principal bookseller in the city, and he
afterward transferred young Edwards to Hugh Gaine,
the publisher of the New York *Mercury*, who taught
him the printing business. David became a member
of a secret association called the "Liberty Boys," of
whom Isaac Lean was at the head, and was the
author of most of the political squibs circulated by
them in the city. He was an active participator in
the stamp and tea-act troubles, and was wounded
on January 18th, 1770, in the fray which occurred
between the citizens and soldiers on Golden Hill (John
Street, between Gold and Cliff streets), since known as
the " Battle of Golden Hill," and which action, instead
of that at Lexington, caused the first bloodshed in the
war of the American Revolution. He remained in
the city until its occupation by the British, in 1776,
when he went with his employer to Newark, and
remained there a week, during which time Gaine made
his terms with Howe, and returned to New York and
became a rank Tory. David, however, refused to ac-
company him, and, going to Trenton, was at once em-
ployed by Isaac Collins, the printer of the New Jersey
Gazette, in whose employ he continued until the close
of the war. In 1784 he returned to New York and

The drowsy Premier, starting, cries,
    'Tis well, my liege, there are not *two !*

.IV.

OUR COMMANDERS.†

GAGE nothing did, and went to pot ;
Howe lost one town, another got ;
Guy ‡ nothing lost, and nothing won ;
Dunmore was homewards forced to run ;
Clinton was beat, and got a garter,
And bouncing Burgoyne catch'd a Tartar;
Thus all we gain for millions spent
Is to be laugh'd at, and repent.

---

worked for Samuel London until his death, which occur-
red in 1794. The greater part of the poetical effusions
which appeared in Collins's paper were attributed to
Edwards. For a portion of the above sketch I am in-
debted to Albert J. Disney, in the *Historical Maga-
zine,* Vol. III., page 350.

Another version of the authorship of the verses—
doubtless without foundation—is that it was composed
by a student at the Westminster School, who wrote it
in Latin as an epigrammatic couplet upon the subject
" Saratoga"—that being the word selected for the day's
exercises. So at least says the " Chaplet of Comus."

* Epigram from the New York *Public Advertiser* of
December 5th, 1777. Walpole, in his " Last Journals,"
II., page 159, says that it was written by Arnold him-
self, as a parody of one of Burgoyne's manifestoes.

† This epigram is from the London *Evening Post.*

‡ Sir Guy Carleton, by far the ablest general and
most humane officer that England ever sent out to the
colonies.

THE HALCYON DAYS OF OLD ENGLAND;

OR,

WISDOM OF ADMINISTRATION DEMON-STRATED.*

(*To the tune of " Ye Medley of Mortals.*")

GIVE ear to my song, I'll now tell you a story,
This is the bright era of Old England's glory ;
And though some may think us in pitiful plight,
I'll swear they're mistaken, for matters go right !
    Sing tantarara, wise all, wise all,
    Sing tantarara, wise all.

Let us laugh at the cavils of weak silly elves !
Our statesmen are wise men !—they say so them-
    selves !
And though little mortals may hear it with wonder,
'Tis consummate wisdom that causes each blunder !
    Sing tantarara, etc.

---

* On December 2d, 1777, an express arrived in London from Carleton saying that he had learned by deserters and believed that the Provincials had taken Burgoyne and his whole army prisoners. On the 15th this unwelcome news was confirmed by Captain Craig, as Walpole writes, "after great slaughter and desertion of the Germans." This charge against Burgoyne's German allies is in the highest degree unjust, since, had it not been for them, it is exceedingly doubtful if Burgoyne would have had any army to surrender. The Brunswickers, under the brave Riedesel, prevented the utter rout of Burgoyne on September 19th, and saved his army from annihilation on October 7th. At the end of December Walpole wrote and published the above ballad. Walpole's " Last Journals," Vol. II., page 187.

They now are conducting a glorious war !
(It began about tea, about feathers, and tar !)
With spirit they pushed what they planned with sense !
Forty millions they've spent for a tax of three pence !
            Sing tantarara, etc.

The debts of the nation do grieve them so sore,
To lighten our burden—they load us the more !
They aim at the American cash, my dear honey !
Yet beggar this kingdom and send them the money.
            Sing tantarara, etc.

What honors we're gaining by taking their forts,
Destroying bateaux and blocking up ports ;
Burgoyne would have worked them—but for a mishap,
By Gates and one Arnold he's caught in a trap !
            Sing tantarara, etc.

But Howe was more cautious and prudent by far,
He sailed with his fleet up the great Delaware ;
All summer he struggled and strove to undo them,
But the plague of it was that he could not get to them.
            Sing tantarara, etc.

Oh, think us not cruel because our allies
Are savagely scalping men, women, and boys !
Natural affection to this step doth move us—
The more they are scalped, the more they will love us !
            Sing tantarara, etc.

Some folks are uneasy and make a great pother,
For the loss of one army and half of another ;
But, sirs, next campaign by ten thousands we'll slay
            them,
If we can but find soldiers and money to pay them !
            Sing tantarara, etc.

I've sung you my song, now I'll give you a pray'r :
May peace soon succeed to this horrible war !
Again may we live with our brethren in concord !
And the authors of mischief all hang in a strong cord !

   Sing tantarara, etc.

TWO BURGOYNE DITTIES.

I.

FATHER and I went down to camp,
 Along with Captain Goodwin ;
There we saw the men and boys
 As thick as hasty pudding.
And there we saw a deucéd gun,
 As big as tree of maple,
'Twas on a deucéd little cart,
 A load for father's cattle !

II.*

John Burgine's a mighty big man.
" Give me five thousand men," says he,
" And I'll clean out the rebel clan ;
Give me five thousand men," says he,

---

* Mr. Jared C. Markham, in sending me the above
ditty, writes as follows : " The enclosed verses, as near
as I can remember, were those that my grandfather,
Asa Markham, used to sing to me when I was a
child, sixty years ago. Asa Markham, a great-grandson
of Daniel Markham, who was the first of the family to
come to the colonies, in 1666. Daniel Markham was
an own cousin to Major William Markham, the father
of William Markham, who was archbishop of York,
and one of the private council of George III. (p. 3), at

" And we'll march the country through.
The rebels are cowards, you'll see,
The people are loyal and true."
The men are raised, and on comes John,
With red-coats and Hessians in plenty.
The Tories and Indians fall in
In regiments and battalion,
And 'mong them was seen grim Gov'nor Skene*
Upon his old blundering stallion.
But let them all j'ine and come on,
With all their big lords and ladies,
And all their gew-gaws and laces,
All got with their taxes on tea,
And everything else they can see.
Of the tax we won't pay a penny.
We ask no " protection" of George,
And of John we do not expect any,
With all his grand proclamations!

---

the time of the American Revolution. So, while
the archbishop was luxuriating at the British court,
and encouraging by his advice his king to war upon
the colonies, his second cousin was enjoying the
freedom of colonial rebellion and revolution. Again,
a great-grandson of the archbishop, Clements R.
Markham, is now the secretary of the Royal Geo-
graphical Society in London, while, on this side, in
the United States, the present writer is the architect
of the Saratoga Monument—a structure which com-
memorates the surrender of Burgoyne—an event
which was the turning-point of the Revolution."

   * Governor Skene was always during the Revo-
lution a *bête noir*. To him were ascribed by the
settlers many of the annoyances and troubles of the
day. Hence this allusion.

Of pardon and fine " protection,"
He's 'listed the whole Six Nations
To bring us into subjection.
But let the poor devils come on,
The Indians and Tories and John,
We'll learn them a trick they don't know !

AN OLD VERSE.

THE following specimen of ingenious versification
was published in a Philadelphia paper while the fate
of Burgoyne was in doubt. It may be read three dif-
ferent ways : First, let the whole be read in the order
in which i was written ; second, read the lines down-
ward on the left of each comma in every line ; third,
in the same manner on the right of each comma. In
the first reading the Revolutionary cause is condemned,
and by the others it is encouraged and lauded.

Hark ! hark ! the trumpet sounds, the din of war's
      alarms,
O'er seas and solid grounds, doth call us all to arms ;
Who for King George doth stand, their honors soon
      shall shine ;
Their ruin is at hand, who with the congress join.
The acts of parliament, in them I much delight,
I hate their cursed intent, who for the congress fight ;
The Tories of to-day, they are my daily toast,
They soon will sneak away, who independence boast ;
Who non-resistance hold, they have my hand and heart,
May they for slaves be sold, who act a Whiggish part ;
On Mansfield, North and Bute, may daily blessings
      pour,
Confusion and dispute, on congress evermore,
To North and British lord, may honors still be done,
I wish a block or cord, to Gen. Washington.

EPITAPH

On two American officers who were killed and scalped
by the Indians in the employ of the British at Isle aux
Noix, where the tombstone is still to be seen :

" Sons of America, rest in quiet here,
  Britannia, blush, Burgoyne, let fall a tear ;
  And tremble, Europe, sons with savage case [*sic*],
  Death and Revenge await you with disgrace."

MERZ KATER.

[A BURLESQUE song and popular air, which the
Brunswick officers (captured at Saratoga), in their
quarters at Bethlehem, Pa., in 1779, used to sing :]

" IST es nicht ein rechter Scherz
  Wenn ein Kater in den Merz
  Auf den Dash, ruft seiner Frau
  Und beshudz schreyt Mi-au !" *

* This first stanza is the only one preserved in the
traditions of the captive "Convention troops," still
preserved among the old inhabitants of Bethlehem, Pa.

TRANSLATION.

" Is it not a rare delight,
  When a tom-cat in the night,
  On the roof tree makes his bow,
  Calling to his wife, Mi-au !"

ANECDOTE.

In August of 1777, and for a period of ten months
thereafter, the minister's house of the Lebanon, Pa.,
Moravian congregation was the abode of Hessian pris-

TO THE RELICS OF MY BRITISH GREN-
ADIER.

By E. W. B. Canning.*

I HAVE in my possession a portion of the skeleton of
a British officer of the grenadiers, who was killed in

---

oners. The pastor of the congregation has made the
following entry in his diary, under date of February
4th, 1778:

"To-day a rifleman from Ausbach and a corporal
visited me. They related that recently General Howe
had written a letter to Washington, containing merely
a transcript of chapter 7 of the prophet Ezekiel, and
that Washington had replied by an epistle embodying
chapter 4 of the Book of Baruch."

Communicated to the author by Mr. John W. Jor-
dan, of Philadelphia, Pa.

* Edward W. B. Canning, poet and author, was
born in Gill, Mass., November 8th, 1813; and after
graduating from Williams College he taught school
in Western Virginia, but removed to Stockbridge,
where he became principal of the Williams Academy.
In 1854 he founded a family school, which he
continued until 1858. He always took great inter-
est in anything pertaining to our Revolutionary his-
tory, especially that relating to our border warfare.
He was mainly instrumental in having placed the
unique memorial to the Stockbridge Indians in the
naval cemetery of Stockbridge, and also in procuring
the erection of the monument which now (1893) marks
the site of the fall of Colonel Ephraim Williams (the
founder of Williams College) at the battle of Lake
George, September, 1755; and Mr. Canning's name is

the battle of October 5th, 1777, which was accidentally
exhumed in the spring of 1852.   The skull has a per-
foration through the right temple, and the bullet that
made it was found inside.   A portion of his uniform
coat bears the color and texture of the cloth and two
heavily gold-plated buttons, after a burial of seventy-
five years.—*Canning.*

> Strange bivouac, old Grenadier,
> Thou in my quiet study here,
>   Hast found at last;
> While I, who life's campaign began
> When thou for forty years hadst done,
>   Patrol the past.
>
> O had your hollow skull a brain,
> Your bony mouth a tongue again,
>   I know full well
> In *why's* and *when's* and *how's* you'd find
> A Yankee of the bluest kind
>   Your sentinel.

very appropriately inscribed on the monument as one
of the originators of that tribute to a most distin-
guished man in colonial times.   He was also, until his
death, a valued trustee of the Saratoga Monument
Association, and until a few years since—when his
many engagements forced him to resign—its corre-
sponding secretary.   During the time that Mr. Canning
held the position of deputy naval officer of the port
of New York, it was the writer's good fortune to be
associated with him; during all of which time he was
constantly struck with his loving graciousness of
manner, which, combined with rare dignity and ex-
ecutive ability, made him not only respected but
revered.   He died August 12th, 1890.

I *guess* for many an hour we'd join
In talk about Sir John Burgoyne,
      And the " whole boodle,"
Who 'gan their game of brag in June,
But on one bright October noon
Laid pride and arms down to the tune
      Of " Yankee Doodle."

Just as old Dido ached of old
To be by brave Æneas told
      Quantus Achilles—
Quales"—but I can't write it all—
So I am prurient to recall
How once our fathers pounded small
      King George's follies.

I long for more about that day
When Rebels met in grim array
      The Regulars:
When trumpet clang and plunging shot
And shouting made the battle hot
      About their ears.

When Dearborn,* Poor,† and Paterson,‡

---

* Major-General Henry Dearborn, born in North
Hampton, N. H., February 23d, 1751; died in Rox-
bury, Mass., June 6th, 1829. He served with bravery
at the battles of Bunker Hill (where he caused the
retreat) and Saratoga, and accompanied Arnold in his
expedition to Canada in 1775. He was appointed by
Jefferson Secretary of War—an office he held from
1793 to 1797. He was appointed senior major-
general in the United States Army January 27th,
1812, and assigned to the command of the Northern
Department. He published an account of the battle

And Cilley, Brooks* and Livingston,
    With hearts of steel,
Met Phillips, Fraser, Hamilton,
Rolling the tide of slaughter on,
    And made them reel.

When Morgan and his riflemen
" Bearded the lion in his den,"
    And signed his name ;
While Arnold—battle's thunderbolt—
Flashed, like a comet on a colt,
    About the plain—

I'd ask what gallant Fraser said,
When bullet from the tree-top sped,

---

of Bunker Hill and wrote a journal of his expedition
to Canada. He was also a minister to Portugal from
1822 to 1824. Fort Dearborn (the site of Chicago,
Ill.) was named after him.

† General Enoch Poor, born in Andover, Mass.,
June 21st, 1736, died near Hackensack, N. J., Septem-
ber 8th, 1780. He served with great distinction
till near the close of the Revolutionary War ; and in
announcing his death, General Washington declared
him to be " an officer of distinguished merit, who as a
citizen and a soldier had every claim to the esteem of
his country."

‡ Major-General John Paterson, distinguished for
bravery and patriotism during Daniel Shays's Rebellion
in 1786, he commanded a detachment of Berkshire
militia that was ordered out to suppress the rising.
M. C. during 1803 to 1805.

* Afterward governor of Massachusetts.

Its work had done:
How stout old Earl Balcarras tore,
When Yankees "true to Freedom swore"
      His twelve pound gun.

How many inches on that day
The visage of Burgoyne, I pray,
      A lengthening went?
Didst hear him say—as once before—
That with ten thousand men—no more—
He'd conquering walk from shore to shore
      The continent?

But I forget, old Grenadier,
You never lived yourself, to hear
      What others said:
A luckless missile found you out,
And, killing instantly no doubt,
      It bored your head.

For seventy-five long years, old brave,
You occupied your shallow grave—
      No gun to stir;
At length by plough and not by drum
Disturbed your huge wreck has become
      My prisoner.

And now I'll keep you guarding there
All of your coat the mould could spare,
      And darkling worm;
With the gashed ball by which you died,
And buttons, too, that lit with pride
      Your uniform.

To those infused with martial leaven,
Of Bemus's Heights in '77

You'll tell for long;
Aye—and perchance some bard may troll
From out that ragged bullet hole,
Another song.

BURGOYNE'S DEFEAT.

An Ancient Ditty.

Come, all you valiant soldiers that's courage stout
and bold,
Who scorn as long as life doth last, ever to be con-
troll'd;
Come listen to my ditty, and the truth to you I'll tell,
Concerning many a soldier, who for his country fell.

Brave General Burgoyne from Canada set sail,
'Twas with eight thousand regulars, he thought would
never fail;
With Hessians, Canadians and Tories, as we hear,
Beside a fleet of shipping, o'er Lake Champlain did
steer.

Before Ticonderoga, the first day of July,
Their fleet and army did appear, and we did them
espy;
Their motions we observed full well both night and
day,
And our brave boys prepared all for the bloody fray.

Our garrison they viewed, and soon their troops did
land;
When General St. Clair, he came to understand,
That the great Mount Defiance they soon would
fortify,
He found that he must quit his lines, or every man
must die.

July the fourth we had orders to retreat,
And the next morning left our fort, Burgoyne he tho't
     us beat;
So closely they pursued us, 'twas nigh to Hubbarton;
Our rear guard they'd defeated, they tho't they'd
     gain'd renown.

And when our congress came to hear that we our
     lines had left,
And had retreated near to Albany to rest,
Brave Gen. Gates they sent us our country to relieve,
With shouts of acclamation of joy we him receiv'd.

Burgoyne sent out a party of fifteen hundred men,
Of Hessians and Canadians, came near to Benning-
     ton,
With savages and Tories, our cattle for to steal,
Commanded by a Tory, they call'd him Col. Skein.

And when brave Gates came to hear of Col. Skein's
     conduct,
Sent out a small party, his march for to obstruct;
They took all his artillery, and Skein his flight may
     mourn,
'Twas out of fifteen hundred men but four hundred
     return'd.

And when Burgoyne he came to hear that Skein did
     not succeed,
With his army and artillery Burgoyne he did proceed,
Thinking therefore to frighten us and make us fly;
But soon he found out his mistake, he found we'd
     sooner die.

July the fourteenth, that morning being clear,
Brave Gates unto his men did say, my boys be of
     good cheer,

For Burgoyne, my lads, is advancing, and we will
    never fly,
To maintain our country's rights, we'll fight until we
    die.

And soon the news was brought us their army, it
    was near;
And then, my boys, we met them, 'twas without dread
    or fear,
And 'twas nigh unto Stillwater, and there about
    noon-day,
And quick as you shall hear, my boys, began the
    bloody fray.

We fought them full six hours, like valiant hearts of
    gold,
Each party scorning to give way, we fought like lions
    bold,
Until the leaves with blood are stained; our generals
    they did cry;
It's diamonds cut diamonds, we'll fight until we die.

Night came on, from our lines we did retreat,
Which made the Britons for to think our army it was
    beat;
But early the next morning, we held before their eyes,
As ready to engage again, which did them much
    surprise.

Of fighting they seemed tired, to work they then
    did go,
In burying of their dead men, entrenchments up did
    throw;
Thinking therefore with shot and shell our army to
    destroy,
But brave Gates he gave such orders, he did them
    all defy!

At length our gracious Lord inspired our noble
      Gates' mind,
To send out Gen. Arnold,* to see if he could find

---

* A bitter controversy has been carried on for the
last few years as to whether General Arnold was
an actual participant in the battle of September
19th. After carefully weighing the arguments brought
forward on both sides, I believe this to be the fact—
viz., that while Arnold may not have been during
the action itself actually on the battle-field in person
(though this, even, is by no means proved), yet he was
during the entire action close at hand, superintending
and directing, under his own immediate eye, every
manœuvre of the different regiments, thus causing
them to act as one harmonious whole. Hence, that
in this sense he was a virtual and an active partici-
pant in the battle of the 19th admits of no manner
of doubt. Wilkinson, the only original authority on the
American side who deprives Arnold of the credit of
the success of the action, and who was, also, doubtless,
the " informant" of Gordon & Marshall, is *entirely
worthless and unreliable* in all his statements whenever
his jealousy (as in this case) is aroused, and hence
should not for a moment be believed in this matter
against the concurrent testimony of many of the
survivors of that action, who, after death, left on record
the statement that Arnold was an active participant
in the battle. Among these is an order of General
Riedesel, first given to the public in Hadden's
" Journal and Orderly Book" (edited by General
Rogers), upon which the editor comments as fol-
lows : " Now, how Arnold could have observed these
things on the part of his troops when, according to
Wilkinson, he was 'calmly sitting on his horse a mile

A passage thro' the enemy, and make them for to flee :
Which quickly he obtained, and set his country free.

---

and a half away from the action, it is very difficult to
understand !' " Steadman, a most reliable authority
also, states the fact that Arnold was in the action.
But besides all this, the following, from an Orderly
Book kept by Colonel Thaddeus Cook, of Walling-
ford, Conn., now in possession of the American Anti-
quarian Society of Worcester, Mass., should set the
matter beyond all doubt, even to professional carpers
and cavillers. Here it is :

"Division Orders, 20th Sept., A.D. 1777. Genl.
Arnold returns his thanks to the officers and soldiers
of his division for their brave, spirited conduct yester-
day, in withstanding the force of the whole British
Army, whose loss a Deserter from their army says is
upward of one thousand men killed and wounded—
while ours is very trifling, not one fourth Part of the
enemies—a convincing proof of the mercifull Inter-
position of Heaven in covering our heads in the day
of Battle, and loudly calls for our gratefull acknowledge-
ments.

"The Genl. observed yesterday that two many offi-
cers that zeal and spirit pushed on in the front of
their companies, whose business it was to have brought
up those in the rear, and hopes they will in future ob-
serve their proper stations and suffer no man to retreat
until an order is given by the Commanding Officer of
the Regts. on Detachments—those who are found to
have deserted their posts in time of Action may ex-
pect Instant Death.—

"The Genl. makes no doubt the Troops will act with
a spirit and firmness becoming free men strugling for
their just Rights and Liberties when they are called out

And burning all their baggage, made off with haste
    and fear,
And up to Saratoga, Burgoyne himself did steer;
Brave Gates, our bold commander, he after him did
    fly,
Resolving for to take them all or every man must
    die.

And soon we overtook them, it was nigh to Saratoga,
A burning all the buildings as they went on the road.
'Twas the 17th of October, they were obliged to
    capitulate,
Burgoyne and his army, our prisoners they were
    made.

Now to conclude my ditty, my song is at an end;
I hope no brave American will slight what I have
    penn'd,
For our cause is just, in God we trust, therefore, my
    boys, don't fear,
For brave Gates will clear America in less than one
    more year.

Now here's a health to congress, and our commander
    Gates,
To officers and soldiers, whom all the Tories hate,
God prosper and succeed them, it's both by land and
    sea,
Success to the brave Americans and sons of liberty.

---

again, which they may expect every moment, and
wishes them to make every necessary preparation."

    Now, how, in the face of this order, any one can say
that Arnold was not an active participator in the action
of the 19th passes comprehension.

THE NORTH CAMPAIGN.*

A Song of Saratoga.

Come unto me, ye heroes,
    Whose hearts are true and bold,
Who value more your honor
    Than others do their gold ;
Give ear unto my story,
    And I the truth will tell
Concerning many a soldier
    Who for his country fell.

Burgoyne, the king's commander,
    From Canada set sail
With full eight thousand reg'lars,
    He thought he could not fail ;
With Indians and Canadians,
    And his cursed tory crew,
On board his fleet of shipping
    He up the Champlain flew.

Before Ticonderoga,
    The first day of July,
Appear'd his ships and army,
    And we did them espy.

---

* This ballad was known during the Revolution as
" The North Campaign," " Gates's Song," and "A Song
for the Red-coats," and was for a long period sung
throughout New England. It has been attributed to
a private in Colonel Brooks's regiment and also to
the author of "American Taxation." A portion of it is
changed somewhat by the " *wagoner*" of Dr. Dwight's
story. It would seem, however, that this is a mere
paraphrase of "An Ancient Ditty," also published in
this connection, though under a different title.

Their motions we observed
    Full well both night and day,
And our brave boys prepared
    To have a bloody fray.

Our garrison they viewed them,
    As straight their troops did land,
And when St. Clair, our chieftain,
    The fact did understand
That they the Mount Defiance
    Were bent to fortify,
He found we must surrender,
    Or else prepare to die.

The fifth day of July, then,
    He order'd a retreat,*

---

* The semi-criticism here is most just. St. Clair, although a true patriot, erred most amazingly in not having Mount Defiance, or Sugar-Loaf Hill—as it was also called, from its resemblance to the old-fashioned loaves of sugar—fortified. Especially, too, was he greatly blameworthy from the fact that the great importance of fortifying it had been long previously pointed out. Originally it had been supposed, and, in fact, had been taken for granted, that the crest of Sugar-Loaf Hill was not only inaccessible, but too distant to be of any avail in covering the main fortress—*i. e.*, Fort Ticonderoga. This opinion was, as said, an error, to which the attention of the officers stationed at Ticonderoga had been called the preceding year by Colonel John Trumbull, then adjutant-general for the Northern Department. When Colonel Trumbull made the suggestion, he was laughed at by the mess; but he soon proved the accuracy of his own vision by throwing a cannon-shot to the summit, and subsequently

And when next morn we started,
  Burgoyne thought we were beat.
And closely he pursued us,
  Till when near Hubbardton,
Our rear guards were defeated,
  He thought the country won.

And when it was told in Congress,
  That we our forts had left,
To Albany retreated,
  Of all the North bereft,
Brave General Gates they sent us,
  Our fortunes to retrieve,
And him with shouts of gladness
  The army did receive.*

---

clambered to the top, dragging a cannon after him,
accompanied by Colonels Stevens, Wane, and Arnold.
It was, in fact, a criminal neglect on the part of St.
Clair, that the oversight was not at once corrected by
the construction of a work upon that point, which
would have commanded both the whole post and the
surrounding country. St. Clair was tried afterward
by a court-martial for evacuating Ticonderoga, but he
was acquitted more on account of his tried   iotism
than of his skilful management.   Schuyle , also, had
seen the necessity of occupying M ur. ͞ fiance, and
had urgently requested from Congress re-enforcements
for that purpose.—*Conversations of the Author's
Father with Colonel John Trumbull.*
  * In allusion to the fact that General Schuyler was
most unjustly held in great odium by the New
England troops—a fact which was the cause of his
being superseded by Gates in the command, leaving
Gates to reap the fruits of what Schuyler had, by his

Where first the Mohawk's waters
  Do in the sunshine play,
For Herkimer's brave soldiers
  Sellinger* ambush'd lay :
And them he there defeated,
  But soon he had his due,
And scared† by Brooks and Arnold
  He to the North withdrew.

To take the stores and cattle
  That we had gathered then,
Burgoyne sent a detachment
  Of fifteen hundred men ;

---

wonderful generalship, sown. The cause is not far to
seek. Schuyler was a *strict* disciplinarian, and per-
haps a little too autocratic and unapproachable by his
privates. This manner the New Englanders greatly
resented ; and in Gates, who, for motives of his own—
which were to supplant even Washington himself—they
found a person to listen to all their grievances. Hence
Schuyler was most *unjustly* superseded, chiefly by
the contemptible jealousy of Adams and other New
Englanders in Congress. The same feeling of New
England jealousy against the soldiers of New York
and the South had, however, found expression years
before during the campaign, in 1755, of Sir William
Johnson against Dieskau. This contemptible jealousy
had then been very nearly the cause of defeat.

  * St. Leger.
  † A man employed by the British as a spy was
taken by Arnold, and at the suggestion of Colonel
Brooks sent back to St. Leger with such deceptive
accounts of the strength of the Americans as induced
him to retreat toward Montreal.

By Baum they were commanded,
　To Bennington they went;
To plunder and to murder
　Was fully their intent.

But little did they know then
　With whom they had to deal;
It was not quite so easy
　Our stores and stock to steal;
Bold Stark would give them only
　A portion of his *lead :*
With half his crew ere sunset
　Baum lay among the dead.

The nineteenth of September,
　The morning cool and clear,
Brave Gates rode through our army,
　Each soldier's heart to cheer:
" Burgoyne," he cried, " advances,
　But we will never fly ;
No—rather than surrender,
　We'll fight him till we die."

The news was quickly brought us,
　The enemy was near,
And all along our lines then
　There was no sign of fear;
It was above Stillwater
　We met at noon that day,
And every one expected
　To see a bloody fray.

Six hours the battle lasted,
　Each heart was true as gold,
The British fought like lions,
　And we like Yankees bold ;

The leaves with blood were crimson,
    And then brave Gates did cry—
"'Tis diamond now cut diamond!
    We'll beat them, boys, or die."*

The darkness soon approaching,
    It forced us to retreat
Into our lines till morning,
    Which made them think us beat;
But ere the sun was risen,
    They saw before their eyes
Us ready to engage them,
    Which did them much surprise.

Of fighting they seem'd weary,
    Therefore to work they go
Their thousand dead to bury,
    And breastworks up to throw:
With grape and bombs intending
    Our army to destroy,
Or from our works our forces
    By stratagem decoy.

The seventh day of October
    The British tried again,
Shells from their cannon throwing,
    Which fell on us like rain,
To drive us from our stations
    That they might thus retreat;
For now Burgoyne saw plainly
    He never us could beat.

---

* This of course is "bosh," or, perhaps, we may charitably call it "poetical license," as Gates acted in both actions the roll of a coward. See my "Burgoyne's Campaign."

But vain was his endeavor
    Our men to terrify;
Though death was all around us,
    Not one of us would fly.
But when an hour we'd fought them,
    And they began to yield,
Along our lines the cry ran,
    "The *next* blow wins the field."

Great God who won their battles,
    Whose cause is just and true,
Inspired our bold commander
    The course he should pursue.
He order'd Arnold forward,
    And Brooks* to follow on;
The enemy were routed,
    Our liberty was won!

Then, burning all their luggage,
    They fled with haste and fear,
Burgoyne with all his forces
    To Saratogue did steer;
And Gates our brave commander,
    Soon after him did hie,
Resolving he would take them
    Or in the effort die.

---

*John Brooks, governor of Massachusetts, born in Medford, Mass., May 31st, 1752; died March 1st, 1825. He assisted in fortifying Breed's Hill. In the second battle of Saratoga, on October 7th, he stormed and carried the German intrenchments at the head of his regiment. He greatly assisted Baron Steuben in his tactics, and was a very valued officer of the Revolution.

As we came nigh the village,
  We overtook the foe;
They'd burned each house to ashes,
  Like all where'er they go.
The seventeenth of October,
  They did capitulate;
Burgoyne and his proud army
  Did we our pris'ners make.

Now here's a health to Arnold,
  And our commander Gates;
To Lincoln* and to Washington,
  Whom ev'ry Tory hates;
Likewise unto our Congress,
  God grant it long to reign,
Our Country, Right and Justice
  For ever to maintain.

Now finish'd is my story,
  My song is at end;
The freedom we're enjoying
  We're ready to defend;
For while our cause is righteous,
  Heaven nerves the soldier's arm,
And vain is their endeavor
  Who strive to do us harm.

THE CARPET KNIGHT.

By Joseph Stansbury.†

LATE a council of gods from their heavenly abodes
  Were call'd on Olympus to meet;

---

* General Lincoln behaved bravely in this battle;
and to him is due the credit of creating a diversion in
favor of Gates by his assault on Ticonderoga.

†Joseph Stansbury, merchant, born in England in

Jove gave his commands from his throne in the
　　clouds :
　　Attend, and his words I'll repeat.
Ye know, all ye pow'rs that attend my high throne,
　　Your will to my pleasure must bow ;
I will that those gifts which you prize as your own
　　Shall now be bestowed on my *Howe.*

Astræa, who long since had quitted the earth,
　　Presented her balance and sword ;
The honors derived from titles and birth
　　By *Juno* were instant conferred ;

1750 ; died in New York City in 1809.　Emigrating
to Philadelphia, he became an importing merchant, and
held a high position as a man of integrity and an up-
right and high-minded citizen.　In 1776 he was im-
prisoned in Burlington, N. J., for having sung in his
house " God Save the King."　He was again, in 1780,
imprisoned by the Whigs in Philadelphia.　Upon his
liberation his property was restored, and with his family
he resided in New York during the remainder of the
war, but returned to Philadelphia in 1785, after a brief
residence in Nova Scotia.　Threatened again in that city
with violence, he gave up his former occupation and,
removing to New York, became secretary of an insur-
ance company.　He wrote in support of the crown,
and his verses were edited by Winthrop Sargent,
under the title of " Stansbury's and Odell's Loyal
Verses" (Munsell, Albany, 1860)—verses which at the
time they were first written obtained considerable
popularity among the adherents of the crown.　The
date of this song, says Mr. Sargent, seems to be De-
cember 24th, 1777, shortly after Howe's return to
Philadelphia, from his idle attempt to surprise Wash-
ington's army at Whitemarsh.

Fierce *Mars* gave his chariot; gay *Hermes* his wand;
　Alcides, his club and his bow;
Sweet *Peace* with her olive-branch graced his hand;
　And *Venus* herself did bestow.

Thus enrich'd with such gifts as the gods can impart
　The hero by *Jove* was address'd;
As you wish to reclaim each American heart,
　Let justice preside in your breast;
Exhibit the blessings of order and peace
　As wide as your conquests shall spread;
Let your promise be sacred—rebellion shall cease,
　And the laurel shall bloom round your head.

I know that fell *Discord*, your zeal to oppose,
　Will nourish Sedition and Hate;
Mistakes may occur, and friends suffer with foes;
　Yet your wish is confirmed by fate.
Sweet Peace shall revive from the horrors of war,
　Her empire again be restor'd;
Affection and duty shall cover each scar,
　And *Howe* by the world be ador'd!

Now with shame must the muse the sad sequel display;
　With sorrow, and shame, and surprise:
The gifts of *Astræa* he lost by the way,
　And her fillet he plac'd o'er his eyes.
The arms of *Alcides* he sent to Burgoyne,
　And with them the chariot of *Mars;*
For what but assistance and weapons divine
　Could finish such Quixotic wars?

Hermes' wand was now useless; no snakes would
　unite;*

---

* Perhaps in allusion to the broken snake, with the
motto "Unite or die," so much in vogue at the time

The olive in vain was display'd ;
For blessings no longer attended the fight,
And loyalty fled from its shade.

---

as a patriotic device.   John Holt, editor of the New
York *Journal or General Advertiser*, a stanch friend
of the Whigs in 1774, discarded the king's arms from
the title of his paper, and substituted in place of it a
serpent, cut in pieces, with the expressive motto,
" Unite or die."   In January, 1775, the snake was
united and coiled, with the tail in his mouth, forming a
double ring.   On the body of the snake, beginning at
the head, were the following lines :

> " United now, alive and free,
>   Firm on this basis Liberty shall stand ;
>   And thus supported ever bless our land
> Till time becomes eternity."

The designs both of 1774 and 1775 were excellent
—the first, by a visible illustration, showing the dis-
jointed state of the colonies, and the second present-
ing an emblem of their strength when united.   Holt
maintained his integrity to the last.   When the British
took possession of New York, he removed to Æsopus
(now Kingston, N. Y.) and revived his paper.   On the
burning of that village by the British, in 1777, he re-
moved to Poughkeepsie, and published the journal
there until the peace of 1783, when he returned to New
York.   Holt was an unflinching patriot—very dif-
ferent in this respect from his contemporary editor,
James Rivington, who turned his coat to suit every
change of mind, but did not long survive the achieve-
ment of his country's freedom, having fallen a victim
to the yellow fever in 1798.

The gifts sent to Burgoyne return'd to the skies—
Despairing he yielded his arms;
And fair *Venus*, disgusted, beheld with surprise
A mortal preferr'd to her charms.*

THE CHURCH AND KING CLUB.†

By Joseph Stansbury.

Come, honest Tories, a truce with your politics;
  Hoc age tells you in Latin as much;
Drink and be merry and—*à melancholy, nix!*
'Tis de same ting, do I speaks it in Dutch.

---

* The mortal whose charms were preferred, according to the song, to those of Venus herself, was probably a married lady from Jamaica Plains, near Boston, who is named in the same connection, but in rather broader phrase, by Francis Hopkinson, in his "Battle of the Kegs."

† Written by Stansbury, apparently in the latter part of 1778, for a festive meeting of a loyal association. Such associations as the Church and King Club, says Mr. Sargent, were not of unusual occurrence with the Loyalists. They were generally designed to bring together at the festive board a party of men whose political sentiments were in unison—similar, in fact, to the Union League Club (Republican) and the Manhattan (Democratic) of New York City. In this instance, the members were probably Philadelphians, who had followed the royal standard to New York. The phrase, "'Tis all the same in Dutch," was probably a local expression arising from the numbers of German settlers in Pennsylvania.

If old Diogenes lov'd altercation,
   Had he, sir, a drop of good wine in his tub?
Mirth and good humor is *our* occupation;
   Let this be the rule of the Church and King Club.

Well do we know the Adelphi's miscarriages,
   And the disasters of Johnny Burgoyne;
As to beefsteaks, no good fellow disparages
   One who in *battles* finds *leisure to dine.**

Congo pretends (O good Lord, what a fibber 'tis!)
   Now to *feel bold*, and to fear no mischance;
As well might he say that he fights *for their liberties*
   Whom he hath sold in a *mortgage* to France !†

---

  * This is undoubtedly in allusion both to Burgoyne supping merrily with his mistress just before his surrender and while his army were in great distress for food (see Stone's " Memoirs of Mrs. General Riedesel," Munsell, Albany, N. Y.), and to his dinner with General Gates immediately after the capitulation.

  † It was frequently declared at this period by the advocates of England that the American Congress had given secretly some sort of a lien upon a part of the American territories to France, as a security for the assistance afforded us by that power. There was probably no truth in this report, though this cannot be said positively, in view of the fact that documents are yet unquestionably to be discovered in the French archives. The exultations of the Americans, and of Congress in particular, were, however, naturally and justifiably, as after events proved, very great at the prospects of the results to flow from the alliance with France whicht he Confederation had now entered into. The first anniversary of the day on which the treaty was signed was celebrated by a banquet given by Congress

Soon shall you see a *rebellious minority*
  Blush for the part they have acted so long;
Britain shall rouse and regain her authority;
  Come then, a bumper and call t'other song.

If old Diogenes lov'd altercation, etc.

SATIRICAL VERSES IN HONOR OF SIR JOHN BURGOYNE.*

PATENTE DE LORD-DUC POUR JOHN BURGOYNE.

Nous, le Parlement d'Angleterre,
Souverain par mer and par terre
D'Empereurs, Rois and Potentats,
Corsaires, insulaires, and soubas,
A tous Rois, Etats monarchiques
Margraves, Electeurs, Républiques

---

to the French minister, at which the King and Queen of France, the King of Spain and all the princes of the House of Bourbon were formally toasted amid salvos of artillery. On May 8th, 1778, Congress had issued an address to the people, in which the certainty of victory over England was proclaimed, and a vivid picture given of the prosperity which would then attend the destinies of the United States—a picture, as the result proved, not overdrawn.

* Extract from "Correspondance secrete politique et littéraire ou mémoires pour servir à l'histoire des cours, des sociétés et de la littérature en France, depuis la mort de Louis XV. Tome Cinquième, pp. 51–53.

This work, "Correspondance secrete," according to Barbier, "Dictionnaire des ouvrages anonymes," was edited by Métra and others.

Salut N'ayant rien plus à cœur
Que de combler de biens, d'honneur,
Tous ceux qui par action belle,
Se couvrent de gloire immortelle,
Ayant à toutes bonnes fins
Examiné tous les bultins
Qui sont venus de l'Amérique
Et autres lieux rimans en *ique:*
Ayant enfin oui le rapport
Présenté par Suffolk and Nort
Sur les hauts faits de Jean Burgoyne
Voulons que ce grand Capitaine
Dont on veut dénigrer le nom,
En le traitant de fanfaron,
Soit accordé toute justice ;
Et pour confondre la malice
De Burke and Pitt ses ennemis
Et d'autres tortueux esprits ;
Mandons à notre secrétaire
D'expédier en beau caractere
A ce General fameux
Brevets and titres glorieux
Pour rétablir sa renommée
Fort injustement attaquée
En maints lieux and pays divers
Tant déça que delà les mers.

A ces causes, par ces présentes
Authentiques lettres-patentes ;
Nous and le Roi, nous le nommons
Duc and Milord de Bennington :
Permettons qu'en ses armoiries
Pour supports soient deux batteries
Des canons qu' à Saratoga
Ce général abandonna.

En faisant si belle retraite,
Quand son armée fut défaite
Par ces insurgens, ces poltrons
Et ces François vrais fanfarons
Qui n'auront jamais en partage
De nos Allemands le courage,
N'en déplaise au comte Turpin
Qui l'un de nous, provoque en vain . . .
Ayant le tout considéré
Et mûrement delibéré
Avons, sous le grand sceau de cire
Et le cachet de notre *Sire*,
Expédié le présent brevet
De Duc Pair, même Baronnet
Pour le Général Jean Burgoyne,
Signé Bute, Nort and Germaine
Trente Janvier avant minuit
Mil sept cent soixante dix-huit.

*Translation of the above by Bauman L. Belden.**

PATENT OF LORD DUKE BURGOYNE.

WE, the Parliament of England,
Sovereign over sea and land,—

---

* Bauman L. Belden, *littérateur*, born in Brooklyn, N. Y., November 23d, 1862. Studied at New Brunswick, N. J. His great-great-grandfather, on the maternal side, was Colonel Sebastian Bauman. Colonel Bauman served through the Revolution as major in Colonel Lamb's regiment of artillery, and at the evacuation of New York by the Americans, in 1776, was the last officer to leave the city. In October, 1789, he was appointed postmaster of New York City, which position he held until his death, October 19th,

Over emperors and over kings
    And potentates most grand,

And islanders and devils
    And the rovers of the seas—
To all kings, margraves, electors,
    Republics and monarchies.

Greeting !

Our hearts' desire being to reward
    All who, amid war's alarms,
Have won immortal glory
    By splendid feats of arms,

And having well examined
    All the bulletins which came
From America, and countries
    Too numerous to name,

And having also heard reports,
    From Suffolk and from North,
Of the mighty deeds of John Burgoyne,
    That soldier of great worth,

And wishing this great captain—
    Whose fame they seek to dim,
By calling him a boaster—
    Should have justice done to him,

1803. As might be inferred from his ancestry, Mr. Belden takes great interest in all matters pertaining to our Revolutionary history. He is (1893) librarian of the American Numismatic and Archæological Society, and resides at Elizabeth, N. J. The reader, especially one acquainted with the French idiom, cannot fail to see how admirably this ballad has been rendered into English by Mr. Belden. Each shade of thought is preserved, while the feet of the verses is almost exact.

And to confound the malice
　　Of his foes, Pitt and Burke,
And other crooked spirits
　　Who his ruin seek to work.

Now therefore, our secretary
　　We do herewith command
To send a beautiful parchment,
　　With brevets and titles grand,

To this most famous general,
　　That thereby his fair fame
May be fully re-established,
　　And honors crown his name.

His fame unjustly was attacked
　　In very many places,
As well here as beyond the sea
　　They covered it with disgraces.

For these reasons, by these presents—
　　Honors he has fairly won—
We, and the King, do hereby name him
　　Lord and *Duke* of *Bennington*.

And also on his coat of arms,
　　The supporters to the shield,
Shall be two batteries of cannon,
　　Left on Saratoga's field—*

---

* This is about as keen and delightful a piece
of satire as we have ever chanced to meet with, es-
pecially the permission of the patentors, Bute, etc., to
Burgoyne, who is here dubbed " Duke of Bennington,"
to use as supporters on his coat of arms the two bat-

Abandoned by this famous general
    In that beautiful retreat,
When his brave and splendid army
    Suffered such a dire defeat

At the hands of those French braggarts,
    Those rebels, cowards and poltroons,
Who have not a portion of the courage
    Of our brave German dragoons.

So, after mature consideration
    We have made this matter plain.
Nor should this displease Count Turpin,*
    Whom one of us provoked in vain.†

Under our Sires' great waxen seal,
    We hereby confirm the brevet
Of the great John Burgoyne,
    Duke, Peer and even Baronet.

Signed.—Bute, North, Germaine,
    Thirtieth of January—very late—
Just before midnight
    Seventeen hundred and seventy-eight.

---

teries of cannon captured by the Americans at Sara-
toga. These bronze cannon, by the way, have, by an act
of Congress, lately been loaned to the trustees of the
Saratoga Monument, to be placed at the base of the
monument.
    * The famous highwayman.
    † The point of this allusion is not plain. However
this is the literal translation.

PART OF AN OLD SONG SUNG BY THE WAGONERS
OF GATES'S ARMY FOR MANY YEARS AFTER THE
BATTLES OF SARATOGA. FROM DR. DWIGHT'S
"NORTHERN TRAVELLER."*

THAT the great Mount Defiance
They soon would fortify :—
We found that we must quit our lines,
Or ev'ry man must die.

Which soon we did in haste perform,
And went to Sarritoag,
A burning all the buildings
We found along the road.

'Twas then the gen'rous thought inspir'd
The noble Gates's mind,
For to send out Gin'ral Arnold,
To see if he could find

A passage through the inimy,
Wherever he might be ;
Which soon he did accomplish,
And set the country free.

---

* Dr. Dwight tells us that once, while travelling by
stage from Caldwell to Ticonderoga, he heard the
driver, an old wagoner in Gates's army, sing the above
song, these four verses being all that Dr. Dwight
remembered. These verses are, however, but an
adulterated form of the ballad on "The North
Campaign," elsewhere given.

THE RESTORED CAPTIVE.

(*An incident of the Burgoyne Campaign.*)

By COLONEL WILLIAM L. STONE.*

IN yonder sylvan dale,
 The hills and woods among,
Bright as the fairest vale
 The poets e'er have sung,

---

* William Leete Stone, a distinguished American journalist and author, was born at New Paltz, Ulster County, N. Y., April 20th, 1792, and died at Saratoga Springs, N. Y., August 15th, 1844. His wife was a sister of President Wayland, of Brown University, and a daughter of the Rev. Francis Wayland, the pioneer minister of the Baptist Church at Saratoga Springs. When a child, his father removed into the valley of the Susquehanna, and subsequently to Sodus, N. Y., on the shore of Lake Ontario. The son received from the father thorough instruction in Latin and Greek—the latter having himself graduated with high honor at Yale —and at the age of seventeen entered the newspaper office of Colonel Prentiss, at Cooperstown, N. Y., to learn the printer's trade, and soon began to write newspaper paragraphs. In 1813 he became the editor of the *Herkimer American*, subsequently editing political newspapers at Hudson, Albany and Hartford —in the latter town succeeding Theodore Dwight in the editorship of the *Hartford Mirror*. In the spring of 1821 he became editor and one of the proprietors of the New York *Commercial Advertiser*, which position he retained until his death. Though possessing decided ability as a political writer, "Colonel" Stone

Where Hudson's silver tide
　Adorns the fairy scene,
Rejoicing in his pride,
　'Mid groves forever green ;
There, dark as clouds of night,
　The lurking savage came,
With hatchet burnished bright,
　And torch of lurid flame ;
To wake with horrid yell
　The hamlet's sweet repose
By deeds no tongue can tell,
　The deeds of savage foes !

(as he was always called, from having held that rank on the military staff of his intimate personal and political friend, Governor De Witt Clinton) preferred literary pursuits to partisanship. In 1825 he was appointed by the corporation of New York City to write "The Narrative of the Grand Erie Canal Celebration." His short stories, written for the different annuals of the United States and England, were subsequently collected and published in two volumes, under the title of "Tales and Sketches." "Ups and Downs in the Life of a Distressed Gentleman" (1836), a satirical novel on the follies of the day, was very successful. Among his more elaborate works were: "Letters on Masonry and Anti-Masonry" (New York, 1832), "Border Wars of the American Revolution" (2 vols., 1834), "Matthias and his Impostures" (1835), "The Life of Maria Monk" (1832), "The Life of Joseph Brant, Thayendanegea" (2 vols., Cooperstown, 1838), "Life and Times of Red Jacket" (New York, 1840), "The Poetry and History of Wyoming" (Wiley & Putnam, 1840), and "Uncas and Miantonomah" (1842). He was the first super-

II.

The war-whoop, shrill and wild,
　　Through darkest gloom was heard ;
The mother clasped her child,*
　　The father grasped his sword ;
But ere the morning's dawn,
　　The cruel work was o'er :
The dusky foe was gone.
　　The vale was steep'd in gore.
The dying and the dead,
　　Were strew'd along the plain,
And fewer those who fled,
　　Than those among the slain ;
And loud the plaintive cry,
　　Broke on the saddened ear,
With many a heaving sigh,
　　And many a scalding tear.

---

intendent of public schools of the city of New
York, and his great controversy with Archbishop
Hughes, in regard to the reading of the Bible in
the public schools of that city, will long be remem-
bered, the last letter to whom, occupying six col-
umns in the *Commercial Advertiser*, was written by
him, by dictation, on his death-bed but a week before
his decease.   At the time of his death he was engaged
upon a life of Sir William Johnson, which was com-
pleted by his son, William L. Stone, Jr.   The above
MS., written about 1819, was found by his son among
his unpublished MS. after his death.

　* In this connection the reader is referred to the
alto rilievo in the Saratoga Monument at Schuylerville,
N. Y., " Burgoyne reprimanding the Indians for their
barbarities," for the picture of the mother holding her
babe to her breast—on which this ballad is founded.

III.

With throbbing bosoms there,
  Amid the field of blood,
Engaged in silent prayer,
  Full many a woman stood,
With swimming eyes, disturb'd,
  Transfixed as by a spell,
The maiden smote her breast,
  With grief she could not tell.
A mother, there was one,
  A widow—and she wept
Her darling infant son,
  That in the cradle slept:
The babe, the eve before,
  Had sweetly sunk to rest,
Alas! to smile no more
  Upon a mother's breast.

IV.

But see! what form is there
  Thus bounding from the wood,
Like panther from his lair,
  Back on the trail of blood:
A chieftain by his mien,
  Of noble form is he;
A prouder ne'er was seen,
  In chase o'er dell and lea.
Swift as the arrow's flight,
  He speeds his course along,
With eye of burning light,
  To reach the weeping throng.
And o'er his eagle crest,
  A banner white he waves,

As though to make request
  Of good intent he craves.

V.

Wrapped in his blanket warm,
  Loose o'er his shoulder flung,
Yet guarded safe from harm,
  A lovely infant hung.
On, on with breathless strife,
  The warrior held his way.
Quick at the mother's side,
  Her own lost infant lay !
The babe look'd up and smiled *
  And sweet the thrill of joy,
As now with transports wild,
  She clasped her darling boy;
While rapid as the light,
  The warrior leaped the flood,
Sprang swiftly from their sight,
  And vanished in the wood!

---

* Some reader may recall a similar line in "The Snow Storm," by, I believe, Hawthorne: "The babe looked up and sweetly smiled." But as this ballad was written by Colonel Stone when Hawthorne was a mere lad, no one will suspect plagiarism.

BALLADS ON THE DEATH OF GENERAL FRASER.

THE DEATH AND BURIAL OF GENERAL FRASER.

By way of explanation of the many allusions in the following ballads, a short sketch of General Fraser and the circumstances of his burial may not be inappropriate.

Simon Fraser, British soldier, born in 1729 ; died in Saratoga, N. Y., October 8th, 1777. He was the youngest son of Alexander Fraser, of Baluaire and Glendo, of the Lovat family, by a daughter of Angus Mackintosh, of Kellady, from whom the celebrated Sir James Mackintosh was directly descended. He entered the army at an early age, and after several promotions became lieutenant-colonel July 14th, 1768. He served with distinction in Holland and Germany, was in the expedition against Louisburg, and accompanied General Wolfe to Quebec. He was afterward stationed in Ireland, whence he embarked for America with the Twenty-fourth Regiment, April 5th, 1776, arriving at Quebec May 28th of that year. He assisted in driving the Americans out of Canada in 1776, and was in command of the severely contested engagement at Three Rivers. Having acquired a high reputation for judgment and cool daring, he was selected by Burgoyne to command the light brigade, which formed the right wing of the British army. He thus was constantly in the advance, rendering most efficient service ; and had his advice been followed, the blunder of advancing on Bennington with heavily mounted dragoons, on an expedition requiring the greatest celerity of movement, would never have been committed. After the evacuation of Ticonderoga he pursued the retreating Americans under St. Clair, and, assisted by his German ally, General Riedesel, gained a signal victory at Hubbardton, July 7th, 1777. He opened the battle of September 19th by engaging Morgan's skirmishers ; and in the action of October 7th was shot and mortally wounded by "Tim" Murphy, one of Morgan's riflemen, in obedience to special instructions from that officer.*   During the succeeding night he was tenderly ministered to by the Baroness Riedesel, who did all in her power to alleviate his sufferings, and at eight o'clock on the following morning he died. As he lay dying he was heard frequently to exclaim : " Oh, fatal ambition ! Oh, my poor wife ! Oh, poor General Burgoyne !" He was buried at sunset, according to his special request, on a knoll overlooking the Hudson River, on which was a battery, Chaplain Brudenell officiating. His remains were attended to the grave at six o'clock in the evening by the general officers ; and the funeral scene is described by Burgoyne, in his " State of the Expedition," and by other contemporaneous writers, as unusually solemn, impressive, and awful, by the voice of the chaplain being accompanied by constant peals from the American artillery, and the cannon-shot which flew thick around and near the funeral cortége as it was ascending the hill. This fire, however, ceased imme-

---

* For an original sketch of Murphy, see Appendix No. IV.

diately as soon as the nature of the gathering was known.

To Burgoyne the loss of Fraser was a severe blow ; and contemporary military writers affirm that, had he lived, the British would have made good their retreat into Canada. Certain it is that had Fraser lived to give his advice to Burgoyne—and it would undoubtedly have been taken—the latter would have avoided the blunders he made, which was the cause of his surrender. Riedesel, it is true, advised the same course which Fraser would have done had he lived. But advice from Riedesel—whom, as a German ally, Burgoyne never liked—would have been a very different thing from Burgoyne's loved friend, Fraser.

It was said of Fraser that he had always shown as great skill in conducting a retreat as bravery in leading an attack, having, during the Seven Years' War, brought off in safety five hundred chasseurs in sight of the French army. General Fraser's temperament was warm, open, and communicative, but reserved in matters of confidence. Burgoyne paid him a touching tribute in his " Narrative," and in his report to Lord George Germaine, dated Albany, October 20th, 1777, said : " The extensive merits which marked the public and private character of Brigadier-General Fraser will long remain upon the memory of this army and make his loss a subject of particular regret." Fraser married, in 1769, Mrs. Grant, of London, who survived him, and who, in 1781, married at Edinburgh an advocate named George Buchan Hepburn. The statement that the remains of General Fraser were removed to England after the Revolution is without foundation. For more about Fraser, see Stone's " Burgoyne's Campaign" and General Rope's " Hadden's Journal," both published by Munsell's Sons, Albany, N. Y. In " Burgoyne's Campaign" will be found an interesting account of the death of Fraser, with reflections on that event, written by Professer Lilliman during the night he stopped in the house where Fraser died.

THE BURIAL OF GEN. FRASER.

Read before the Annual Meeting of the Saratoga Monument Association, 1874, by E. W. B. Canning, Esq.

On Saratoga's crimsoned field,
　　When battle's volleyed roar was done,
Mild autumn's mellow light revealed
　　The glories of the setting sun.
On furrow, fence and tree that bear
　　The iron marks of battling men,
The radiance burneth calm and fair,
　　As tho' earth aye had sinless been.
The gory sods, all scathed and scarred,
　　And piled in trenched mounds declare
That mutual foeman, fallen, marred,
　　Have found a final bivouac there.
And list! from yonder bulwarked height
　　The faint-heard martial signals come:
For those who keep the watch to-night
　　Are gathering at the evening drum.

So, Saratoga, lay thy field
　　When freedom, 'mid the shock of steel,
Made Britain's rampant lion yield,
　　And crushed his terrors 'neath her heel.
Proudly the freeman points to thee,
　　And speaks thy unforgotten name;

While on her page bright history
  For children's children writes thy fame.

As the last sunbeam kissed the trees
  That sighed amid its dying glow,
Borne softly on the evening breeze
  Floated the soldier's note of woe.
From out the Briton's guarded lines,
  With wailing fife and muffled drum,
While gleaming gold with scarlet shines,
  A band of mourning warriors come.
With arms reversed, all sad and slow,
  And measured tread of martial men,
Forth on their lengthened path they go,
  But not to wake the strife again.
No plunging haste of battles there,
  No serried ranks or bristling lines;
No furious coursers headlong bear
  Their riders where the death flash shines.
The pennon is the soldiers' pall,
  The battery for the bier is changed,
And plumes of nodding sable all
  On chieftains' brows are round it ranged.
The noblest leader of the host
  They carry to his dreamless sleep;
The heart of British hope is lost,
  And vain the tears that Britons weep.
Thine arm of valor, proud Burgoyne,
  Is paralyzed for ever now;
While sorrow-stricken comrades join
  Fondly to wreathe dead Fraser's brow.

On yonder hill that skirts the plain,
  A lone redoubt with haste upraised

O'erlooks around the trampled grain,
　Where oft the dying hero gazed.
" Bury me there at set of sun,"
　(His latest words of ebbing life)
" 'Tis mine to see no triumph won,
　Or mingle with the final strife.
If gloom awaits our path of fame,
　I die before the ill befalls ;
These ears shall tingle not with shame,
　Nor longer list when glory calls.
At set of sun, in yon redoubt,
　Lay me to rest as rest the brave."
The flickering lamp of life went out,
　And strangers' land must yield a grave.

Slowly in mournful march they wend
　Their upward pathway to the tomb ;
Unwittingly the foemen send
　Their shots around amid the gloom.*
They reach the height, commit their trust,
　And reverent all uncovered stand ;
While booming shots updash the dust
　In clouds about the listening band.
Robed and with dignity serene,
　The man of God reads calmly on ;

---

　* This refers to the shots which were at first sent
by the Americans at the funeral cortége which was
ascending the hill to bury General Fraser.   Although
it has often been explained that the Americans, as
soon as they ascertained that the procession was to the
funeral of Fraser, ceased *at once* to fire on the party,
yet by prejudiced English historians this fiction has
still been kept up.   See preceding note.

No terror marks his quiet mien,
  As hoarse responds the distant gun.
" Earth to earth and dust to dust:"
  Thus the solemn accents fall ;
Each receives her precious trust,
  Evening saddens over all.
Pile the mound ; no living form
  Nobler soul enshrines than he,
Now bequeathed the darkling worm—
  Pride of Albion's chivalry !
All is done : there wait for thee,
  Fallen chief, no more alarms ;
But thy peers anon must see
  Hapless " field of grounded arms."

*   *   *   *   *

Years have trolled their changes by ;
  Harvests oft have robed the plain ;
And the leafy honors high
  Sigh no more above the slain.
Sons of sires who in the black,
  Doleful days of '77
Rolled the tide of battle back,
  Seeking hope and strength in Heaven,
Wondering tread the storied ground,
  And with glowing accents tell
How their fathers victory found,
  And the spot where Fraser fell.
Gallant chieftain, nobler song
  Ought to speak thy honored name ;
But our sons remembering long,
  Worthier tribute pay thy fame !

THE BURIAL OF GENERAL FRASER,

AT SUNSET, OCTOBER 8, 1777.

BY E. W. B. CANNING.

[*Dedicated to the trustees of the Saratoga Monument association.*]

THERE was mourning at the eventide that sad October
day,
There was mourning in the camp wherein the hosts of
Britain lay ;
For the sun that glanced so proudly on their bayonets
at dawn
Behind the ling'ring battle clouds of rout and wreck
had gone.

As the stern sergeant's tones, amid the day's decline,
Called the thinned muster roll along the martial line,
How eloquent the silence fell, and, ah ! how frequent!
when
A comrade's name was spoken who should answer
not again !

But deeper gloom than wont befell when battle's
crash was o'er,
For he who led the foremost ranks should lead them
nevermore—
The leader round whose knightly brows the oak and
laurel join—
The bravest chieftain of the brave—the right arm of
Burgoyne.

" Bury me"—said the hero, as the spark of life went
out—
" At sunset, where your banner waves above the
' Great Redoubt';

Believe my soul is with you yet, and be my memory
Still cherished in your valiant hearts whate'er the end
    may be."

And in the misty gloaming went a sad procession
    forth,
With solemn step and muffled drums and thoughts of
    fallen worth,
While foeman's guns, unwittingly, upon the hills afar
Roared out, amid the gathering gloom, the thunder
    tones of war.

And as the mournful multitude the yawning grave
    surround,
Fiercely the iron messengers updash the sodded
    ground :
But not a coward cheek was blanched; no hurried
    word was said
Of service due the holy man rehearsed above the dead.

So laid they gallant Fraser in his chosen place to rest,
And warriors' tears bedewed the sod that hid his
    manly breast.
Peace to the ashes of the brave ! For him no more
    alarms,
No grief, anon, of comrades on "The Field of Grounded
    Arms."

THE BURIAL OF GENERAL FRASER.

By Lura A. Boies.*

HE fell, the bold hero! low lay the proud form
That braved the red wrath of the battle's wild storm,

* Lura A. Boies, daughter of Jerome and Hannah
G. (Gillette) Boies, was born in the town of Moreau,

When dark hung the cloud of the furious fray
O'er the fell hights of Bemis, they bore him away.

He spoke, and his heart for a moment beat high,
The fire of his spirit flashed forth from his eye,
"When the terrible voice of the conflict is still,
Lay me down in the sunset to rest on the hill."

They saw the fierce gleam of the battle light fade,
And faint grew the roar of the fell cannonade,
When the wing of the night fluttered down o'er the
      west,
They laid the brave warrior away to his rest.

> Proud day, Columbia, for thee,
> When upward soared thine eagle FREE!
> Proud day, when from the hills of strife
>   The sullen war cloud rolled away,
> And Triumph waved her peaceful wing
>   Above the fell and fatal fray.
> Glad millions shouted then " 'TIS DONE!"

Saratoga County, N. Y., on May 2d, 1835. Like the
Davidson sisters (Lucretia and Margaret Miller), she
at a very early age developed precocious intellectual
abilities "which her pen shaped from 'airy nothings'
and formed 'a local habitation and a name.'" Devoting
the leisure hours of a busy life to literary pursuits,
she, while yet in mere girlhood, accumulated the
materials for a graceful volume of poems, which, after
her death, through the indefatigable efforts of the late
Judge Hay, of Saratoga Springs, were published under
the title of "Rural Rhymes." She died April 15th,
1859, and is buried near her heroine, Jane McCrea,
in the Union Cemetery between Fort Edward and
Sandy Hill.

And high hearts hailed the victory won,
    And clear the exulting strain,
In one loud peal of lofty song,
    Went o'er the heaving main.

Oh, there was grief and anguish then
In the bowed hearts of Albion's men,
And dark as night the wing of woe,
Brooded above the vanquished foe !
Not as when girded for the strife,
In the full flush of daring life,
    With glowing hopes all vain,
Through the dim silence, hushed and still,
At sunset up the chosen hill,
    Wound the slow funeral train.
Oh, not as marshaled for the field,
With burnished lance and gleaming shield,
    And scarlet banners flame,
That stricken band of warriors brave
    To the lone burial came ;
Nor yet, with death-flag's ebon wave
    And sound of muffled drum,
As conquering heroes to the grave
    Of martial glory come.
No plaintive dirge rose on the air,
No sable plumes drooped darkly there,
But with hushed hearts and mournful tread
They bore away their gallant dead.

More awful than the battle's roll
The gloom that bowed each haughty soul,
And wilder was the storm within
Than the fierce conflict's raging din,
    Where he, the hero, fell,
'Mid clash of arms and ring of steel,
And brazen trumpet's clarion peal,
    And noise of bursting shell.

Hark! from the hills a sudden sound
Trembles along the startled ground,
    And slowly dies away—
'Tis from the bosom of the free,
The mighty heart of victory
Throbs in that solemn, mourning gun,
And thus to Albion's fallen son
    The brave their tribute pay.

'Tis beautiful, when those who met
In dire and dreadful strife, forget
    Their hatred, dark and deep;
And when the tide of life swells high,
Lay all their full rejoicing by,
    To weep with those who weep!

Oh, grateful in that hour of woe
    To those whose light had fled,
The homage of the conquering foe,
    To him their noble dead!

And many a stern heart's mute despair,
Was melted into softness there,
    And hot tears fell like rain,
O'er the bold soldier's coffined form,
    The gallant Fraser slain!

The night came down in silence grand
    Above the hero's grave;
They turned away that mournful band—
    They left the sleeping brave
Far from his own, his native land,
    Beyond the deep blue wave,
And cloud and storm and gathering gloom,
Were mourners at the warrior's tomb!
    *   *   *   *   *
'Twas the wild eve of that dread day
    When Albion's haughty standard fell,

Red lightnings flashed above the slain,
   And thunders tolled a fearful knell.
The dying wail, the hollow groan
Blent strangely with the hoarse wind's moan
And darkly o'er the fatal Hights
   Where cold the ghastly fallen slept,
Black clouds hung like a sable pall,
   And sad the pitying heavens wept.

Out in the deep night's starless gloom,
   Like a white angel in the storm,
Moved by her pure heart's deathless love,
   Stole woman's frail and tender form.
Above her burst the tempest's wrath,
And shadows gathered o'er her path,
And yet the hurtling, shrieking blast
   Swept all unheeded by;
For colder than the blinding rain,
The weary weight of grief and pain,
   That on her soul did lie.
With falling tears her face grew damp,
   A mist came o'er her clear blue eye;
Her love, her light, her spirit's pride,
He whose low voice had called her, *bride*,
Bound bleeding in the foeman's camp,
   Had laid him down to die.
Oh, stronger in that awful hour,
   And mightier than the strife,
He tried affection's holy power,
That lofty inspiration gave,
And nerved with courage, calm and brave,
   The true, high-hearted wife!
She in her fearless faith would seek
   The proud, victorious foe,
The chilling grief that blanched her cheek,

To the stern hearts of men should speak :
The strong should bow before the weak,
　　And pity her wild woe.
Her love the stricken one should bless,
Her lips the brow of pain should press,
By all her soul's deep tenderness,
　　She to her lord would go !

Down by the surging river's shore,
　　Lashed by the foaming spray,
With spreading sail and waiting oar,
　　The frail boat ready lay—
And thither with light step and fleet,
Her fond heart winging her fast feet,
　　The brave wife bent her way.
A moment's pause, a brief space o'er,
And swift the light, careering barque,
Launched out upon the waters dark,
And closer round her shivering form,
Fell the cold mantle of the storm.

Oh, strengthened by the holy flame,
　　That glows within her breast,
And nerves with power her gentle frame,
When clouds come o'er her heaven fair,
What will not woman do and dare
　　For those her love hath blest !

THE BURIAL OF GEN. FRASER.

From Theodore Dwight's " Northern Traveller."*

I.

The warrior sleeps, he wakes no more,
　　At glory's voice of chivalry ;

---

*Theodore Dwight, author and editor, was born

His part amid the strife is o'er
He starts not at the cannon's roar,
Nor rolling drum, nor musketry.

---

in Hartford, Conn., March 3d, 1796. In 1833, he re-
moved to Brooklyn, N. Y., and engaged in various
public and philanthropic enterprises, becoming a direct-
or in numerous religious and educational societies. In
1854-8 he, with George Walker, was active in a
systematic effort to send free-soil settlers to Kansas;
and it is estimated that 9000 persons were induced by
them to go to that State. He was at different times
engaged in an editorial capacity on several newspapers
and magazines, and he was at one time chief editor
and publisher of the New York *Presbyterian*. He
published a number of works, one of which was "The
Northern Traveller," from which the above verses are
taken. He was a grandson of the Rev. Dr. Timothy,
who served in the army of General Gates in Parsons'
Brigade of the Connecticut line, and who, a few days
before the battles of Saratoga, preached from the text:
"*I will remove far from me the Northern army.*"
At the time of his death Mr. Dwight was translating
educational works into Spanish, for introduction into
Spanish-American countries. He was an exceedingly
active man, bearing his age wonderfully well. Indeed,
this very activity was the direct cause of his death,
which occurred in 1866. Shortly before his decease
he called on me at the *Journal of Commerce*, of
which paper I was then city editor, and coming up to
the fifth floor—it was before the days of elevators—
he fairly bounded into my room, exclaiming: "Mr.
Stone, I have run up your stairs as easily and with no
more effort than as if I were a boy again!" Some
four days later, while attempting to board a Pennsyl-

II.

No more the soldier leads the band
  Of Britain's warlike infantry,
They hear no more his stern command
Nor gleams his sword, nor waves his hand
  Urging to death or victory!

III.

The rifle lays the chieftain low
  By Morgan aimed so fatally.
He falls where streams of life blood flow,
Where comrades 'neath the deadly blow
  Have fallen wounded mortally.

IV.

So "Glory leads but to the grave"
  Such was the soldier's destiny
To meet his doom he crossed the wave,
His life-blood flowed, his deeds so brave,
  Were given for chains and slavery.

V.

In evening shadows sinks the sun,
  And life departs thus mournfully,
Its brightness fades in shadows dun,
And so the hero's course was run,
  And ended thus in tragedy.

---

vania Railroad train in motion—relying upon this
same activity—he was thrown under the wheels and
instantly killed!

VI.

His lifeless form is borne on high,
   In solemn martial pageantry
While threat'ning clouds obscure the sky,
And fires of death are flashing nigh
   And roar of dread artillery.

BALLADS ON THE DEATH OF JANE McCREA.

SKETCH OF JANE McCREA.

THERE have been so many different versions of the tragic death of Jane McCrea put forth, both at the time of the occurrence and since, that it seems only proper to give, as a preface to the numerous poems and ballads on this subject, the true version as gathered by myself after much research.

Jane McCrea was born in Bedminster (now Lamington), N. J., in 1753, and was killed near Fort Edward, N. Y., July 27th, 1777. She was the second daughter of Rev. James McCrea, a Presbyterian clergyman of Scotch descent, whose father, William, was an elder in White Clay Creek Church, near Newark, Del. After his death she made her home with her brother John at Fort Edward, N. Y.* It is safe to

---

* John McCrea, the brother of Jane, was a patriot. He had been with the unfortunate expedition of General Montgomery and fought in the battle of Quebec; and when General Schuyler, in command at Fort Edward, called on the militia to take the field,

say that no event, either in ancient or modern warfare, has received more versions than that of her death. It has been commemorated in story and in song, and narrated in grave histories in as many different ways as there have been writers on the subject. The facts appear to be as follows:

David Jones, her lover, an officer in Burgoyne's army, then lying four miles from Fort Edward, sent a party of Indians, under Duluth, a half-breed, to escort his betrothed to the British camp, where they were to be at once married by Chaplain Brudenell,* Lady

---

he promptly obeyed the summons. Between him and David Jones there had arisen an estrangement, growing out of their opposite sympathies in relation to the war. But Jane still clung to her betrothed, notwithstanding her brother's dislike for him.

* There is also much probability that Jane received communications from her lover at intervals, especially after the British army left Skenesborough. The following original letter from Jones to Jenny bears out this view:

"SKENESBORO', July 11, 1777.

"*Dear Friend:* I have ye opportunity to send you this by William Bamsy, hoping through Freel it will come safe to hand. Since last writing, Ty has been taken, and we have had a battle, which no doubt you have been informed of before this. Through God's mercy I escaped destruction, and am now well at this place, for which thanks be to Him. The rebels cannot recover from the blow yt has been struck, and no doubt the war will soon end. Such should be the prayer of all of us. Dear Jenny, I do not forget you, though

Harriet Acland * and Madame Riedesel (the wife of
General Riedesel, in command of the Brunswick con-
tingent) having good-naturedly consented to grace the
nuptials by their presence.   Duluth, having arrived
within a quarter of a mile of the house of a Mrs. McNeil,
a cousin of General Fraser (where Jane was waiting),
halted in the woods until he should be joined by her by
preconcerted arrangement.   Meanwhile, another body
of Indians from the British camp, under Le Loup, a
fierce Wyandotte chief, returning from a marauding

---

much there is to distract in these days, and hope I am
remembered by you as formerly.   In a few days we
will march to Ft. Edward, for which I am anxious,
where I shall have the happiness to meet you, after
long absence.   I hear from Isaac Vaughn, who has
just come in, that the people on the river are moving
to Albany.   I hope if your brother John goes, you
will not go with him, but stay at Mrs. McNeil's, to
whom and Miss Hunter give my dutiful respects.
There I will join you.   My dear Jenny, these are sad
times, but I think the war will end this year, as the
rebels cannot hold out, and will see their error.   By
the blessing of Providence I trust we shall yet pass
many years together in peace.   Shall write on every
occasion that offers, and hope to find you at Mrs.
McNeil's.   No more at present; but believe me yours
affectionately till death.

DAVID JONES."

* For a sketch of Lady Acland, explaining the fab-
ulous account of her marriage with Parson Brudenell,
etc., see Appendix No. V. I do not give one of Madame
Riedesel, as that is found in my " Memoirs of General
and Madame Riedesel," Munsell's Sons, Albany, N. Y.

expedition in the vicinity, drove in a scout of Americans, and stopping, on their return, at Mrs. McNeil's, took her and Jane captive, with the intention of bringing them into the British camp. On their way back they encountered Duluth's party, when the half-breed claimed Jane as being under his protection. Le Loup being unwilling to surrender his prisoner—himself wishing the honor of being her escort—high words ensued between the two leaders, when Le Loup, enraged at being opposed, in a fit of violent passion, shot her through the heart. Then, having scalped his victim, he carried the reeking scalp into the British camp, where it was immediately recognized, by its long and beautiful tresses, by Mrs. McNeil, who, having been separated from Jane before the catastrophe, had arrived at Burgoyne's headquarters a little in advance. The next day her mangled body was conveyed by her brother, Colonel John McCrea, to the camp-ground of the fort, and there buried. Her lover, David Jones, it is said, never recovered from the shock thus received. He soon after resigned and left the army, and after many years of melancholy died unmarried.

Miss McCrea is described by those who knew her personally as a young woman of rare accomplishments, great personal attractions, and of a remarkable sweetness of disposition. She was of medium stature, finely formed, and of a delicate blonde complexion. Her hair was of a golden brown and silken lustre, and, when unbound, trailed upon the ground. Her father was devoted to literary pursuits, and she thus had acquired a taste for reading unusual in one of her age in those early times.

The tragic death of Jane McCrea was to the people of New York what the battle of Lexington was to the New England colonies. In each case the effect was to consolidate the inhabitants more firmly against the invaders. The blood of the unfortunate maiden was not shed in vain. Her name was passed as a note of alarm along the banks of the Hudson, and, as a rallying cry among the Green Mountains of Vermont, brought down to the army of Gates her hardy sons. It thus contributed in no slight degree to Burgoyne's defeat, which became a precursor and principal cause of American independence. Descendants of the Mc-Crea family are still (1893) living at Ballston, N. Y., and in other parts of the State of New York, and also in Newport, R. I.

At the time of her death, her mangled and disfigured body was conveyed by her brother, Colonel John Mc-Crea, and sympathizing friends to Moses Kill, where a fortified camp-ground, laid out by the celebrated Polish engineer Kosciusko, was then occupied by the rear guard of the American army, under the command of General Arnold. Here, after some preparation, her body, together with that of the fated Van Vecten, was committed to a common grave. On April 22d, 1822, these remains were removed to the old burial-ground near the fort, at the lower end of the village of Fort Edward. The ceremonial was attended with unusual pomp and display for those early days—the celebrated and afterward unfortunate Hooper Cummings, of Albany, preaching upon that occasion from Micah 2 : 10 so impressive and pathetic a sermon that many of his audience were convulsed with sobs and weeping.

The remains of Miss McCrea were, in 1852, again removed to the Union Cemetery between Fort Edward and Sandy Hill, the McCrea lot being near the main entrance. The marble slab which marks the spot bears the following inscription :

HERE REST THE REMAINS OF
JANE McCREA
AGED I7
MADE CAPTIVE AND MURDERED
BY A BAND OF INDIANS
WHILE ON A VISIT TO A RELATIVE IN
THIS NEIGHBORHOOD
A.D. I777
TO COMMEMORATE
ONE OF THE MOST THRILLING INCIDENTS
IN THE ANNALS OF THE AMERICAN REVOLUTION
TO DO JUSTICE TO THE FAME OF THE GALLANT
BRITISH OFFICER TO WHOM SHE WAS AFFIANCED
AND AS A SIMPLE TRIBUTE TO THE
MEMORY OF THE DEPARTED
THIS STONE IS ERECTED
BY HER NIECE
SARAH HANNA PAYNE
A.D. I852.

"There is at present" (1893), writes to me Mrs. Charles Stone, of Sandy Hill, who, with most praiseworthy zeal, has taken a deep interest in the matter "a chain fence with stone posts around the lot. The marble slab bears the coat-of-arms of the relic-hunter! being nicked at every point, except possibly beneath the soil. The whole has the appearance of great neglect. There is, however, a fund now being raised to put it in much better condition. The public schools of Sandy Hill and Glens Falls have sent penny donations, and Fort E. has promised to do likewise. It is the intention of the trustees of the cemetery to have the improvements made this spring. They wish to erect a substantial fence, ornamental, of iron, but to be kept impenetrable from the chisel of the relic-hunter. Referring again to the fund, several of our citizens have given ; others are only waiting to be called upon. Ex-Mayor Henry Bedlow, of Newport, on learning the facts and of the fund, sent immediately fifty dollars. Mr. Bedlow has among his family deeds those of the McCreas, Jane having been his great-aunt. The treasurer of the Union Cemetery is Ashiel Irving, cashier of the First National Bank of Fort Edward, and he will take pleasure in receiving contributions toward this end. In short, Jane McCrea's romantic and tragic death is of national importance, and means should be taken to let the public know of the fund now being raised. A certain portion of the fund will be kept in trust continually to improve, adorn, and keep in order the lot."*

THE EPISODE OF JANE McCREA.

(*Samuel Standish narrator*).

By Rev. O. C. Auringer.†

To A. W. Holden, A.M., M.D., Scholar, Physician, and Friend, this poem is gratefully dedicated.

Part I.

We left the camp behind us locked in sleep,
And marched with silent footsteps to the plain.

---

* For an account of the latter days of Lieutenant David Jones, her betrothed, see Appendix No. VI.

† Obadiah Cyrus Auringer, one of the most brilliant of the later-day exponents of the poetry of nature and nature's God, a most clever sonneteer and a writer of the sweetest, most taking, and elevating verse, was born in Glens Falls, Warren County, N. Y.,

We paused a moment at the sentry's hail,
And answering passed on. Quitting the road—

June 4th, 1849, of German-French parents. He
was educated in the local schools, studied litera-
ture and science for several years under various tutors,
and began contributing articles in prose and verse to
New York papers at the age of eighteen. Since then
his name has become well known to readers of peri-
odical literature, and his poems have been considered
worthy of place in such standard works as Stedman
& Hutchinson's "Library of American Literature,"
Sharp's "American Sonnets" (London), Crandall's
"Representative Sonnets" and Higginson & Big-
elow's "American Sonnets," as well as many other
collections of high standing and similar nature. He
entered the United States Navy at the age of twenty-
two, and for three years was attached to the "Worces-
ter" on the West Indian station, where he studied life
in the tropics, and contributed to journals North and
South. He left the navy in the summer of 1875, and
spent several subsequent years on the family estate on
Glen Lake, Warren County—as he says, "cultivating
strawberries and poetry with considerable success."
He was married in 1875 to Mrs. Eva Hendryx.
While at Glen Lake he issued two volumes of poetry,
contributed to leading papers and magazines, and
began the study of theology, preparatory to entering
the ministry. He was ordained in 1890 as a minister
in the Presbyterian church. He removed to North-
wood, N. Y., where he published another volume
of verse. He was successful in his chosen profession,
built up the church, and was, in 1893, called to the
Third Presbyterian church of Troy, N. Y., over which
he is now pastor. Mr. Auringer has published the fol-

The broad way from the fortress leading north—
We fell in file along a narrow path
That lay across the plain and river marsh,
O'ertopped a bluff by shaggy growths o'erspread,
And crowned with pines and silence, leading thence
Still on amid the wildwood's tangled glooms,
Straight toward an ancient blockhouse on the hill.
There lay the posts we were to seize and keep
'Gainst scout or foray from the British line,
Encamped upon the high plains to the north.

Eighteen good men we were, armed woodman-like
With musket, knife and hatchet, every man
A chosen soldier seasoned in the wars—
Sons of the sword, all eager for the work,—
Led by a dark lieutenant, silent, stern,
Yet true as steel and loved by every man—
The trustiest in the camp.

                                   Without a word
We moved in line along the narrow path,
Crossed the flat plain, crossed the low river marsh,
And steeped in moonshine and hot airs of night,
Set knees against the rough acclivity,
And gave ourselves to the wild wilderness.

---

lowing volumes of poetry : " Voice of a Shell," 1883;
" Scythe and Sword," 1887; " Heart of the Golden
Roan," 1891. He has now in preparation for early
publication the " Episode of Jane McCrea," a nar-
rative poem ; and a volume of minor verse.—*Sketch*
by J. A. HOLDEN, of Glens Falls, N. Y.

   This poem was originally published in the Glens
Falls *Messenger*, of December, 1888, a few years before
Dr. Holden's death.   A sketch of this lamented gentle-
man, by his son, J. A. Holden, will be found in Ap-
pendix No. XI.

We climbed the steep ascent with guns atrail,
Picking our steps among the roots and stones
That hid along the pathway. Now and then
A musket breech would clink against a stone,
Sending a sudden thrill along the file ;
And then again some careless-falling foot
Would slip and bring a soldier to his knee,
Or send him reeling sidelong from the path,
Where he would catch and cling by branch or limb,
And sway his body back in line again,
And onward as before. Then suddenly
Some man would stop stock still along the file,
Smote in the face by some lithe hazel rod
That, carried out of place and springing back,
Stung like a whip. Then would an oath break forth,
Strangled at birth ; and followed in its turn
A laugh or joke in smothered undertones
At his expense who suffered from the blow—
Danger just seasoned by a spice of fun,
And no one made the worse, so all was still.
For we were men trained not to utter sound
Above necessity when foes were nigh
Like those that hemmed us now. Because one day
While hunting deer among the mountain glens
Round old Ticonderoga in the north,
And lying hushed and breathless with suspense,
Hid in a rocky hollow, while our foes
Drew ever closer round their secret snares,
An Irishman, o'erfull of bubbling fun
And mirth,—the wit and spirit of the camp,—
Possessed by some rash madness of the brain,
Let loose his tongue with such garrulity
That all the woods heard, and within an hour
Revealed our hiding-place, and brought the foe
Around us, roaring like a rush of wolves.

And in the wildwood battle waged that day
From tree to tree along that rugged ground,
A feathered arrow from a warrior's bow
Pierced both poor Michael's cheeks, transfixed the
      tongue,
And silenced it forever.
                              O'er the plain
Two hills arose, abrupt and difficult
To master—one above the other piled
Like cloud on mountain, blotting out the stars
And sky-gleams on the north.   And on the crown
Of the first height lay shelved a little plot,
By jealous fairies stolen from the wilds,
Gone bare of trees, but richly carpeted
With soft green moss and silent, and it lay
Walled three sides round by netted hazelwood
Impenetrable.   And there by the hill's sheer brow
Where mingled earth with rock sprang one great pine,
Whose black bulk carved on darkness towered in air
In rugged perpendicular, and thence
Branching, spread broad a dark green canopy,
Mysterious, o'er the moss-soft forest floor,
And down amid its roots a forest spring,
Alive and cool, broke through the leaves and moss,
Filling its shadowy basin to the brim,
And then o'erflowing, broke o'er the hill's brow,
Streaking the hillside with a vein of pearl.
This was the ancient pine, and this the spring,
And here the spot renowned in all the world,
And here we halted, breathing hard, and here,
With studied charge and order from the chief,
Low spoken in the dark, distinct and short,
I took my stand beneath the ancient pine
To watch till morning.   And my friends filed on,
Vague bulks in darkness, laboring up the path,

Across the plot, and up the next ascent,
On toward the ruined blockhouse on the hill.

A long and lonesome watch beneath that tree—
Long watch and lonesome ; wide in darkness spread
The night-lone landscape round, behind, before—
A wilderness gone dreaming, with the moon,
Stars, silent-pacing clouds and stealthy airs
Alert above it ; and below, alert,
Their fellow-guard and watchman of the night,
I, with my weapon and a lonely heart,
But unafraid, kept watch, obedient,
For our dear country's sake and liberty.

The night hung slumberous, but one must keep
His senses bound about him—no light charge,
With naught to keep him wakeful but to watch,
Just watch and wait the sluggish hours away,
And listen. And to move beyond a small
Circle well worn of safe and level ground,
To stir about and feel one's self at large—
Strictly forbid ! To make companionship
With one's own pleasant inward impulses
By singing songs, as soldiers love to do,
Or whistling to call up the merry thoughts,
To charm an idle watch—most perilous !
Our foes were wary ears, and there was cause
To fear some few red warriors from the camp
Above us lurked about the fort that night.

A soldier's mind hoards small philosophy
Among its treasures, woo it as he will ;
A life of shocks breaks up the course of thought,
And checks it midway. Contemplation, shy,
Recluse and sensitive, starts from the sound
Of war's oncoming murmur militant,

And 'mid the roar of his impetuous rush
Gathers her things about her daintily,
And vanishes;—Guard! is the soldier's watchword.
And yet he has his fancies, often sweet,
Dreams dreams, and has ambitions of his own,
Most welcome, though so oft they come to naught;
He has his store of stirring memories
Laid up through years of strange experience,
Of camps and marches, bloody battle-fields,
Shipwrecks at sea, and perils on the shore,
Hair-breadth escapes—all memorable things
To lighten up the long hours of a watch.
All these my mind tossed o'er, then fled away,
Heart-piloted beyond the wilderness,
And visited beside the eastern sea
A humble fisher town 'twixt sands and crags
Clustered apart, a butt for bluff sea winds,
And salt-sharp storms hurled inland from the main.
There stood a house I knew of, with its door
Opening upon the wild sea waves, with sand,
And wreck, and waste of many a stormy tide
Spread near it.   And I saw upon the beach
My three sweet motherless children hard at play
With all their little sea things—fairy boats
Freighted with fairy thoughts imaginative
Launched bravely from their hands, with mingled cries
Of joy and apprehension—" See, she floats !"
" She's down ! she's gone !"   " Nay, there she comes
        again !
How sweetly she sails on now !   We will call
Her name the Lucky Sailor, for good luck."
And then they wave their hands and cry in the wind :
" Luck to the Lucky Sailor !" o'er the foam.

Back flashed my thought, and then forth out of earth,
Or visionary starlight, airy space,

Or fairyland of beauty none knows where,
A maid's sweet face rose on my heart, distinct
With light more real than reality,
And warm as coming sunrise when far off
It lingers half reluctant.   Ah, such grace !
Fairer for loveliness than eye beholds
Ever amid these desert solitudes
Forsaken of fair things !   And it appeared,
Arrayed for wonder and for loveliness,
In one long downward flood of yellow hair,
Like that which flows 'mid webs of charmed romance,
Magical tales and legends all forlorn
Imagined in old time, to net the heart,
And bear it happy captive through the tale.
Whereat my lips obedient spoke aloud
A name in the darkness with such vehemence
As made me start alarmed, and cast around
Eyes apprehensive.   But the loyal night,
Kindly discreet, gave not the sound away
To alien senseless ears.   It was a name
Since famous in the annals of the land
That heard it cried round its circumference,
Till it became a sign to conjure with,
A watchword and a symbol.   It had power
So that a banner blazoned with that name,
And borne from town to town through the broad land,
Might by its magic gather to itself
How many a thousand gallant hearts and swords,
Fast pledged to all heroic sacrifice,
For vengeance and our land's dear liberties !
And in that name deeds deemed incredible,
Opposed to all the precedents of war,
Were yearly done and recorded by fame,
Until the land breathed free, and we beheld
Our flag triumphant wave from every hill.

And in that name what individual acts
Have been accomplished ! I have known the soul,
Lukewarm in hope and courage, take quick fire,
And burn to noble death beneath its spell.
And I have known the base and dissolute—
The wretch that fought for plunder, hardened men,
Cold soldiers by profession, shallow souls—
Burlesques of heroes, liors in the camp,
And lambs in battle—I have known all these
To change their very nature at that name,
And in the day of opportunity
Prove Romans all ; and terrible in fight,
Heap fame and honor and proud victory
Upon themselves and country !

        But these things
Were yet unknown, unborn. The burning deed
Yet lingered that would consecrate that name,
Baptize it in warm blood, and send it forth
On its miraculous mission through the world.
As yet the name of maiden Jane McCrea
Was but a synonym of beauty, grace,
And worth, and all things rare and excellent
In maidenhood's domain. And in that realm
She ruled supreme and only. It was she
Who reigned the belle of all the border land,
The boast and toast of all the gallant souls
In camp and garrison, the old man's cheer,
The light of every young man's heart and eyes ;
A queenly creature, governing her world
By right supreme of beauty and excellence,
Who moved among her people royally,
Regarded now with fond solicitude,
Because 'twas whispered that she was in love—
Love makes a maiden sacred, so they say.

Among the people there's a story told
About a soldier wounded in the war,
Who fled through weary leagues of wilderness
'Mid wild and secret perils of the woods,
Hunger and beasts and foes inveterate,
Seeking the camp ; and how at length he reached it—
Only to lay him down a broken man
In mind and body in a hospital,
Along with more of war's unfortunates,
To be born back with pain ; and how our Jane,
Then but a tender bud of maidenhood,
From sacred pity that he had no friend
To nurse him in his sickness, took the place
Of the restoring angel by his bed,
And came and went a sunbeam in the gloom
Of that dark hospital ; and how at length,
Amid the feeble glimmerings of his mind,
He knew her face alone among the many
That passed before him daily.   And 'tis said
That when the lamp of mind burned clear once more
And he could rise and walk with growing strength,
And feel his heart returning through her care,
From long beholding her he came to love her ;—
The gentle looks, the touch of soothing hands,
And all the nameless magic of a voice
Attuned to sympathy, so wrought upon him
That when he rose again, a man restored,
His heart had all gone forth to the restorer.
And then they tell how he delayed to speak
The passion that possessed him, hiding it
And hoarding it for awe and sacredness,
Apart within his breast ; till learning late
By chance report of love already pledged
By her to some first lover long preferred,
In manly silence, but with broken looks,

He went away, leaving due recompense
Of gratitude for all the faithfulness
That wrought his restoration. So he passed
From living sight and knowledge of his friends,
And half from their remembrance as the days,
Burdened with anxious cares of war, went by,
And strife of factions. Then at last came one
Who brought the tidings of a battle fought
Out somewhere in the West, who told the tale
That when 'twas o'er and won, among the slain
They found a soldier, propped against a wall,
Still grasping his red blade, and round his feet,
Fallen in a horrid heap, full many a foe
Lay weltering, gashed with many a fearful wound,
As from a madman's fury. And they found,
When they approached to bear him from that post
Of death and valor to a soldier's grave,
Pressed to dead lips with war-ensanguined hand
A lock of golden hair, that could have grown
On but one lovely head in all the world.

Ah, such a girl! Ah me, had I been young!—
Had I been young and free, as once I'd been,
With all the virgin hunger of the heart,
And all the headlong fire and fantasy
That heavenly beauty kindles in the brain,
What soul can tell what might have been? Ah well,
Her heart had built its nest in another tree!
Her smile, that would have overflowed with light
Of glory and gladness some proud patriot's soul,
Love-darkened all for her, had lit amiss
Upon a Royalist! And truly 'twas
A time of strange affections, lives perplexed,
And lives run all to random! Ere the war
Broke o'er our land for life and liberty,

While peace prolific tended at the plough,
And heaped the grain in autumn well content,
Walking thus largely liberal through the year,
A youth, young, gay, and handsome, choicely bred,
With mind and manners shaped in city schools,
Whose stock had taken root in border soil,
And flourished into fair prosperity
With lands and cattle, saw our forest rose
Brightening the borders of his daily path,
And stopped, admired and plucked it. And the maid,
Whose kin were friends of freedom, first of those
Who voiced in the assemblies of the people
Those thoughts deemed treason by the power o'er seas
Ruling our land, became his promised bride—
And he a Royalist! By what mad chance,
Or what wild tossing of the dice of fate,
While wild war-spirits laughed, that stroke befell,
Predicting strange confusion in the event,
And necessary vengeance—who can say !
Were there not gallant fellows mad to woo,
And just as gallant fellows mad to win,
Among her near and loyal countrymen,
Who blessed the ground she trod on, air she breathed,
And made her queen and goddess of their thoughts,
That she should cast her treasure all away
Upon a counterfeit of royalty,
That royalty despises in its heart—
A foolish boy mad for a uniform
Of scarlet—scarlet as the hue of shame
That mantled honest faces when his act
Of treason stirred the border ! Many a curse
Lit on the act and actor, out of lips
Thin drawn with bitterness ; and many a brow
Knit hard, and many an eye flashed sullen fire ;
And many a nail bit flesh of palm, as men

Thought on his deed and its significance—
The torture and the peril of the time,
Chiefly endured because of treachery,
Betrayals by false friends, who underground
Set traps to catch their neighbors unawares,
Invoking all the arms of foreign foes,
Leagued with the hatchet and the incessant torch
Of pitiless heathen for our overthrow.
How we remembered all the suffering,
The ceaseless roar of war waves round our shores,
Breeding anxieties, reports extreme
Of battle and disaster day by day,
On sea and land, and all the multitude
Of harrying disquiets poured upon us !
At home, the frequent midnight burnings, raids,
And sudden slaughters, and a land laid waste,
Fast slipping back to savagery, with life
Cheapened to competition with the brutes,
Our fellow-sufferers.   And everywhere,
Suspended over every household hearth,
Forever in the trembling thoughts and dreams
Of helpless grandsire, maiden, wife and babe,
Scaring the dove of peace from every home,
The fearful image of the tomahawk !
Was it so strange, remembering such things,
A fire of hate should spring from this small spark
Dropped on such fuel !   Then to think that one
Who bartered honor for a piece of tape
To wear upon his shoulder should have won
And held so sweet a treasure, 'twas enough
To roil men's thoughts, and stir their passions up
To protestation—powerless enough,
Because love makes a mockery of us all.
But while they flung him hate and burning scorn
As his right portion, still they loved the maid,
Because she was so rare and beautiful.

But by and by the morning! 'Twas the pipe
Of bird, I think, that first announced the dawn
From some near tree—a sweet and slender strain,
Inquisitive, as if the dear musician
Were doubtful if he caught the scent of dawn,
And hesitated in his song. But now
Upon that note pipe after pipe broke forth
In choral harmony from all the hill,
Until a thousand joyous voices blent
Were making fairy music to the dawn!
It ceased; and then appeared a narrow line
Of mellow light low on the eastern sky,
Beyond the distant hill lines as they lay
Crouched on the horizon, silent, saturnine,
And then a deeper glow warmed the same hills,
That rose, unmasked, and showed their visages
Beaming with genial light. And the same splendor
Made pale the lustre of the summer stars
Sprinkled along the east, and sent the darkness,
Broken and pierced with many a kindling shaft,
In broad retreat, until the orient
Shone with red glory, though the sun delayed.
The heavens waxed warm and bright, but all the earth
Slept, in that latter deep and dreamless slumber
That aye precedes the waking. Silent all
The endless forest lay, except perchance,
Unceasing, as the sweet breeze played, arose
The sigh and murmur of a million leaves
Shaken o'erhead; the hum of rushing waves;
And sounding on in endless monotone,
The surge and rumble of the cataract
Far northward. And below along the plain
Reposed the fortress ramparts coiled in dusk,
Girdled with scattered huts; and on the right
Beneath the walls the eager Hudson flowed,

Marching with all his thousands from the hills,
With rustle and murmur of his million feet,
Passing unseen beneath his cloud of mist
That overhung him, seen for many a mile
Tracking the forest with a trail of fleece.
But brighter grew the red along the sky,
And thinner grew the veil that wrapped the woods,
As marched the light to westward o'er the world ;
And then a bow of ruddy fire appeared,
Crowning the far-off topmost eastern hill,
And in a moment o'er the wilderness
Broke the broad sun !—a swimming fount of fire,
Pouring its streams across the solitudes,
Kindling the world to beauty with his blaze.
His rays fired up the fog along the stream,
And set the water sparkling, gilt the sands,
Hung webs of yellow gauze about the hills,
And woke the merry music of the birds
In thicket deep and treetop everywhere.
Oh, 'twas a sight worth one long watch to see,
That world-old battle of the day with night,
In which the day is glorious conqueror !
And while I gazed, and silent blessed the light
For all its bounteous life and cheerfulness,
A lengthened drum-pulse throbbed along the plain,
That chorused with my heart-pulse pleasantly.
It ceased. A wreath fantastic of fierce smoke .
Rolled from the fort's low eastern parapet,
And lo ! the fort spoke from her early gun,
Telling the world of morning ! And the sound,
Recoiling, passed, and fell among the hills
Crashing ; as when a storm cloud from the west
Opens its first hoarse volley o'er the hills,
That cracking rends the arches of the woods,
Making the heart leap up in bird and beast

And man, and striking silent all the trees
In all their leaves. And then in mimicry,
A hundred echoes, seizing on the theme,
Ran babbling it the forest arches through,
Hither and thither flying through the wilds,
With voices blowing ever faint and fainter,
Far off and farther, dying on the wind
That blew from out the solitudes.

        For me,
Yet one long hour before relief would come.

I leaned upon my weapon, looking down
Upon the narrow vista of the plain,
Where war had drawn a furrow of dark earth,
And planted it with cannon. There had men
Reared for themselves rude homes in which to dwell,
And till their narrow strip of backward soil,
And hunt and fish and barter, nestled there
Beneath the fostering pinions of the fort ;
Each cottage with its tributary lawn,
Beds of rare roses, yellow marigolds,
And lilacs shadowing doorways with their green
Blossoms just fallen—haunts of friendly birds,
That made their homes in summer 'mid the boughs.
I saw the people stirring out of doors,
About their morning tasks—a pleasant sight,
As I remember how it moved me then—
Some bringing wood to light their morning fires,
And some with yoke and bucket, toilsomely,
That brought fresh water from the river's brink ;
Or driving forth their cattle 'mid the dew
To some deep forest pasture out of sight.
I saw the soldiers moving in the fort,
A few from cabined quarters just emerged,
Greeting the morning from the low dark walls ;

Half-naked gunners on the parapets,
Swabbing away like demons in the light
Of the red sun; and creeping on his post,
The sleepy watch with gun and bayonet;
Or servants from the stables leading forth,
With halters slack, the train of thirsty beasts
To water where the river lapped the sand.
And I remember most especially
How good the cook house smoke seemed to my eyes,
And how the thought of breakfast cheered me up,
And all the genial mess-room company
One has in barracks.

      But in seeing this
I saw not all. And truly such a morning—
So flush, so rich—was pledge of fairer things
Than visions of rough, kindly cottagers
And war-stained soldiers—something for a crown
To this fair morning kingdom. And that pledge
Was now redeemed. Upon the southern edge
Of the high forest wall that girt the camp,
A something, charmed with airy grace and motion,
Something akin to sunrise and fresh dews,
And winds, and blowing roses of the wilds—
A waft of morning—crossed my longing sight,
Brightly advancing. Where the river waves,
Penned in a cove that balked their onward rush,
Like sheep pressed in confusion and complained,
Striking the sand and shrinking in recoil,
Pressing back on their fellows suddenly,
As if they feared to tread the shining sands
That bore their foot-prints of unnumbered years,
I saw it break the shadows of the wood,
And dawn another sunrise on the camp,
Just touching it in passing. Where the fort

Thrust out a threatening angle toward the stream,
It lightly turned and took the narrow path—
The path that we had taken—moving on
Across the plain, across the river marsh,
Threading the gleaming ribbon of the path
Dry shod, as light and dainty as a fawn
That trips the forest pasture. And I leaned
And watched it hushed, as one so often will
Who stands and cranes his neck, and holds his breath,
To note the outcome of some ventured guess,
As if 'twere life or death. And so my heart
Laid wager with my eyes who this might be
Coming so lightly. 'Twas a woman's form
Coming so sweetly—sight in soldier's eyes
Most prized of all in this great wilderness,
Because so rare and transient. On it came
Until it reached a cabin reared of logs
Piled roughly in their bark, and covered o'er
With faded forest branches that crouched low
Within the outer circle of low huts—
A lonely little dwelling, with its door
Swung open to the morning, and a curl
Of friendly smoke above its chimney stack.
And to its door the maid of morning came,
And paused. And from the cabin came a dame
Of stanch and portly frame, and courteously
Took the fair morning stranger by the hand,
And led her in ; and both were lost to sight.
They passed away from sight, but ere they went
A breath of laughter floated up to me,
Upon the air of morning sweetly borne.
And then my heart laid claim upon my eyes
For one more wager won—'twas lovely Jane,
Even as my heart had said ! And this was she—
The famous, lovely, luckless Jane McCrea,

Whose face had set such martial hearts aflame,
Whose mournful fate has set the world on fire !
And I was glad at heart to have her near,
And blessed the sunny morning in my soul,
Praised the soft wind, the flashing river, and
The songs of birds and forms of fellow-men,
And all the forest scene.   But suddenly
All gladness died within me as my soul,
By some mysterious instinct like a hound,
Caught a fleet scent of evil in the air,
Far off or hovering.   There was lovely Jane,
Arrayed as for her bridal, with the sun
Seeking a Tory's house—I knew the dame,
A brave Scotch lady, but in sentiment
A Royalist as rank as ever breathed.*
Here was our maiden nested in that lodge
Of treason, with her lover hovering nigh,
Hawk-like and watchful, in the English camp,
Perhaps prepared to march with horse and foot
Against her friends and mine, the feeble few
Who held the fort, for 'twas a conquered land.
What fate had lured her forth at such a time
Of watch and danger ?   Was it possible
She dreamed to quit the shelter of the camp,
And home and friends, and all the gallant guard
Of hearts and weapons leagued in her defence,
For that dark league of wilderness, beset
By such two well-known dangers, all for a sight
Of one mad boy in uniform ?   Alas !
If she had only known—had only known !
If she had only kept at home that day !
But there too late was she !
                              Then like a peal
Of trumpet to a soldier in his dreams,

_____

* Mrs. McNeil, a cousin of General Simon Fraser.

There spake our foes! There came a deadly crash
Of rifles from the summit of the hill,
A burst of smoke, and then a cry so wild
And savage that the heart stopped at the sound
An instant in its beating, and then leapt,
Making the brain swim. 'Twas the battle shout
Of twice a score of savage enemies
Launching from ambush in a dim ravine
That split the upper hilltop with a gash
From some old torrent stroke, now flowing o'er
With a roaring tide of red ferocity
Upon my hapless comrades of the guard.

Downward the cloud of battle swept the hill,
Shooting its smothered lightnings as it went,
With thunder and sound of voices wildly blent,
Fierce yells, and short sharp cries from here and
        there,
Where a shot struck the life, and laid on earth
A soldier quivering. And on its edge
Now and again lithe figures sprang to sight
And vanished 'mong the tree boles here and there;
And then there passed the fleeting pantomime
Of clenched and struggling forms that rolled on earth,
With nimble limbs like serpents writhed and tossed,
Knit in the last great grapple breast to breast.

The first live thing I saw break from that cloud
Was one poor soldier fleeing from his foes,
Wild-eyed, bareheaded, wounded, weaponless,
All blind with blood and terror, leaping out
From the upper bluff, who fell, and gathering, came,
Now stumbling more than running, toward the spot
Where I stood roused and watching.
                                On he came,

But a clear streak of fire broke from above
And downward, and he stopped with staring eyes
A moment, and then dropped a clod beside me,
Pierced through the breast; and at his fall his foe,
A tall fantastic warrior grim as hate,
Launched at him from the bluff, with pealing cries
Of triumph, waving high a glancing blade,
To bear away the trophy of his deed.
He never reached it!   Swifter than the lightning
My weapon rose and spoke, and at the word
Down rolled the heathen howling, clutching earth,
And showering leaves in agony—a stroke
Well struck, and yet, alas! the only one
That fate permitted me to deal that day.
For lo! the hanging bluff was all alive
With gliding forms and fearful visages,
And streaming scalp-locks! Then I knew in soul
The fatal issue of that dark surprise,
And fight so quickly finished—naught, alas!
Save sudden death or capture to my friends,
Whose weapons spoke no more, whose shouts were
          still,
Whose enemies in insolent victory
Ranged everywhere.
                    One instant desperate
Wherein to fight or flee—to die or flee—
That was the choice.   With madness in my soul,
Yet loving life, I laid my gun aside,
That death to many a foeman, and my friend
Trusted and true, gift of my ancestor,
Whose deeds in former wars had made it famous—
Famed weapon, famous fighter; cast beside it
My oxhorn flask, and leathern pouch with balls;
Plucked out the heavy war-axe from my belt,
Grasped firm my knife, and glancing everywhere

For lurking foes, slid snake-like down the path,
Brushing the foliage lightly ; then leapt out,
Long like a hunted deer, when stretch the hounds
Red-mouthed upon his track.   And running raised
My voice, and rang aloud along the plain—
" Fly for your lives, the foe is at your doors !
Fly to the fort !" to warn the villagers.
I never reached the fort though ; luck, or fate,
Or some ill influence that dogs men's steps,
Had writ me down unfortunate that day.
For scarce my feet had carried me 'mid plain,
Running with every nerve stretched, arms a-play,
My spirits up and dancing, courage roused,
And passions all enlisted in the race,
When suddenly a thicket by the path
Let out three lurking heathen on my front,
And cut the glorious race short.   One of the three,
A hunched black warrior with a spiteful eye,
Thrust out a fire-arm in malignant rage.
And as I bounded onward, fired, and I
Plunged forward to the earth, stung in the heel
By hissing lead—a moment shocked, surprised,
Not knowing well my hurt—fell, but arose,
Hot-faced with rage, and met my foeman there
With one slim blade, but panting for the strife
Of strength and warrior courage to the end.
But ere a blow was struck, amid the pause
Defiant, filled with flying hateful glances,
A tall wild warrior, limbed like Hercules,
And slippery as a serpent from the fens
Of his old forests, flung his gun to earth,
Leapt lightly on me, coiled himself about me,
Tying my limbs with tangles of lithe strength,
And bore me down to earth tied motionless ;
And his companion, greedily with his hands

Tied fast my limbs with cords. Then both arose,
And looked on me. Then the hunched heathen took
My blade, torn from my grasp, and whetted it
Upon his earth-soiled moccasin awhile,
Eying me as a butcher eyes a sheep
Laid bound for slaughter. Ceasing, up he sprang,
And flashed the steel in my eyes, extravagant
In cries and shows of triumph.

                     So I lay
Bound in the presence of my enemies,
It was a thing most wonderfully done—
I never saw aught like it in my time,
'Mid all the cunning arts and sleights of fight
Long practised in the handicraft of war !
My heart cried shame upon me then, and tears,
The first to dim my eyes for many a year,
Flowed to reproach my fallen estate, that I,
A famous wrestler in my college days,
And man of action, and on many a field
Since then triumphant in my strength of arm,
At last should yield my prestige in the art
To that wild fellow of the woods, untaught,
With naught but simple nature for his friend.
And yet amid my sharp humility
I did admire the deed !   It pleased me so
That I forgave the fellow on the spot
With all my heart, it was so bravely done !

A few swift words in their ungentle tongue,
Complete with glancing eyes and waving arms,
Passed 'twixt my captors. Then the champion took
His weapons, beckoned to his chosen mate —
A lean and sinewy warrior, like a wolf—
Who followed, and the pair with secret steps
Passed silently from sight. And then approached

My foe, that piece of fierce deformity,
And bade me rise.   And I arose and went,
Having no choice, before him up the slope,
Printing the path with blood, but with the sun
Warm on my back ; and soon, with bounden limbs,
In pain lay stretched beneath the ancient pine
Where gushed the spring of water from the bank—
A vein of pearl by moonshine, but in the sun
A darting snake of gold that rustling ran
Down briary cleft of hillslope to the plain.
I lay and watched it from my rugged couch
Awhile, half pleased and soothed to see it flow,
Bearing my thought a moment on its wave.

Then sounds were heard above me on the rock,
Voices confused, and tread of many feet,
And ring of arm that clashed on fellow arm
Cast on the earth.   But all I heard unmoved,
Being downcast and captive.   But my guard
Grew restless at the sounds, and flew aside
Often to view the scene, as oft returned
With looks more dark and threatening ; till at last,
O'ercome by restless longing like a child,
Fretful of aught that bars him from his wish,
He vanished up the rock, leaving behind
His spear, and one wild warning glance of eye
Shot backward as he passed.   I heeded not,
But lay until his last limb disappeared,
Withdrawn above the brink !   'Twas then with pain
And utmost struggle that I rose and stood,
Supported by the pine tree's friendly bulk—
Ah, how the cords did eat into my flesh !—
And looked with sharpened eyes across the plot
Brought level with my gaze.   It was a sight
To stir the heart with wrath, disgust, and hate,

To fill the soul with curses 'stead of prayer,
The mouth with prayers that were naught else but
        curses ;
And stir a sleeping demon in the breast
To thrills of fiendishness that puts to shame
The thing divine in man.   A company
Red-handed from the slaughter clustered there,
Astir with dark exultance round a heap
Of ghastly battle trophies, which their hands
Had stripped from murdered bodies of brave men,
And they my comrades !   Garments bathed in blood
Were there ; and many a weapon with its steel
Dimmed with the smoke of conflict, as it fell
From some strong soldier's grasp struck in mid course
Of fiery onset.   One slim blade I saw
Snapped at the point and crimsoned to the haft.
Among the throng were some that crawled along
On wounded limbs, the furnace of their hate
Seven times more heated by the fires of pain ;
And now and then a hand amid the throng
Would pluck a loathly object from a girdle,
And whirl the fearful trophy high in air,
Whereon triumphant cries broke from the throng,
That filled my soul with loathing.   Back I sank
Upon the kindlier earth, all sick at soul,
With nature shocked, offended at the sight
Of triumph more degrading than defeat.

Now sounds of coming footsteps caught my ear
Climbing the path beneath me ; though the leaves
Hung thick before the way, and mixed o'erhead,
Shut out the panting climbers from my sight,
A hope my soul had harbored while I lay
Helpless, with prayers for vengeance on my foes,
Sprang up alive at these oncoming sounds,

And broke the dear news to my panting heart,
This was the longed-for succor from the fort—
Alas, that never came! The foliage
That closed the path, just where it took its plunge
Sheer to the plain, was shaken for a space,
Then parted, and my conqueror stood in view,
With some behind him. It was then I saw
The first true act of savage gallantry
My eyes had ever seen. A step aside
He made, and paused, and gracefully with his hand
Drew back the plaited foliage from the path,
And let two ladies through. The first that came
Was Jennie, issuing from the leafy shade
In all her maiden glory—like the sun,
O'ermounting in its course victorious
Through heaven the cloud that barred his early beams.
The morning's exercise had put a flush
Of rosy warmth upon her countenance ;
Her bonnet now was off, and from her head—
That strong proud head she carried like a queen—
Even from the low brow backward o'er her crown,
Along her back until its crinkled gold
Streaked bright the path behind her as she walked,
Rolled down in glorious billows that great hair
Whose match was never seen in all the world !
I looked upon her face—there was no shade
Of fear that troubled her fair countenance ;
But in her sweet blue eyes a pointed light
Quivered ; and on her cheek, and in her lips,
Proud curled and beautiful, a fire and sting
Of lovely indignation burned, that told
A world of things by tongue unspeakable,
In judgment from a proud imperial soul
Offended. Painfully behind her came
Her friend and hostess, great in flesh and frame,

On whom the heat and toil pressed wearily;
And o'er her shoulder as she came two eyes
Shone baleful, of a captor at her back.

Scarce had they issued ere the maiden's eyes
Beheld me lying helpless in my bonds.
She thrust aside with an imperious hand
And glance of scorn, her captor from her path,
And came close to my side, knew me and smiled,
And spoke a pleasant word to cheer me up,
Bending above till her fallen hair
Touched my prone breast with blessing—in her care
For me forgetful of her greater woe.
O tender light of woman's sympathy,
Shining in that dark place!

                              A moment more
And all were passing onward up the path,
Round the rock's angle, climbing toward the plot—
A rugged path for tender feet to tread,
Rough, hard and stony cruel! Oh, I wished—
I wished and longed, but could not, being bound—
To ease them on—it was but natural—
One loves to smooth the pathway for a friend!
And as they vanished, winding round the rock,
I felt that awful sinking of the heart
Suddenly take me, that I oft had felt,
Sometimes on battle-fields, sometimes in camps,
And often on the waters of the deep,
Forerunning some disaster, woe or death
To one I loved the best in all the world.
They reached the plot and halted; then a shout
Vociferous from savage throats arose
In greeting to their chief.   And then the chiefs,
Grave and subdued, apart upon the rock,
Assembled in dark conclave, motionless

Except for lips and eyes unresting moved
In energy of speech, and glances shot
Oft toward the fort with sign significant,
And oft upon the captives.   And among them,
Chief in authority and eloquence,
Presided my wild captor.   Brief the council,
And soon dissolved; and mixing with the men,
By swift and subtle signs the chiefs made known
Their will.   And then stepped forth two warriors,
      strong
Of limb and innocent of battle stain
Or reek of human trophy, and addressed
In broken tongue, but still unbroken signs,
And not ungentle art and emphasis
The elder captive, pointing toward the north
With often outstretched arm and liberal air
Of signified assurance.   But the dame
Returned no word nor stirred, but stood bowed down
As if absorbed in her calamity.
And oft she sighed and deep, like one o'erspent
With toil or utmost grief.   A little while
Remained she thus, and then she raised her head,
With stern and flashing eyes fixed on her foes,
And opening at once her heart and lips,
Poured out with marvellous mastery of tongue
A rain of indignation on her foes.
And all the band shrank awestruck from that speech,
Whose fire and thrust wrought havoc with their wits,
And overthrew each warrior where he stood
With fear and admiration.   Cowed, subdued,
By such unwonted thunder in their ears,
They changed—unchanged in purpose still—their arts
To win obedience to their designs
From their reluctant captive—cringed and crawled
In awkward forms of savage blandishment,

And flatteries unpractised by their kind.
Their rude persuasions triumphed ; and the two
Took her between them, moving leisurely.*
And sought the broader highway pointing east
Along the hill's foot.   Winding toward the plain
They pressed along, appearing in and out
Among the hazel shoots and pine-tree boles
That clustered thick between us, and were gone.

---

* At this point it would seem that Mrs. McNeil
lost sight of Jenny, "who," to use the language of
Mrs. McNeil, in relating the circumstances afterward,
"was there ahead of me, and appeared to be firmly
seated on the saddle, and held the rein, while several
Indians seemed to guard her—the 'Wyandotte Panther'
still ascending the hill and pulling along by bridle-bit
the affrighted horse upon which poor Jenny rode."
Mrs. McNeil, however, was soon separated from
Jenny and carried off to "Griffith's House," and there
kept by the Indians until the next day, when she was
ransomed and taken to the British camp.   "I never
saw Jenny afterward," says Mrs. McNeil, "nor any-
thing that appertained to her person, until my arrival
in the British camp, when an aide-de-camp showed me
a fresh scalp-lock which I could not mistake.   Till
that evidence of her death was exhibited, I hoped
almost against hope that poor Jenny had been either
rescued or brought by our captors to some part of the
British encampment."   While at "Griffith's House,"
Mrs. McNeil endeavored to hire an Indian, named
Captain Tommo, to go back and search for her com-
panion; but neither he nor any of the Indians could be
prevailed upon to venture even as far back as the brow
of Fort Edward Hill to look down it for the
"White Squaw," as they called Jenny.

And as they passed, my eyes from the pursuit
Flew back to the rock where hovered all my fears,
Like birds among the branches when the snake
Comes crawling toward the nest.   Upon that rock,
Conspicuous amid the wilderness,
With these wild scenes and faces witnessing,
Those children of two races, white and red,
The maiden and the warrior, with a sword
Extinguishing between them, stood apart
And gazed upon each other. . . . May his race
Fade from the white man's face as sank his gaze
Before those eyes of steadfast innocence,
Judging his lawless soul !

                        Meanwhile, the sun,
All bright till then, and shining in his strength,
Making the whole world beautiful with light,
Suddenly darkened, and a wind arose,
Silent till then, and wailing filled the woods
With mournful sounds, and sinking swept the ground,
Shaking the leaves and trailers on the stones,
And whispering round the tree trunks drearily,
As if it knew and grieved.   And in the trees
The sweet birds ceased their songs, and suddenly
With piercing cries fled through the lowering air,
Whirling in frightened bevies out of sight.
Away in forest depths some wandering wolf
Howled and was still ; and some distressèd beast
In some far border farmyard raised its voice
And lowed disconsolate to the darkened sky.
And through my heart and blood a dull chill crept,
And o'er my mind a dark foreboding cloud
Closed by degrees, and was not lifted more
Till that dark evil drawing to a head
Discharged itself in blood upon the land.

There rose a sudden tumult on the rock,
Like shouts of drunken soldiers when a town
Is sacked, and riot howls amid the streets,
Urged on by lust and passion and vile drink
Concocted by the devil.   And I saw
The fit of lawless passion break and rage,
'Mid brutal violence and strife of tongues,
Not wanting coarsest poison ; gestures mad,
Flashing of hate-hot eyes, hands clenched and tossed
In desperate menace, weapons seized and drawn,
And all the tumult of a savage strife
Swelling to blows.   And I stood trembling, stayed
Against my bulwark tree, with all the man
Within me crying out against my bonds,
No power of mine could rend, although I strove
With strength by rage made desperate—all in vain !—
The cord was trusty and the knot made sure
Beyond all rending.

                         Suddenly as I gazed,
A rifle barrel gleamed amid the throng,
Hung there a moment set and ominous,
Ere the wild shot screamed out.   Then I beheld
The maid start suddenly, as if surprised
At the hurt dòne her, saw her shining head
Sink, with its weight of tresses, to her breast ;
I heard a long deep sigh, as of a soul
Passing to quiet rest ; and sinking down
She lay a lovely ruin on the earth,
All overflowed with her great wave of hair.
And then I saw a hatchet whirl in air,
And fall upon that poor defenceless head
Scarce yet insensible.   These eyes did see
A savage hand twined in that sacred hair,
A hell-lit face above, a glitter of steel,

And then—and then I saw no more! I barred
With burning lids my eyes against the sight,
And turned and laid me on the earth and wept—
As I weep now. Forgive me if I weep,
It helps the heart to grieve a little while—
The flow of tears turns off the flood of woe,
And saves the heart from too much memory—
The memory of that deed unparalleled
In all the annals of this bloody land
Since history began. . . .
                               Oh, there goes forth
A cry that shall be quiet nevermore,
A voice to speak unto the years unborn,
A voice proclaiming judgment, and a power
To trouble thrones, cast reputations down
Beyond wide seas, in other, alien lands
Our arms can never reach, our laws o'erawe,
Our justice rectify. That voice was heard
A war cry thrilling through the patriot hosts
On Saratoga's field. And flying on,
It sounded wild o'er Yorktown, and gave back
The eagle to our hosts. On ocean's wave
It sounded suddenly amid the roar
Combined of wind and wave and bellowing guns;
Filled with heroic madness the strong souls
Of seamen, till another answering shout,
This time of victory, ran on the waves
Which bore the news to all the nations. So
Our flag triumphant waves from every hill.

And when at length I looked abroad again,
Another change had come upon the scene;
The summer sky was blue and bright again,
Now that the evil shadow of that cloud
Had broken up, and passing left it clear.

For that mysterious darkness now was gone;
Again the sun shone o'er the wilderness,
Again the merry birds sang in the trees,
The squirrel skipped and sported on his limb,
And cast the empty refuse of his feast
With mocking gibes upon me as I lay,
Then sped with nimble scamperings out of sight.
A pleasant breeze hummed quaintly in my ears,
Making the leaves shake lightly, while the sun
Speckled the rich turf under them with gold.
Nature, who closed her eyes on that dark deed,
Refusing to behold it, now was gay,
And made her Sabbath music as before.

Part II.

Ah well! I scarcely knew what next they did,
Except they spared me—spared my worthless life,
Though they had torn my heart, and stunned my brain,
And stabbed my suffering spirit through and through
With thrice the pangs of death.   They loosed my
      bonds,
And bade me rise—not spitefully indeed—
Even a little pitifully it seemed.
And I arose and made essay to walk,
With such poor progress as my stumbling limbs
Might make along a path so blind and rough.
For I was stunned, benumbed in head and limb,
And moved as one that walks but half awake,
Scarce feeling pain or pleasure.   Everything
Seemed strangely dim and dusky round me now,
And faint and dream-like.   All the pleasant sounds
And gladsome sights that filled the Sabbath woods
Came to me through some dusky medium
That cloaked the senses.

So we passed along,
My captors strangely temperate with me
In my loose walk, and stumblings to and fro,
With feet benumbed and bleeding. Yet they kept
Ever beside me, gliding dim and dark,
Like demons in a nightmare—creeping, creeping—
So dumb and death-like—it was terrible!
Truly they seemed like devils!
Slow we went
Under the cooling shade, o'er leaf-beds spread
To deaden more our footsteps; when erelong
We overtook the dame and her two guards—
Travellers more slow than we—journeying on
Their road laboriously. And yet the dame
Failed not of spirit, but brave and bright of eye,
And stout of heart, toiled on complainingless.
I thought she paled a little when she saw
Our band appear with but one prisoner,
And that the one least present in her thoughts;
Perhaps she questioned me by some mute sign—
But I was stunned and dreaming, knowing naught,
And she bore stoutly onward as before.

At last we reached a cabin hid in woods,
Log-built and brown, with hospitable look—
A sort of inn, with loungers round the door—
White men and red, who roused them as we came
Up to the porch, and gazed, but said no word—
And dogs and children playing round the porch.
And here we paused and rested for awhile,
Took food, and such rough comfort as we might,
Being downcast and captive, and reserved
For what dark fate we knew not—nay, and I—
At least I cared not! Fate had naught for me
I even cared to question or to know,

So weary was my soul of all this strife.
We gathered up, and took our road again,
Something improved in spirit and in limb,
For the brief tarry and the food we took.
And now our captors grew more kind, and turned
Often, and spoke to us in broken words,
And not ungently.   Tried to cheer us up,
Speaking in words and signs of camp and friends,
Of ransoms and of coming liberty—
Themes, to be sure, to buoy a captive up,
And start a peering hope within the heart
Of black misfortune—all in vain to me,
Too heart-sick to revive at anything ;
Too worn of all this seeming senseless strife,
Of all this noisy war of arms and tongues—
These endless themes of battles, battles, battles !
Of marches, sallies, camps and victories
Forever on men's tongues !   Sick of this land—
Sick of the land and all its miseries,
And even of life and all that life contains.
And my brave comrade in captivity—
She was too angry still to heed them much,
Or answer if she heeded.
                              When the sun
Had dipped below the fringe of forest trees
Far on the skirts of that green lonely world,
And half the summer afternoon had waned,
Slow fading toward the west, we reached a place
Where the high plain around us and behind
Ceased suddenly, and the land fell away
To northward with a plunge, into a stretch
Of dark and sunken soil, with cedar shades
O'erspread, that girt the highlands like a girdle.
And in its very coil the British camp,
Dotting a low knoll with its clustered tents,

Like cones of fleece amid the blackened stumps
And black earth scorched with fire. And round it,
  walls
Of cedar woods impenetrable, wild,
And dim and lonesome. 'Twas a pretty sight,
That touched the soul with a reviving sense
Of hope and cheer and human fellowship,
After that dim and ghostly march, with souls
Bowed 'neath their burden of captivity.
And as we looked, it seemed as if I saw,
Instead of tents that sheltered mortal foes,
A camp of angels, with celestial tents
Pitched in the heart of the great wilderness,
Gleaming a moment, soon to be withdrawn.
Our captors saw, and shouting swung in air
Their bloody relics ; for their march was done,
Their danger past, their triumph nigh complete.
They shouted, and an answering cry arose
From the camp's rear. And then a troop of friends—
Friends of our foes, God help us, not of ours—
Sprang forth to meet them, like a pack of dogs
Flying with yelps and gambollings of joy
To meet their kind returning from a raid
Upon some innocent sheepfold, bathed in blood,
And mad with gust of slaughter—so they came.
A file of soldiers too were soon on foot,
Flashing in steel and scarlet up the path,
And as they came the clamorous dogs grew mute,
Ceased their vile gambollings, and slunk away
O'erawed and cowed—except, indeed, the few
Whose game we were. And these restrained them-
  selves,
Submitting while the King's men, filing round,
Enclosed and drew us from them. Silently,
With stately tread, they marched us down the hill,

And with no further parley or delay
Drew toward a log-reared cabin, roofed with bark,
That stood the centre of the clustered tents
That flecked the knoll.   A sentry in the path
Saluted, and our leader touched his cap,
And on we passed, dogged by our dusky foes,
Sliding along like shadows, and as still,
Suffered to pass with that mute tolerance
Which shadows claim that dog us everywhere—
Nay, worse, scorned and detested, so it seemed,
With silent and significant neglect
By these their bounden patrons, paymasters,
And nominal fair friends.   Erelong we stood
Around the door of the great general's tent
Commanding these strong legions—men and arms—
Marching with purple pride and waving flags
To crush the weak and miserable few
Who bore the burden of this mighty cause,
And the freedom of our people on their swords.
The red guard parted right and left, and we
Filed in between them through the open door,
My captive friend and I, and following still,
Our foes, subdued and watchful.   Then the guard
Wheeled and marched off, a sergeant, proud and tall,
Stepping with stately motion in our rear.

A low rude room it was wherein we stood,
Divided in the midst by dropping walls
Of painted curtains, looped in heavy folds,
Like banners o'er an archway.   All the walls
Were cedar beams yet shaggy with the bark
Wherein they grew; and for a floor our feet
Stood ankle-deep in bearskins loosely laid
Upon the bare and rugged earth beneath.
Around the room were banners, weapons, chests

Carved, and with mighty clasps of brass thereon,
Ancient, from over seas; and everywhere
The all select and choice appurtenance
Of a great general's tent. There stood a desk,
Whereat a pale clerk in half uniform
Sat busy working at his documents,
His head upon one side, with sidelong eye
Upon the lines made by his running quill.
He quit his task, half wheeling in his seat,
Eying us sharply; then smiled, half in scorn,
At such extreme dejection. "Ah," he said,
"Prisoners, I see! Go, orderly, report
Two prisoners to the general, and return."
And turning to his documents again,
Wrote on. And the proud sergeant at the door
Stalked out, his sabre clanking as he went.

Then passed a scene I never shall forget,
The strangest scene, considering time and place,
My eyes have ever seen. Entered the tent
Two officers in royal uniform—
One, middle-aged and careworn, moving slow;
One, young, built like a prince, with flashing eyes,
And with the name and character complete
Of soldier and brave man inscribed upon him—
A fine, dark fellow. Then the elder paused,
Scarce yet within the tent door, with his eyes
Upon the wretched dame, and suddenly,
With dubious voice, "Why, madam!" he exclaimed.
And, "General!" she replied, distinct and short;
And flash upon that greeting there arose
A storm of tongue and temper, unapproached
In all my memory of wordy wars—
The crown and flower of female raillery,
Saved by just rage from mere vulgarity

Detestable to see.   Oh, it was rare,
To see that haughty English general,
Great lord of hosts, and conqueror of realms,
Who never bowed before an enemy,
Whipped in his tent by one wronged woman's tongue!
And that same woman his own cousin born—
His kinswoman according to the flesh;
And more than that, in soul and sentiment,
A partner in the cause for which he fought—
A royalist as rank as ever breathed.
A doting lion, hungering for prey,
Had pounced upon and caught—a lioness!
And now, Sir Lion, look you out for claws!
Oh, and the claws were there!   And suddenly
Unsheathed, made havoc more complete than swords
Of twice a score of alien adversaries,
Whom courage might o'ercome.   " Sir, stand and look!
This is a precious piece of gallantry,
Right worthy of a Royal officer
And gentleman!"   'Twas thus the gale begun,
And waxed anon until it blew great guns,
Drowning all opposition.   " On my word!"
" Upon the honor of a gentleman!"
" Madam, I swear"—" Permit me, but a word!"
" I never knew—indeed, how could I know!—
I beg you stop and let me say a word."
Straws to the wind!   'Twas wonderful to hear
What gusts of words, what flashes scintillant
Of keen sarcastic lightning, stormy bursts
Of most authentic thunder, what keen thrusts
Of deadly irony, dealt thick and fast,
One following on another like a glance,
Poured from the fiery heart and stormy lungs
Of that great titaness!   And ended all
With one great cry that filled the tent, and shrilled,

Piercing all ears. "Oh, there stand murderers here!
Ask them of Jenny—ask of Jane McCrea!"
And then the true warm woman in her heart
O'ermatched at last her rage, and down she sank,
O'ercome, and, like a woman, all in tears.
And thereupon the mighty general
Brought out a soldier's cloak of ample breadth,
And gallantly as ever soldier could
Spread it about the shoulders of the dame,
And smiling besought her wear it for awhile,
Until a fitting robe be found for her,
To better clothe her form. And she arose,
Muttering short thanks, and shaking down the folds,
Sat down again, wrapped up from head to heel.
And then the clerk, whose pen had quit its task
Upon the outbreak of that wordy war,
His eyes meanwhile brimful of sparkling fun,
And overbubbling humor scarce restrained,
Resumed his quill, and scratched on as before.
The general, mild and all obsequious,
Complacent with his tact and management,
Stood rubbing hands vivaciously.
                                        Behind,
Unmoved and sullen, ranged along the wall,
The Indians stood, like shadows darkly limned,
But shadows with fierce eyeballs now and then
Slanting their dusky glimmer, half at rest,
Patient, on foot, taking their wonted ease.
And every mind took on a sense of calm
How grateful; and each heart conceived a touch
Of human fellowship; and every face
Assumed a look of comfort and content
At this subsidence—every face save one,
And that was white and anxious, as the man
Measured the cabin's length from end to end

With restless strides.   A panther might have moved
Thus while the brush stirred with the hunter's steps,
Closing the hunt around him.   As he paced
His glances played in an incessant search
Betwixt the dame and those dumb witnesses
Ranged 'gainst the wall with looks inscrutable.
It was that princely soldier whom my eye
Had marked with admiration,—a moment since
Careless and graceful in his mien, but now
With soul strained like a bowstring while it trembles
Tense for the shaft.   Then suddenly he ceased
His pacings, and strode straight up to the dame,
And on her shoulder laid a hand, and bent
With burning eyes above her, and at her ear—
Heard by all ears beside : " Tell me of Jane ;
Something you said of Jenny—Jane McCrea."
And then the answer came, but not from lips
Of any living being.   While he spoke,
Three wild and warlike figures foul with dust,
And soil of darker stain, came gliding in,
And halting, rolled their snaky eyes around,—
Silent, and weary with their forest march
And wild work of the morning ; yet no less
Elate with triumph cunningly concealed.
And as the soldier turned and faced them there,
One, a wild, brawny creature like a wolf,
Raised a strange thing he held, shook it aloft,
And with a red forefinger significantly
Tapped it and smiled—a grim, ferocious smile—
Even for a savage, grim and hideous.
Then from behind there rose a fearful cry,
A woman's cry of anger and despair ;
As when a lioness returned from hunt
All day, for prey to feed her little ones,
Hungry within their covert, comes at night

And scents the bodies of her little ones
Slaughtered by hunters, and in rage and grief
Peals through the woods her solitary cry.
So cried the dame and rose, her mighty bulk
Aquiver and her eyes aflame, her hand
Pointing—" O see ! that is our Jenny's hair.
O, they have slain—have slain our innocent !"
" That thing my Jenny's hair !" these were the words
I heard that poor bewildered lover say—
Bewildered for a moment, but no more.
And then there came a blow, swift, deadly, sure,
That rolled the savage headlong to the earth.
There like a whirlwind passed a furious strife
Betwixt those fiery warriors white and red ;
One bent on vengeance deadly in its aim,
And one, with wily art and ready tact,
Evading that dread issue.   From side to side,
Over and over they rolled, until the tent
Shook, and the bearskins flew this way and that
Among the circling spectators, disturbed
With panic, this way dodging and then that,
To evade the writhing bodies.   Thus the fight
Went on.   And when 'twas finished there arose
A soldier breathless, haggard, wild and torn,
And in his hand grasped tight that ghastly thing,
And it was piteous how on fumbling feet
He staggered, blind and panting, through the tent
And sank upon a seat with face bowed down
And sunken in his hands in utter grief.
And thus he stayed awhile ; then stirred, and passed
His hand along his brow and o'er his face,
And groaned aloud in mighty agony
Of spirit.   Suddenly he started up
And groped toward the tent door till an arm
Was lent in pity, and he leaned on that

And passed the tent door, groaning as he passed,
" Oh, my poor lost belovèd ! my poor Jane !"
And thus with feeble footsteps, stunned and blind,
Tottering like age and palsy—piteously
He passed from sight a broken, ruined man.
And when we quit the tent at dusk that night,
And passed into the moonlight, with the stars
Above that dark and deadly wilderness
Flashing their kindly beacons through the night,
And the wind sighing mournful 'mid the tents,
And the far panther screaming in the wilds—
Upon the outmost edge of clustering tents,
Where the black earth fell off to blacker depths
Of dense morass and denser cedar shades,
We saw against the red orb of the moon
An unknown wandering figure cross our path,
And seek the shelter of a neighboring tent.
And as a wave of night-wind swept along
We seemed to hear that cry disconsolate
Pass on the night air, piercing every soul—
"Oh, my poor lost belovèd ! my poor Jane !"

THE END.

JANE McCREA.
By Lura A. Boies.*

'Twas in the gorgeous summer time,
The vesper bells with mellow chime
    Rang out the golden day.
Along the distant mountain's height,
And o'er the Hudson, flashing bright,
In purple floods of dazzling light,
    The sunset glory lay ;

---

* For sketch of Miss Boies, see note, *ante.*

The crimson of the western fires
Glowed redly on Fort Edward's spires,
    And deeper splendors burned,
'Till Earth, with all her lakes and rills,
Her waving woods and towering hills,
    To burnished gold was turned.

I had been listening to the chimes,
And thinking of the stirring times,
    When hill and lonely glen
'Woke to the thunder tones of yore,
The sounds that rolled from shore to shore,
The deep-mouthed cannon's sullen roar,
    The tramp of mail-clad men ;
I had been thinking of the days
When the fierce battle's lurid blaze
    Hung like a fiery cloud
O'er rock and river, wood and dell,
Where now the radiant sunset fell
    And I had left the crowd,
And sought, with hushed and reverent tread,
That pleasant city of the dead,
    Where the wild wind-harps play,
And pine trees wave and willows weep,
Above her in her dreamless sleep,
    The hapless Jane McCrea.

Silent, as if on holy ground,
I neared that angel-guarded mound,
    Where white wings viewless wave ;
An aged man, with hoary hair,
And rude scars on his forehead bare,
Was kneeling in the sunset there,
    Upon the maiden's grave.
Was it some risen chief I saw,
That o'er me came that breathless awe—

Was it some warrior bold?
Whose hand had grasped the ringing steel,
Whose soul had thrilled to Freedom's peal,
    In the wild strife of old?

With sudden tears mine eyes grew dim,
Nearer I drew and questioned him
    Of all the storied past;
Of the fierce days when roused our sires
    To the shrill trumpet's blast,
And the red light of battle fires
    Upon our free hills lay;
I asked him of the green arcade,
Where gleamed that savage chieftain's blade,
I asked of her, the Scottish maid,
    The fated Jane McCrea!

Then did the veteran warrior speak,
And down his pale and furrowed cheek
    The hot tears glistening ran;
Then with the old fire flashed his eye,
His trembling tones rose clear and high,
    And thus his tale began.

PART I.

The booming guns of Lexington
Had 'roused both gallant sire and son,
And louder than the trumpet's clang
The notes of wild alarum rang.
The dawning light of Freedom's star
Shone dimly in the skies afar,
Where veiled in the black night of war
    The sun of peace went down.
And by that faint and flickering glow
The brave of heart and broad of brow

Had boldly sworn they would not bow
    To England's regal crown.

A thrill went through Columbia's soul,
An alien sound went o'er the sea,
Majestic as an anthem's roll,
    The DECLARATION of the free !
Earth's startled minions wondering heard,
Britannia, to her proud heart stirr'd,
Hurl'd back the bold, defiant word,
And drew in wrath her flaming sword ;
Fiercely the hostile nations met,
And yonder sun in darkness set
    On many a fatal day ;
In scenes of blood and carnage din,
'Mid hissing balls the gray-haired sire
Fought with the youthful warrior's fire
    In many a deadly fray ;
Still 'rose the red war's fiery form,
Still rag'd the furious battle storm,
    When Burgoyne's haughty hosts,
Breaking the waves with mighty sweep,
Came o'er the waters blue and deep,
    And landed on our coasts.

Clad in the battle's bright array,
With waving plumes and pennons gay,
    And flaming banners spread,
And arms that in the sunlight glanced,
Forward the British ranks advanced
    With slow and measured tread ;
Then rose a swift and rushing sound,
That woke the hills and shook the ground,
    Then freemen fought and fell.
The redder gushed the crimson flood,
Then was our land baptized in blood—

Of all the strife that followed then,
That thrilled the hearts of mighty men,
   Ah me! I may not tell!

The spirit of that warlike age
I feel its fires within me rage,
My bosom heaves, my old heart swells,
I feel it now, the evening bells
   Ring out the dying day.
I hear the sound of martial strains,
   I hear the war-horse neigh;
I see the smoke of battle plains,
The swift blood courses through my veins,
   I plunge into the fray.
I feel the scorching, burning blaze,
I live again those stirring days,
   The days of Jane McCrea.

PART II.

'Twas morning.—Rich and radiant dyes
Flamed in the gorgeous orient skies;
Draped in the purple of his throne
The royal sun resplendent shone.
The broad, blue Hudson, blazing bright,
Glowed like a line of liquid light,
A wave of glory rippled o'er
The hills along the eastern shore,
And waving wood and fortress gray,
Blushing in rosy splendor lay,
Kissed by the red lips of the day,
And glittering spear and lances' gleam
Flashed back again the rising beam.

On the broad lands beyond the wood,
   Now bright with harvest sheaves,

The solid lines of Albion stood
    As thick as forest leaves;
Hot haste and consternation then
Spread through the ranks of our bravest men,
A clear blast rang throughout the glen,
    Louder than hunter's horn,
And the quick tramp of hurrying feet,
The drum's deep bass that rapid beat,
The gathering din of swift retreat,
    Rose on the summer morn.

From many a lowly woodland home
Went up the cry "The foe! they come!"
And warm young hearts grew faint with fear,
And little children clustered near,
    And blushing cheeks grew pale;
And many a form with noiseless glide
Stole to the gallant warrior's side,
And fluttering garments, white and fair,
Were blent, in strange confusion there,
    With coats of burnished mail.

Aside, that morn, from all the crowd,
In earnest thought her young head bowed,
    The Scottish maiden stood,
With downcast face and lips apart,
A new joy thrilling in her heart,
That gave her cheeks a warmer glow,
And brought unto its stainless snow
    The quick o'ermantling blood.
Thus stood she bound as by a spell,
    Oh, in that hour how wondrous fair!
Around her like a glory fell
    The rich veil of her raven hair,
The fearless spirit throbbing high
Lit up her clear, calm hazel eye,

And lent the face bowed meekly there
    A beauty such as angels wear.

Oh, human love! what strange divine,
What strange mysterious power is thine;
It was thy light that inward shone
And bound her in its radiant zone;
It was thy low, melodious lay
That charmed her soul from earth away,
Till mindless of the outward din
She only heard the voice within,
And listened to the silver tone,
That whispered of the chosen one
To whom her plighted troth was given,
Who filled her deepest heart with heaven!
By thee, a willing captive led,
The maiden knew no secret dread,
    Nor felt a boding fear;
Nor heard the Indian's stealthy tread,
    Nor saw the danger near.

A sudden shriek, a piercing cry,
That seemed to rend the bending sky,
Went up that morn so shrill and high,
It made the sternest soldier start,
    And chilled and froze the circling blood,
And sent it curdling to his heart,
    That still with terror stood;
Then rose a wild demoniac yell,
A sound our brave men knew too well!

Each soul had felt the sickening fear,
Each hand had grasped the gleaming spear,
When on the air, distinct and clear,
The tramp of falling hoof drew near,

And with thin nostrils spreading wide,
The ringing spur plunged in his side,
With headlong fury rushing fast,
A foaming courser darted past.
Ha! 'twas the chieftain held the rein
And goaded on the steed amain,
And one, a gentle girl, was there,
With hazel eyes and flowing hair;
Grasped in his sinewy arm, and press'd
Rudely upon his brawny chest,
     The frail form helpless lay.
Alas! for thee, thou captured maid,
Oh, that some hand thy doom had stayed,
     Thou fated Jane McCrea!

A voice went up from mighty men,
     A loud and stirring cry,
And the bold warrior shouted then,
     "Mount! to the rescue fly!"
They rose, a brave and gallant few,
And o'er the ground the swift steeds flew,
     Winged with the lightning's speed;
Till in that green and shady dell,
Where the clear waters sparkling well,
Where towers the tall and stately pine,
And the light falls with softer shine,
The savage gave a fiercer yell,
     And reined his panting steed.
Forth from the leafy woodland shades
     Leaped many a painted warrior's form,
And brightly glanced their murderous blades,
     And wildly rose the battle's storm.
Hot balls hissed through the summer sheen,
     And haughty plumes and crests bent low;

Then darker grew the fearful scene,
    And waves of blood surged to and fro.
Before the shower of fiery hail,
The chieftain saw his numbers fall ;
With ire his swarthy cheeks grew pale,
And turning from the fell strife there,
    He stood by her, the Scottish maid.
He seized her long and flowing hair,
    And o'er her gleamed his naked blade ;
And reeking from the tide of life,
Back flashed the long and glittering knife ;
A fiendish sneer upon his lip,
    A strange wild triumph in his eye,
The chieftain saw the red blood drip,
    And held the ghastly trophy high ;
Then round him drew his blanket-plaid,
And plunged into the forest shade.

The strong, stern man—the warrior true—
Felt in his eye the gathering dew,
When with hushed tread he nearer drew,
    To the still form beneath the pine—
The maiden on the dewy green ;
    For ne'er did morning sunlight shine
Upon a stranger, sadder scene.
The warm bright life-tide's crimson flow
Dyed deep her graceful garment's snow
And mingled with the waters clear,
That in the glad light sparkled near.

The heart that thrilled to love before,
To love's soft strain would thrill no more ;
The light of her young life had fled,
Too well they knew that she was dead ;
Yet better far thus to have died
Than to have been a Tory's bride.

Now oft besides that cooling spring,
The little children play and sing,
    And in that sylvan dell
Full many a form of maiden grace
Treads lightly o'er the hallowed place
    Where she, the fated, fell.

On Saratoga's battle plains,
    Where low the British standard lay,
The murdered maiden's gory stains,
    In British blood were washed away.
The glory of that triumph day
Avenged the death of Jane McCrea.

The old man paused; the trembling tones,
    That woke the bright unconscious tear,
Sad as the low wind's music moans,
    Died on my rapt and listening ear.
Then in the solemn evening time,
When vesper bells had ceased to chime,
    And all the quiet air
Was hushed, as if this world of ours
Had closer clasped the trees and flowers,
And whispered peace through all her bowers,
    And bowed her heart in prayer;
A hush upon my reverent soul,
An awe that o'er my being stole,
    Mournful I turned away,
And left the worn old soldier there,
His white locks streaming in the air,
The dew upon his forehead bare,
And left the consecrated ground
Where holy memories clustered round
    The grave of Jane McCrea.

JANE McCREA.

By Henry William Herbert.*

It was brilliant autumn time—
The most brilliant time of all,
When the gorgeous woods are gleaming,
Ere the leaves begin to fall ;

---

* Henry William Herbert, author, born in London,
England, April 7th, 1807; died in New York City
May 17th, 1858. His father, Rev. William Herbert,
was a cousin of the Earl of Carnarvon, the nephew of
Lady Harriet Ackland, the heroine, together with
Mrs. General Riedesel, of "Burgoyne's Campaign."
(See Stone's "Burgoyne's Campaign.") He graduated
at Oxford in 1829 with high honors ; but having,
through the dishonesty of a trustee, lost his property,
he came the following year to the United States, sup-
porting himself for several years by teaching Greek
and Latin in Newark and New York. Meanwhile,
he added to his income by literary work for the differ-
ent magazines and newspapers, and finally attained to a
high degree of distinction as a writer. He wrote many
novels and books on the game of the United States,
under the *nom de plume* of Frank Forrester, all of which
were highly praised by the literary critics. During the
last twelve years of his life his home was near Belleville,
N. J., and he lived here, like Charles Lee of Revolu-
tionary fame, surrounded by his favorite dogs, of
which he was especially fond. His end was particu-
larly tragic, he having committed suicide by shooting
himself, after a dinner to which he had invited his
particular friends. A movement (1893) has been set
on foot to erect a monument to his memory. At

When the maple boughs are crimson,
    And the hickory shines like gold,
And the noons are sultry hot,
    And the nights are frosty cold.

When the country has no green,
    Save the sword-grass by the rill,
And the willows in the valley,
    And the pine upon the hill ;
When the pippin leaves the bough,
    And the sumach's fruit is red,
And the quail is piping loud
    From the buckwheat where he fed.

When the sky is blue as steel,
    And the river clear as glass ;
When the mist is on the mountain,
    And the net-work on the grass ;
When the harvests all are housed,
    And the farmer's work is done,
And the stubbles are deserted
    For the fox-hound and the gun.

It was brilliant autumn time
    When the army of the north,
With its cannon and dragoons,
    And its riflemen, came forth ;
Through the country all abroad
    There was spread a mighty fear
Of the Indians in the van,
    And the Hessians in the rear.

---

present a plain stone marks his grave in the Mount
Pleasant Cemetery, and on it is carved, according to
his wishes, the word *Infelicissimus*—a word the signi-
fication of which is a most sad commentary on his life.

There was spread a mighty terror,
  And the bravest souls were faint ;
For the shaven chiefs were mustered,
  In their scalp-locks and their paint;
And the forest was alive—
  And the tramp of warrior men
Scared the eagle from his eyry,
  And the gray wolf from his den.

For the bold Burgoyne was marching—
  With his thousands marching down,
To do battle with the people—
  To do battle for the crown.
But Stark he lay at Bennington,
  By the Hoosic's river bright,
And Arnold and his forces
  Gathered thick on Bemis' height.*

Fort Edward on the Hudson,
  It was guarded night and day,
By Van Vechten and his woodmen—
  Bright sturdy woodmen they !
Fort Edward on the Hudson,
  It was guarded day and night,
Oh ! but in the early morning
  It saw a bitter sight !

A bitter sight, and fearful,
  And a shameful deed of blood !
All the plain was cleared around,
  But the slopes were thick with wood ;
And a mighty pine stood there,
  On the summit of the hill,

---

* For the correct spelling of the name of Bemis, see
Appendix No. III.

And a bright spring rose beneath it,
  With a low and liquid trill;

And a little way below,
  All with vine boughs overrun,
A white-walled cot was sleeping—
  There that shameful deed was done!
Oh! it was the blithest morning
  In the brilliant autumn time;
The sun shone never brighter,
  When the year was in its prime.

But a maiden fair was weeping
  In that cottage day by day,
Woe she was and worn with watching
  For her true love far away.
He was bearing noble arms,
  Noble arms for England's king!
She was watching, sad and tearful,
  Near the pine tree, near the spring!*

Weary waiting for his coming—
  Yet she feared not; for she knew

----

* Until 1855 there stood a clump of primeval giant pines on the rise of a knoll just at the left of the highway leading from Fort Edward to Sandy Hill, N. Y., from the roots of which issued an unfailing spring. By indisputable and unvaried tradition underneath these pines the hapless Jane McCrea was massacred. About this time Mr. George Harvey, the then owner of this classic site, caused the last surviving pine to be turned into canes, as souvenirs of this incident in the Burgoyne campaign.

That her lover's name would guard her,
    That her lover's heart was true.
True he was ; nor did forget,
    As he marched the wildwoods through,
Her to whom his troth was plighted
    By the Hudson's waters blue.*

---

* Mrs. Rachael Ayrs Cook, widow of Ransom Cook, who died at her home in Saratoga aged ninety-two years, was one of the last surviving links that bound the present with what was one of the most romantic and decisive incidents of the American Revolution.   She was the daughter of Robert Ayrs, a Loyalist settler in what is now the town of Saratoga Springs, about midway between this village and Ballston.   It was her father, Robert Ayrs, who carried the message to Jennie McCrea in Fort Edward from her Loyalist lover, Lieutenant David Jones, in Burgoyne's army, encamped on the highlands to the north, requesting her to join him in the camp.   It was while Jennie was on her way to meet her lover that she was tomahawked and scalped by the savage Iroquois chief Le Loup, and that event led many of the Loyalist settlers, including Robert Ayrs himself, to join the patriot army under General Gates at Bemis Heights, and materially aided in the defeat of Burgoyne.   Robert Ayrs continued to reside until his death on the farm where his daughter, Mrs. Cook (who was the last survivor of his family), was born, and he is buried in the old village cemetery at Ballston Spa.   Her husband, Ransom Cook, was the builder and first agent and warden of the State prison at Dannemora.   He was also the inventor of the brace and bit, which brought him and the family a large fortune.

He bethought him of the madness
   And the fury of the strife ;
He bethought him of the peril
   To that dear and precious life,
So he called an Indian chief,
   In his paint and war-array—
Oh ! it was a cursed thought,
   And it was a luckless day.

"'Go !" he said, "and seek my lady,
   By Fort Edward, where she lies;
Have her hither to the camp !
   She shall prove a worthy prize !"
And he charged him with a letter,
   With a letter to his dear,
Bidding her to follow freely,
   And that she should nothing fear

Lightly, brightly, rose the sun ;
   High his heart, and full of mirth ;
Gray and gloomy closed the night ;
   Steamy mists bedewed the earth,
Thence he never ceased to sorrow,
   Till his tedious life was o'er—
For that night he thought to see her ;
   But he never saw her more.

By the pine tree on the hill,
   Armed men were at their post,
While the early sun was low,
   Watching for the royal host.
Came a rifle's sudden crack !
   Rose a wild and fearful yell !
Rushed the Indians from the brake !
   Fled the guard, or fought and fell !

Fought and fell! and fiercely o'er them
　　Rose the hideous death hallo!
One alone was spared of all—
　　Wounded he, and pinioned too!
He it was the deed that saw,
　　As he lay the spring beside—
Had his manly arms been free,
　　He had saved her, or had died!

Up the hill he saw them lead her,
　　And she followed free from fear—
And her beauty blazed the brighter,
　　As she deemed her lover near—
He could read the joyous hope
　　Sparkling in her sunny eyes—
Lo! the sudden strife! the rage!
　　They are battling for the prize!

Guns are brandished—knives are drawn!
　　Flashed the death-shot, flew the ball!
By the chief who should have saved her,
　　Did the lovely victim fall.
Fell, and breathed her lover's name,
　　Blessed him with her latest sigh,
Happier than he surviving,
　　Happier was she to die.

Then the frantic savage seized her
　　By the long and flowing hair,
Bared the keen and deadly knife,
　　Whirled aloft the tresses fair—
Yelled in triumph and retreated,
　　Bearing off that trophy dread—
Think of him who sent them forth!
　　Who received it—reeking red!

He received it, cold as stone,
    With a ghastly, stupid stare,
Shook not, sighed not, questioned not—
    Oh ! he knew that yellow hair !
And he never smiled again,
    Nor was ever seen to weep ;
And he never spoke to name her,
    Save when muttering in his sleep !

Yet he did his duty well,
    With a chill and cheerless heart ;
But he never seemed to know it,
    Though he played a soldier's part.
Years he lived—for grief kills not—
    But his very life was dead ;
Scarcely died he any more
    When the clay was o'er his head !

Would ye further learn of her ?
    Visit then the fatal spot !
There no monument they raised,
    Storied stones they sculptured not ;
But the mighty pine is there—
    Go, and ye may see it still,
Gray and ghostly, but erect,
    On the summit of the hill ;

And the little fount wells out,
    Cold and clear beneath its shade,
Cold and clear as when beside it
    Fell that young and lovely maid.
These shall witness for the tale,
    How, on that accursed day,
Beauty, innocence, and youth
    Died in hapless JANE McCREA.

REFLECTIONS AT THE GRAVE OF JANE McCREA.*

AND thus it is,
The bright and beautiful, and wise,
The puling youngster, and the gray-haired sage,
Manhood and youth, and infancy and age,
Alike yield up their struggling, passing breath—
Alike are subject to the grim fiend Death.

Alike, yet not alike,
For I wist not, that it is death to strike
The sudden blow, beneath some summer flower,
And then transplant it into soil more pure,
That it may waste its fragrant sweetness where
More rare exotics bloom and scent the air.

A lowly mound,
But marked from those that's gathered round,
By slab unstoried all, and neither tells
The name, nor worth, nor fame, of her that dwells
Beneath the sod, within the grave's dark gloom,
Our last-sought resting-place, and common doom.

She fell by hands
Of savage violence ;—the gleaming brands
Of war were gathered far, and near around
And seeking love she fell ;—the lover found
Was Death ; and in one long embrace,
With icy lips, he pressed her marble face.

FORT EDWARD, NOV. 5, 1842.

---

* The above lines were written for, and published in, the Saratoga *Sentinel* at the date herein named. The author is unknown.

JANE McCREA.

Read on the One Hundredth Anniversary of the Massacre of Jane McCrea, July 27, 1877.

BY JOSEPH E. KING.*

WHAT is to-day—is only what hath been,
" One touch of Nature makes us all akin."

---

* Rev. Joseph E. King was born in Laurens, Otsego County, N. Y., November 30th, 1823; the son of Rev. Elijah King, a Methodist clergyman, and a member of the old Genesee Conference.

At the age of thirteen, for a few months in a dry goods store in Albany, he then rejoined the family, who "went west," as far as Girard, Erie County, Pa., where, with an interval of a single term only in a select school, he was kept at the business of clerking in the village store until the age of seventeen. At this period the desire for better educational advantages so inflamed him that he wrote to his parents an argument of four pages of foolscap, which quite convinced them that he must be permitted and encouraged to prepare for and go through college. The preparation was at once begun at the Grand River Institute, Austinburgh, Ohio, whither the family moved, to make for him a home.

The student, in 1843, entered Poultney Academy, N. Y., then under Rev. Jesse T. Peck (now Bishop), to prepare for advanced standing in college. In 1844 admitted to the sophomore class in Wesleyan University, he took rank among the foremost of his class, despite the fact that he had to be absent each winter in the Grammar School of Glastenbury, which he taught. In his senior year he was elected to the Phi Beta

Love well befits the poet's lofty rhyme,
No fairer blossom on the trees of Time.

Kappa, graduating from Wesleyan in 1847, in the class which produced Orange Judd, Senator Cole, of California, and Bishop Andrews.

In 1848 he was made principal of the seminary at Newbury, Vt. Though among his predecessors had been such men as Rev. Doctors Hinman, Adams and Hoyt, and Bishop Osman C. Baker, yet during the reign of Professor King this seminary enjoyed its highest intellectual and financial prosperity. He paid its debts, reconstructed its chapel and class-rooms, built its public fountain, and brought the roll of its adult students up to 325 in attendance at the time of his retiring in November, 1853.

Accepting a call to his native State, he assumed the principalship of Fort Plain Seminary, N. Y., and in November, 1853, five days after his term closed at Newbury, he opened its first term—all its rooms filled with students. During this year at Fort Plain, beside the lecturing of his position, his register shows that he preached 59 times in 23 different pulpits.

It being in contemplation to erect at Fort Edward an institution on a grander scale than any existing boarding seminary, the principal of Fort Plain Seminary was invited to visit the town, with a view to give his advice in the proposed enterprise. In connection with Rev. Henry B. Taylor he matured the plans, assisted at the laying of the corner-stone in May, 1854, and was induced to assume the principalship of Fort Edward Institute for a term of 10 years. December 7, 1854, he opened the first term with 500 students in attendance, and during the 23 years of its subsequent history he has been its sole principal, registering over 10,000

Trampled and bruised, its fragrance yet appears
Despite the havoc of a hundred years !

---

different names, hailing from over 33 of the States of
the Union.   Many of his students have taken conspic-
uous places among the successful men and women of
this generation.   Over 100 of his students joined in
the war for maintaining the Union, of whom 18 gave
their lives that the nation might not die.   A few of
his young men also fought on the Confederate side.
He has sent out 165 clergymen of the various denomi-
nations, of whom already 12 have become Doctors of
Divinity.   The lawyers and physicians have been
almost as numerous.

In 1862 Union College conferred the degree of
D.D. upon Professor King, and in 1873 the Regents
of the University of New York, in recognition of his
efficiency as an educator, conferred upon him the
degree of Ph.D.

In the discharge of his duties as principal of Fort
Edward Institute, he has lectured before the faculty
and students over 300 times, and has found leisure to
deliver outside the walls of the Institute 210 lectures
and addresses, besides having preached 1032 sermons
in 182 different pulpits.   From the sessions of the
conference of clergymen of which he is a member, he
has never been absent for a day.   In 1864 he was
elected by his brethren a delegate to the General
Conference of the M. E. Church at Philadelphia,
having also enjoyed the honor of serving as a delegate
to the General Conference of 1856, representing the
Vermont Conference, from which he was transferred
to the Troy Conference, on a vote of that conference
requesting it.   For two weeks he served as acting
delegate in the General Conference at Chicago, in 1868.

We greet with reverent tenderness to-day
The fond and true, the martyr'd Jane McCrea.

Behold the picture—blond and passing fair,
With twenty summers in her golden hair,
The winsome graces of old Scotia's blood
Blooming afresh in her bright maidenhood.
To see her was to love, and one that saw
Deemed it no violence to Nature's law
To woo and win her as his promised bride,
Elect to him o'er all the world beside.

Once he has been called upon to address the Alumni
of his college, once to deliver the oration before the
convention of Psi Upsilon—his college fraternity—and
twice to deliver the annual poem at Psi Upsilon
conventions.

In 1867 he gave himself a special vacation of about
three months abroad; again in 1889, chiefly in the
British Isles, France and Belgium.

By way of recreation from the severer routine of
his educational and spiritual tasks, he enjoys helping
with his presence and counsels the various institutions
and corporations in which he takes an interest. Be-
sides being a working trustee in Fort Edward Institute,
he is also a trustee or a director in the following cor-
porations: Wesleyan University, Syracuse Univer-
sity, Round Lake Camp Meeting Association, Me-
chanicville Academy, the Union Cemetery Associa-
tion, the National Bank of Fort Edward, two banks
in Iowa, and the Glens Falls Insurance Association.

He aims to set the example to his young men of
rarely being absent from the primary meetings of his
political party, from the home councils of his church
or the convocations of his fellow-workers in the cause
of education.

What though the fates, unequal or malign,
Had cast his lot within the British line?
Can love be gauged by rules of trade or war?
Not Mercury or Mars is man's true ruling star;
When Venus rises, turns each heart to her,
Savage or saint, a willing worshipper.
The patriot maiden pledged her willing troth
To country and to lover—true to both—
And felt no discord in her evening prayer
That heaven the one might bless, the other *spare*.
Nor may we blame our heroine of yore,
If not the less our cause, she loved her hero more.

A message comes: "Why should this dreadful strife
Rob me of mine?　Thou art my promised wife?
The guide is safe, thou'lt reach the camp ere night,
Then I'll protect thee in a husband's right."

Between two camps, awaiting mortal strife,
Why need *she* fear?　Love bears a charmèd life.
Coyly emerging from yon mansion's side,
With springing step she joined the savage guide.
Girt for the perils of the path she trod,
In maiden innocence and faith in God.
The breeze, fair girl, that fans your cheek to-day
Toyed with her tresses on her blithesome way;
The bee saluted with his tiny horn,
Waved in the noontide rays the tasselled corn;
The flowers grew brighter underneath her tread,
Bluer the arching sky above her head.

The hill was gained.　Sudden, the startled guide
Clutched at the girl, now trembling at his side.
A skirmish rages from the opposing lines,
And maddened chiefs contend beneath the pines.
In vain she seeks to flee!　A fatal blow
Pierces her brain.　And *then* the fiendish foe,

As sinks the wretched maiden limp and dead,
Tears off the golden glory from her fallen head!
A thousand curses on that savage hate,
To murder first, and then to mutilate!
Plead beauty, youth and innocence, that day,
But plead in vain for hapless Jane McCrea.
The ruthless fiend, his task yet incomplete,
Dashed down the bloody trophy at her lover's feet.
Unpitying Indian! Heaven shall pay thee back,
Its heavy vengeance marks henceforth thy track.
Pushed ever towards the still receding west
Thy wasting tribes shall plead in vain for rest.

For *her*, what heart withholds a votive sigh?
Poor trampled flower that in the dust doth lie!
Denied her woman's rightful place in life,
To rule her home, a proud and happy wife,
Yet Heaven doth martyred innocence befriend,
And in her fadeless fame a compensation send.
How many gallant youths rushed forth to join
The patriot ranks, and crush the proud Burgoyne!
Ten thousand men, at Saratoga's day,
Struck home for "liberty and Jane McCrea."
Had love coursed smoothly o'er life's pebble stones,
Long since forgot, as "*Mrs. David Jones;*"
Forgot, with every other humble name,
That time erases from the lists of fame.
Now, all the world beholds, serene and fair,
'Graved in the azure of the upper air,
And reads in capitals of flame to-day
One only name, the gentle Jane McCrea.
And David Jones, forsooth, despite his British pride,
Gains fadeless laurels through his Yankee bride.
They're gone! all gone! in vain we search around
Where armies trampled this historic ground;

Fields rent and scarred by war retain no trace,
Which Time's all-lev'ling touch cannot efface.
Of yonder fort, which saw a nation's birth,
Remains alone a ridge of common earth.
Still flows the rippling river to the sea,
The type of loving woman's constancy;
And on its banks do other forts arise,
Churches and schools, the States' best armories.

Nigh to our martyrs' monumental stone
Is "*trysting tree*," to village youths well known;
'Tis there, when lovers plight their sacred troth,
Her guardian presence comes to bless them both.

The hillside pines which saw her fall that day
Themselves have fallen, victims of decay;
But from their roots there flows a living spring,
Whose clear, cool waters, gently murmuring
In sweet and mournful cadence, seem to say,
Here fell the fair and fond but hapless Jane McCrea.

THE TRAGICAL DEATH OF MISS JANE McCREA,

Who was scalped and inhumanly butchered by a scouting party of Burgoyne's army on his way toward Albany.

By Rev. Wheeler Case.

As I was passing thro' a certain wood
I heard a doleful noise; surpris'd I stood—
I lent a list'ning ear—but oh, what moans!
The woods all rang with shrieks and dying groans.
Upon a rising ground I cast my eye
And saw a scouting party passing by,
Some *British* troops, combined with *Indian* bands,
With swords, with knives and tom'hawks in their hands.

They gave a shout and pass'd along the road,
Like beasts of prey in quest of human blood.
I mov'd along where I had heard the cries,
And lo! a bloody scene salutes my eyes ;
Here lies an aged man, roll'd in his gore,
And from his hoary head his scalp is tore.
There lies a woman dead, all gashed her face,
A sucking babe just dropp'd from her embrace.
There lies the slaughter'd infant on a clod,
Its head all bruis'd and face besmear'd with blood.
As I advanc'd along, before me lay
A lady richly dress'd, her name *McCrea ;*
Stretch'd on the ground, and struggling there with
        death,
She cannot live, she must resign her breath.
The cursed *Indian* knife, the cruel blade,
Had cut her scalp, they'd tore it from her head ;
The blood is gushing forth from all her veins,
With bitter groans and sighs she tells her pains.
Is this that blooming fair, is this *McCrea ?*
This was appointed for her nuptial day.
Instead of smiles, and a most brilliant bride,
Her face besmear'd with blood, her raiment dyed.
Instead of pleasure and transporting joys,
There's naught but dying groans and bitter sighs ;
For, overwhelm'd with grief, alas! I faint ;
It is too much for language e'er to paint.
Would heav'n admit of tears her rev'rend sire*
Would now look down and o'er her drop a tear ;
A flood of tears down from his eyes would flow
O'er his dear child, touch'd with her fatal woe.
Methinks he now attempts to speak—too full,
With sighs he tells the anguish of his soul.

* The Rev. Mr. McCrea of New Jersey.

In broken accents now I hear him say,
Is this the plant I raised ?   Is this *McCrea ?*
Is this my *Jenny* roll'd in blood I see,
Whom I caress'd and dandled on my knee?
If e'er she was in pain I felt the smart,
If but her finger ach'd, it pained my heart,
But now she's mangled with the *Indian* knife,
With groans and sighs she's breathing out her life.
Oh, cruel savages ! what hearts of steel !
Oh, cruel *Britons* who no pity feel !
Where did they get the knife, the cruel blade?
From Britain it was sent where it was made.
The tom'hawk and the murdering knife were sent
To barb'rous savages for this intent.
Yes, they were sent e'en from the *British throne.*
Is this for acts of duty I have done?
How oft have I address'd the throne of Grace
For Britain's king and all his rising race !
How oft with tears, that God would be their friend,
That peace and happiness might them attend !

No fiction this, the muse hath seen him stand
With eyes erect, and with uplifted hands
Within the sacred desk ; she'd heard him plead
For *Britain's* king and all the royal seed ;
How oft, with earnest cries and flowing tears,
For blessings on the king and all his heirs.

JANE McCREA.
BY JOEL BARLOW.*

*   *   *   *   *   *   *   *   *
ONE deed shall tell what fame great Albion draws
From those auxiliars in her bar'brous cause—

---

* Joel Barlow, author, born in Redding, Conn.,
March 24th, 1754 ; died near Cracow, Poland, Decem-

Lucinda's fate.   The tale ye nations hear ;
Eternal ages trace it with a tear.

[In searching for her lover, who is designated by
the name of *Heartly* in the narrative, and from whom
she has become separated, she strays into the woods,
and he in turn begins a search for her.]

He hurries to his tent ; oh, rage ! despair !
No glimpse, no tidings of the frantic fair ;
Save that some car-men, as a-camp they drove,
Had seen her coursing for the western grove.
Faint with fatigue, and chok'd with burning thirst,
Forth from his friends with bounding leap he burst,
Vaults o'er the palisade, with eyes on flame,
And fills the welkin with Lucinda's name.

---

ber 24th, 1812.   Graduated from Yale in 1778, deliver-
ing the commencement poem, " Prospect of Peace"
(published in "American Poems," Litchfield, Conn.,
1793).   In 1787 he published at Hartford his epic
poem, "The Vision of Columbus," which made him
famous, and afterward his most popular poem, the
" Hasty Pudding."   He was United States Consul at
Algiers in 1795.   He resided afterward for eight
years at Paris, living the life of a man of letters, and
writing there his poem, " The Columbiad," and making
extensive preparations for a history of the American
Revolution and one work on the French Revolution.
He was also, like Freneau, one of the most prolific and
famous writers of the Revolutionary period.   He
introduces the subject of the Jane McCrea massacre
as above, presenting Jane McCrea under the name of
" Lucinda."   In a note accompanying the poem, the
author states that the tragical story of Miss McCrea is
narrated almost literally.

The fair one, too, of every aid forlorn,
Had raved and wandered, till officious morn
Awaked the Mohawks from their short repose,
To glean the plunder ere their comrades 'rose.
Two Mohawks met the maid—historian, hold!
Alas! that such a tale should e'er be told.

She starts—with eyes upturn'd and fleeting breath,
In their raised axes views her instant death,
Her hair, half lost along the shrubs she passed,
Rolls in loose tangles 'round her lovely waist;
Her kerchief torn betrays the globes of snow,
That heave responsive to her weight of woe.

With calculating pause and demon grin
They seize her hands, and through her face divine
Drive the descending axe!—The shriek she sent
Attained her lover's ear; he thither bent
With all the speed his wearied limbs could yield,
Whirled his keen blade, and stretched upon the field
The yelling fiends, who there disputing stood
Her gory scalp, their horrid prize of blood!
He sank, delirious on her lifeless clay,
And passed in starts of sense, the dreadful day.

* * * * * * * * *

LINES ON JANE McCREA.

By Mrs. Sarah J. Hale.*

Oh! very beautiful was she,
A loveliness most rare to see.

* Mrs. Sarah Josepha Hale, authoress, born in New-
port, N. H., October 24th, 1788; died in Philadelphia

Her eyes were like the ethereal hue
From Chimborazo's skyward view,
When stars begin to tremble through,
And not a vapor dims the blue ;
And clustering curls of soft blonde hair*
Around her throat and shoulders flow,
Like morning light on mountain snow ;
And face so delicately fair !

April 30th, 1879. She edited the *Ladies' Magazine*, in Boston, which she conducted till 1837. In that year it was united with *Godey's Lady's Book*, published in Philadelphia, and Mrs. Hale became editor of that periodical, removing to that city in 1841. She was chiefly instrumental in raising funds to complete the Bunker Hill Monument, and also in bringing about the change of Thanksgiving Day from a State festival to a National one—President Lincoln being the first one to adopt her suggestion, in 1864. She is the author of many works and poems, among the latter of which are the well-known ones of " Mary's Lamb" and " It Snows."

 * Although Jenny's hair was said to have been " dark as a raven's wing," yet she has also been described by those who knew her as " a young woman of fine commanding form, rare beauty, delicate blonde complexion, and glossy, golden-brown hair of silken lustre and of unusual length." The weight of evidence and the probabilities, it must be said, are largely in favor of the description as above quoted. Nor must it be forgotten that Jenny was of pure Scotch blood, and the Scotch are noted the world over for their fair complexion, blue eyes, and light hair. Mrs. Hale is, therefore, probably entirely correct in describing her as a blonde.

'Twas like a lily newly blown,
Or like the breathing Parian stone,
Softened by a heart within,
Sending love-light through the skin !
Ay! the soul's transparent vase
Seemed that pure, pale, loving face.

BALLADS ON THE BATTLE OF ORISKANY.

ORISKANY.

By General J. Watts de Peyster.*

OLD Seventeen hundred and Seventy-seven,
Of Liberty's throes, was the crown and the leaven.
Just a century since, August Sixth, was the day
When Great Britain's control was first stricken away.
Let us sing then the field where the Yeomen of York
Met the Lion and Wolf on their slaughterous stalk;
When Oriskany's ripples were crimson'd with blood;
And when strife fratricidal polluted its flood.
Oh, glorious collision, forever renowned!
While America lives should its praises resound,
And stout Harkeimer's name be the theme of the song,
Who with Mohawk's brave sons broke the strength
     of the strong.

To relief of Fort Stanwix New Yorkers drew nigh,
To succor stout Gansevoort, conquer or die;
And if unwise the counsels that brought on the fight,
In the battle was shown that their hearts were all right.
If their chief seemed so prudent that "subs" looked
     askance,
Still one shout proved their feeling, their courage—
     " Advance !"
Most unfortunate counsel! The ambush was set,
Leaving one passage *in* but none *out* of the net,—
Of outlets, not one, unless 'twas made by the sword,
Through encompassing ranks of the pitiless horde.

---

* For sketch of General de Peyster, see Appendix
No. VII.

Sure never was column so terribly caught,
Nor ever has column more fearlessly fought :—
Thus Harkeimer's Mohawkers made victory theirs,
For St. Leger was foiled in spite of his snares.

The loud braggarts who'd taunted Harkeimer so free,
Ere the fight had begun, were from fight first to flee ;
While the stalwart old chief, who a father had proved,
And his life offered up for the cause that he loved,
'Mid the war-whirl of Death still directed each move,
'Mid the rain from the clouds and from more fatal
      groove
Of the deadlier rifle,—and object assured,
To him Palm, both as victor and martyr, inured.

Search the annals of War and examine with care
If a parallel fight can discovered be, there,
When eight hundred green soldiers beset in a wood
Their assailants, as numerous, boldly withstood ;
And while death sleeted in from environing screens
Of the forest and underbrush, Indians and "Greens"—
'Gainst the circle without, took to cover within,
Formed a circle as deadly—which as it grew thin
Into still smaller circles then broke, until each
Presented a *round* that no foeman could breach,
Neither boldest of savage nor disciplined troops :—
Thus they fought and they fell in heroical groups—
But though falling still fighting they wrench'd from
      the foe
The great object they marched to attain, and altho'
The whole vale of the Mohawk was shrouded in woe,
Fort Stanwix was saved by Oriskany's throe.

No New Birth, no advance in the Progress of Man,
Has occurred since the tale of his suff'rings began,
Without anguish unspeakable, deluge of blood.

The Past's buried deep 'neath incarnadine flood.
So, when, at Oriskany, slaughter had done
Its fell work with the tomahawk, hunting-knife, gun ;
From the earth soaked with blood, and the whirlwind
of fire
Rose the living's reward and the fallen's desire.
Independence!
For there on Oriskany's shore,
Was fought out the death-wrestle deciding the war!

If our country is free and its flag, first displayed
On the ramparts of Stanwix, in glories arrayed ;
If the old " Thirteen Colonies" won the renown
"*Sic semper tyrannis ;*" beat Tyranny down ;
There, there, at Oriskany, the wedge first was driven,
By which British invasion was splintered and riven,
Though at Hoosic and " Saratog" the work was com-
pleted,
The end was made clear with St. Leger defeated ;
Nor can boast be disproved, on Oriskany's shore
Was worked out the grim problem involved in the
war.

---

3. Die Schlacht von Oriskany.

By Gen. J. Watts de Peyster.

Ins Deutsche übersetzt von Marie Blöbe.

When through dense woods primeval bower'd,	Als durch des Urwalds laub'gen Gang
A perfect hail of bullets shower'd,	Einst prasselnd Kugelregen drang —
Where bold Thayendanega tower'd—	Wo Thayendanega's Ruhm erklang —
Good old Harkeimer prov'd no coward,	Da ward auch Harkeimer nicht bang',
Commanding at Oriskany.	Dem Führer von Oriskany.
True to his Teuton lineage,	Treu dem teutonisch-eblen Blut
Foremost amidst the battle's rage,	Voran in des Gefechtes Wuth,
As bold in fight, in council sage,	Im Rathe klug, im Kampf voll Muth
Most glorious as he quit the stage	Und ruhmreich, da er endlich ruht
Of life, by the Oriskany.	Vom Streite bei Oriskany.

Altho' he felt the mortal wound,
Though fell in swathes his soldiers round,
Propp'd 'gainst his saddle, on the ground,
He calmly smok'd, gave counsel sound,
    'Mid war-whirl at Oriskany.

War never fiercer sight has seen
Than when Sir Johnson's cohort green
Charg'd on the Mohawk Rangers keen :
The sole such strife Almanza* 'd been
    As that on the Oriskany.

New York's bold yeomen, Watts at head,
Breasted meet foes—New Yorkers bred,
There, eye to eye, they fought, stabb'd,
    bled,
Bosom to bosom strove, fell dead
    In ambush of Oriskany.

Alone can Berwick's shudder tell,
What fury rul'd that moment fell
When Frenchman's steel hiss'd French-
    man's knell :
Horrent made the sole parallel
    To battle of Oriskany.

Teeth with like frantic fury set,
There Frank died on Frank's bayonet—
Here neighbor death from neighbor
    met,—
With kindred blood both fields were wet,
    Almanza and Oriskany.

And, ceas'd the storm whose rage had
    vied,
With ruthless shock of fratricide,
There lay the Mohawk Valley's pride
Just as they fought, stark, side by side,
    Along the red Oriskany.

Though neither force could triumph claim
In war's dread, dazzling, desp'rate game,
Enkindled there, the smould'ring flame
Of freedom blaz'd, to make thy name
    All glorious, Oriskany.

Er saß getroffen, todeswund,
Ein Heer von Todten um ihn rund,
Im Sattel aufgestützt am Grund,
Gab rauchend Rath, der kerngesund,
    Im Kriegs=Sturm von Oriskany.

Nie schlug ein Heer so grimmig b'rein,
Als da Sir Johnsons grüne Reih'n,
Wild brangen auf die Mohawks ein !
Es kann Almanza's * Streit allein
    Sich messen mit Oriskany.

New=Yorker Landvolk zieht ins Feld
Von Watts geführt und dicht gesellt,
Dort Brust an Brust zum Kampf gestellt,
Manch ein New=Yorker blutend fällt
    Im Vorhalt von Oriskany.

Nur Berwick's Schauder sagt es klar,
Wie graus der Tag des Schreckens war,
Da Franzmann schlug die eig'ne Schaar,
Horrent nur bot ein Gleiches dar,
    Wie die Schlacht von Oriskany.

Hier Zahn um Zahn, gleich zornentbrannt,
Der Franzmann starb durch fränk'sche Hand,
Der Nachbar fiel, wo Nachbar stand,
Und Bruderblut durchnäßt den Sand,
    Almanza und Oriskany.

Und als des Sturmes Toben ruht,
Der Brudermord entfacht mit Wuth,
Lag Mohawk Thales Stolz im Blut,
Dicht wie sie fochten, stark und gut,
    Längs dem rothen Oriskany.

Ob Keinem ward des Sieges Ziel
Im wirren Kampfes Schauerspiel,
Der Freiheit Flamme, die verfiel,
Erstand und machte ruhmreich viel
    Den Namen von Oriskany.

---

* Die Schlacht von Almanza, auf welche hier Bezug genommen wird, fand 1707 zwischen den Truppen Ludwigs XIV. unter dem grausamen Herzog von Berwick gegen die Camisarden unter Cavalier statt.

BALLADS ON THE BATTLE OF ORISKANY.

PÆAN TO ORISKANY.

BY REV. CHARLES DOWNES HELMER, D.D.

BELEAGUERED men of Stanwix, brave as those
Who faced a million of their foes
      At old Thermopylæ;
Good cheer to you upon the wild frontier!
For citizens in arms draw near
      Across Oriskany.

But hark! amidst the forest shades the crash
Of arms, the savage yell—with flash
      Of gory tomahawk;
For Johnson's Royal-Greens, and Leger's men,
And Brant's Red Fiends, are in that glen
      Of dark Oriskany.

From down the valley, where the Mohawk flows,
Were hurrying on to meet their foes
      The patriot yeomanry;
For Gansevoort within his fortress lay,
In peril and besieged that day,
      Beyond Oriskany.

As men who fight for home and child and wife,
As men oblivious of life
      In holy martyrdom,

The Yeomen of the Valley fought that day,
Throughout thy fierce and deadly fray—
    Blood-red Oriskany.

From rock and tree and clump of twisted brush
The hissing gusts of battle rush—
    Hot breathed and horrible!
The roar, and smoke, like mist on stormy seas,
Sweep through thy splintered trees—
    Hard-fought Oriskany.

Heroes are born in such a chosen hour;
From common men they rise and tower,
    Like thee, brave Herkimer!
Who wounded, steedless, still beside the beech
Cheered on thy men, with sword and speech,
    In grim Oriskany.

Now burst the clouds above the battle roar,
And from the pitying skies down pour
    Swift floods tumultuous;
Then fires of strife unquenched flame out again,
Drenching with hot and bloody rain
    Thy soil, Oriskany.

But ere the sun went toward the tardy night,
The valley then beheld the light
    Of freedom's victory;
And wooded Tryon snatched from British arms
The empire of a million farms—
    On bright Oriskany.

The guns of Stanwix thundered to the skies;
The rescued wilderness replies;
    Forth dash the garrison!
And routed Tories, with their savage aids,
Sink reddening through the sullied shades—
    From lost Oriskany.

Behold, Burgoyne! with hot and hating eyes,
The New World's flag at last o'erflies
    Your ancient Heraldry;
For over Stanwix floats triumphantly
The rising Banner of the Free—
    Beyond Oriskany.

A hundred years have passed since then;
And hosts now rally there again—
    To crown the century;
The proud posterity of noble men
Who *conquered* in the bloody glen
    Of famed Oriskany.

BALLADS ON THE BATTLE OF BENNINGTON.

ODE ON THE BATTLE OF BENNINGTON.

By Rev. E. H. Chapin, D.D.*

They came, as brave men ever come,
  To stand, to fight, to die;

* Rev. Edwin Hubbell Chapin, a distinguished Universalist clergyman of New York, and the pastor of Horace Greeley, was born at Union Village, Washington County, N. Y., and died in New York City, December 27th, 1880. He received his early training at the Bennington, Vt., Seminary, and afterward studied law in Troy, N. Y. Subsequently he removed to Utica, and became editor of *The Magazine and Advocate*, a periodical devoted to the interests of the Universalists. He afterward studied for the ministry, and was ordained in 1837. His first settlement was at Richmond, Va.; and in 1848 he was installed as pastor in the Fourth Universalist Church in New York City. Dr. Chapin was long one of the most prominent of metropolitan preachers, and his church soon became one of the most noted in the city, and to which "throngs of both church-goers and non-church-goers resorted whenever it was known that he would speak." He was also a very popular public lecturer, and his services were in

No thought of fear was in the heart
　　No quailing in the eye;
If the lip faltered, 'twas with prayer,
　　Amid those gathering bands;
For the sure rifle kept its poise
　　In strong, untrembling hands.

They came up, at the battle-sound,
　　To old Walloomsack's height;
Behind them were their fields of toil,
　　With harvest promise white;
Before them those who sought to wrest
　　Their hallowed birthright dear,
While through their ranks went fearlessly
　　Their leader's words of cheer.

---

constant demand. As his biographer, in " Appleton's
Biographical Cyclopædia," justly says, " His denomi-
national religious associations were with the Univer-
salists, but his sympathies were of the broadest
character, and he numbered among his personal
friends many of the stanchest advocates of orthodoxy,
who could not but admire his eloquence, however
much they may have dissented from his religious
teaching." In 1872 he succeeded Dr. Emerson in
the editorship of the *Christian Leader.* He was
quite a voluminous writer, and with James G. Adams
as his associate, he compiled " Hymns for Christian
Devotion" (1870).

The above ode is selected from some stanzas on the
battle of Bennington in 1837, and delivered by him
in the Old Academy in Bennington Centre. They
were also published in Rev. Isaac Jennings's admirable
work, " Memorials of a Century" (Boston, 1869).

" My men, there are our freedom's foe,
    And shall they stand or fall ?
Ye have your weapons in your hands,
    Ye know your duty all ;
For we—this day we triumph o'er
    The minions of the crown,
Or Molly Stark's a widowed one
    Ere yonder sun goes down." *

One thought of heaven, one thought of home,
    One thought of hearth and shrine,
Then, rock-like, stood they in their might
    Before the glittering line.
A moment, and each keen eye paused
    The coming foe to mark,
Then downward to his barrel glanced,
    And strife was wild and dark.

It needs no monumental pile
    To tell each storied name,
The fair green hills rise proudly up
    To consecrate their fame.
True to its trust, Walloomsack long
    The record bright shall bear,
Who came up at the battle sound
    And fought for freedom there.

---

* This is in allusion to the tradition that on the eve
of the battle, just as the orders were given and the
combatants were about to engage, General Stark, in
his saddle, pointing in the direction of the enemy,
made this laconic address : " BOYS, THESE ARE THE
RED-COATS ; AND THEY ARE OURS, OR THIS NIGHT MOLLY
STARK SLEEPS A WIDOW !"

THE BATTLE OF BENNINGTON.

By William Cullen Bryant.*

(On the occasion of the centennial of the battle of Bennington.)

On this fair valley's grassy breast
The calm, sweet rays of summer rest,
And dove-like peace benignly broods
On its smooth lawns and solemn woods.

---

* William Cullen Bryant, distinguished journalist and poet, born in Cummington, Mass., November 3d, 1794; died in New York, June 12th, 1878. Of distinguished colonial ancestry, he early developed poetical power, and began at an early age to write short epic and satirical verses for the local newspapers and magazines, especially the Hampshire *Gazette*, although he was at the same time pursuing the study of the law. In his eighteenth year he composed his immortal poem " Thanatopsis," the inspiration of which was given him while wandering through the primeval forests of his native State. After being admitted to the bar, he removed to Great Barrington, Mass. He continued, however, his literary efforts, contributing, meanwhile, to the *North American Review*, and in 1825 removed to New York City, becoming assistant editor of the New York *Review and Athenæum Magazine*. Finally he became the editor-in-chief, with a part ownership, of the New York *Evening Post*, with which influential newspaper he was identified until his death. Although a bitter Democrat, yet upon the opening of the Civil War he laid all partisanship aside, and with true patriotism warmly espoused the cause of the United States.

A century since, in flame and smoke,
The storm of battle o'er it broke,
And ere the invader turned and fled,
These pleasant fields were strewn with dead.

Stark, quick to act and bold to dare,
And Warner's mountain band were there ;
And Allen, who had flung the pen
Aside to lead the Berkshire men.

With fiery onset—blow on blow—
They rushed upon the embattled foe,
And swept his squadrons from the vale,
Like leaves before the autumn gale.

Oh, never may the purple stain
Of combat blot these fields again,
Nor this fair valley ever cease
To wear the placid smile of peace !

Yet here, beside that battle-field,
We plight the vow that, ere we yield
The rights for which our fathers bled,
Our blood shall steep the ground we tread.

And men will hold the memory dear
Of those who fought for freedom here,
And grand the heritage they won
While their green hill-sides feel the sun.

THE BATTLE OF BENNINGTON.
1777–1877.
By Mrs. Julia Fay Waldenburg.*

'Twas the eve of that glorious battle morn,
On Vermont's green mountains, in splendor born !

---

* Julia Fay Waldenburg, daughter of George Barron

Down from the frowning clouds, the rain
In torrents fell over hill and plain ;
It bent the trees and the golden grain,
Beating the roof and the window pane,
While the lightning danced on the mountains far
And the thunder boomed like the guns of war !

Crowning a hill in Bennington town,
Stood a low-browed tavern, broad and brown,
With a novel sign, whose like I ween
In book of heraldry ne'er was seen :
'Twas a catamount, swung from a sapling slight,
Looking alive, as its teeth gleamed white !
When the light from the lonely lantern flared
At the open doorway, its wild eyes glared,
And it seemed through the gloom to keep its watch,
The Hessian or "Yorker" foe to catch !
Within the inn, from the candles tall,
A soft light shone o'er the rooms and hall,
And lingered in many a silvery line
On the carven wainscot of native pine ;
On the musket, and pictures upon the wall ;
O'er the white-haired landlord, grave and tall ;

Fay and Catherine Strong ; born at Albany, N. Y., of
Revolutionary stock ; a great-granddaughter of Captain
John Strong, of Pittsfield, Mass., on the maternal side,
and great-granddaughter of Dr. Jonas Fay, of Benning-
ton, Vt. ; the latter was a son of Stephen Fay, Secretary.
of Council of Safety and surgeon under Ethan Allen
She has written considerably in prose and verse—a
volume of poems published by Joel Munsell in 1878—
and has been at different periods foreign correspondent
of the Albany *Argus.* Married in 1881 Mr. William
Waldenburg, of Brooklyn, and has three children.

On the stalwart forms, that were moving there,
With speech and counsel, oath and prayer.
Here the Council of Safety held their court,
Sentenced the "Tories" with session short,
And framed the laws with a loyal zeal,
Enforced with the stamp of the famed "Beech seal,"*
Vermont's brave sons undaunted, true
As the emerald hills before their view !
Allen the fearless, rough, unmoved ;
Warner the Ranger's colonel loved ;
Robinson, Chittenden, Baker, Fay,
Dewey, Fassett, and such as they,
Whose names are written with deathless pen
On the roll of heroes, revered by men !

On this August night, 'mid rain and gloom,
There was gathered within the council room
An eager, anxious and earnest crowd,
Who with nervous gestures and voices loud,
With solemn purpose and steady plan,
Arranged for the battle, man with man,
And were restless for morning's light to break
To war for right and their country's sake.
They would live in freedom from king and crown,
Or would lay their lives with the foeman down ;
They ask no congress for right to move,
But would follow their leaders brave, through love.
Then with parting word, for the night was spent,
To their homes or the distant camp they went.

---

* This allusion is to the circumstance that those
persons who were not considered loyal to the cause of
the Colonies were often waylaid and taken into the
woods, where they were punished by a flaying on
their backs with "*beech rods*"—called, in the back-
woodsman's parlance of the day, "*beech seals*."—ED.

Bright rose the morning's sun serene,
No lingerings of the storm were seen.
The meadows wore a brighter green,
The swollen river shone between,
And proudly rose the mountains far,
On nature's face no frown of war.
Then lo! From out the forests still,
With stately march and sturdy will,
The gallant columns moved apace,
Toward the " Heights" looked every face!
They came from forge, from shop, from farm;
The " Parson," with his gospel arm
Upraised, was eager for the fight,
Strong in his faith for God and right.
Ranger and volunteer, as one,
Gathered beneath that August sun;
Ununiformed, untried, yet brave,
They knew their power to fight and save!

The miry road they wound along,
And every mile they grew more strong,
'Till soon the foe, with colors bright,
Stood grouped before their waiting sight.
Brave Stark commanding called aloud
Unto his little army, proud,—
" The red-coats! See!!—We win this fight,
Else Molly Stark this very night
Must sleep a widow!" Then to view
The foe's defences burst, clear through
The stubborn outworks on they prest
From northern wing, and from the west;
While from the British breastworks poured
The Hessian fire. The cannon roared;
The line it wavered, comrades fell,
Still pushed they bravely on, and well,

Heedless of hail from rattling shot
Or blistered hand from rifle hot;
They rushed and leaped o'er parapet,
And charged with butt and bayonet.
Wearied and hungry, wounded sore,
With throbbing brows and stained with gore,
They held their posts 'till the fight was done,
The foe was routed, the battle won,
While the rays of the setting sun were shed
O'er a smoking plain, with its pallid dead,
And the twilight shadows reached down upon
The victory field of Bennington!

In Paris proud, 'neath a golden dome,
Where wandering pilgrims ever come;
'Neath massive marble and sculptured stone
Is gathered the dust of Napoleon!
There's a legend told that a mighty host,
Shadowy, ghostly, to vision lost,
Paces ever the tomb, before,
In tattered garments streaked with gore;
Who, pallid and wounded, keep watch and ward.
'Tis the band of the emperor's famous Guard!
They wait his rising who sleeps below,
To follow his form through heat or snow,
'Till he lead to glory and victory ;
And they wait the day and hour to be !

No shadowy, ghostly guard have we
Pacing before dead royalty ;
But giant forms that to-day we see
Uprise in their glorious history!
Oh ye with the clear-eyed sight of seers
Who glanced o'er the wid'ning space of years
And saw a form whose radiance bright
Flooded the western world with light,

Oh, soldiers brave of those mighty days,
Whom we crown with a century's crown of bays,
Keep ye your vigils over our land,
O'er valley and mountain, river and strand !
In rain or sunshine, calm or storm,
Guard ye this beauteous living form,
Warm with the youth of her hundred years,
With her pulsing heart and her shining tears,
Oh, watch our Land in her strength and pride,
Ye loved her fondly and for her died !
So lead her upward, thy guard ne'er cease
'Till she enter the endless years of Peace !

ODE ON THE VETERANS OF THE BATTLE OF BENNINGTON.

By Mrs. Anna C. Botta.*

Our patriot sires are gone ;
The conqueror Death lays low

* Mrs. Anna Charlotte (Lynch) Botta, authoress, born in Bennington, Vt., in 1820. Her father was a native of Dublin, Ireland, who at the age of sixteen joined the rebel forces under Lord Edward Fitzgerald. He was afterward banished to the United States, where he married. His daughter was educated in Albany, N. Y., and at an early age began writing for literary periodicals. Removing to Providence, R. I., she there edited the " Rhode Island Book" (Providence, 1841), containing selections from the authors of Rhode Island. Soon afterward she returned to New York, where she has since resided, and in 1855 married Professor Botta. Among her many works is a " Hand-book of Universal Literature" (New York, 1860), containing concise ac-

Those veterans, one by one,
    Who braved each other foe ;
Though on them rests Death's sable pall,
Yet o'er their deeds no shade shall fall.

No, ye of deathless fame !
    Ye shall not sleep unsung,
While Freedom hath a name,
    Or gratitude a tongue.
Yet shall your names and deeds sublime
Shine brighter through the mists of time.

Oh, keep your armor bright,
    Sons of those mighty dead,
And guard ye well the right
    For which such blood was shed !
Your starry flag should only wave
O'er Freedom's home or o'er your grave.

PARSON ALLEN'S RIDE.*

DELIVERED AT THE CENTENNIAL CELEBRATION OF
THE BATTLE OF BENNINGTON, AUGUST 16, 1877,
BY WALLACE BRUCE.†

The "Catamount Tavern"‡ is lively to-night ;
    The "boys" of Vermont and New Hampshire are
      here,

---

counts of great authors of all ages and their works,
which has been adopted as a text-book in many edu-
cational institutions. Mrs. Botta's style is musical,
elegant, and finished, and her sonnets are especially
successful (" Appleton's Biographical Dictionary").

   * For a sketch of Parson Allen, see Appendix
No. VIII.

   † Wallace Bruce, lecturer, born in Hillsdale, N. Y.,

All drawn up in line in the lingering light
　To greet Parson Allen with shout and with cheer.

Over mountain and valley from Pittsfield Green,
　Through the driving rain of that August day,
The "flock" marched on with martial mien,
　And the Parson rode in his "one horse shay."

"Three cheers for old Berkshire!" the General said,
　As the boys of New England drew up face to face,
"Baum bids us a dinner to-morrow to spread,
　And the Parson is here to say us the grace."

"The lads who are with me have come here to fight,
　And we know of no grace," was the Parson's reply,
"Save the name of Jehovah, our Country and right,
　Which your own Ethan Allen pronounced at Fort
　　Ti."

"To-morrow," said Stark, "there'll be fighting to do
　If you think you can wait for the morning light,
And, Parson, I'll conquer the British with you,
　Or my Molly* will sleep a widow at night."

November 10th, 1844. He graduated from Yale in
1867, and has lectured extensively before lyceums and
associations on literary subjects, especially on Shake-
speare, Scott, Burns, Irving, and Bryant. Among his
works are "The Land of Burns," "Yosemite," "The
Hudson," and "From the Hudson to the Yosemite."
At present (1893) he holds the position of United
States Consul to Edinburgh, Scotland.

‡ For an account of the old Catamount Tavern, see
Appendix No. IX.

* Elizabeth was her name, but General Stark used
"Molly" as a word of endearment. This Mr. Charles
M. Bliss had on the authority of a granddaughter of

What the Parson dreamed in that Bennington camp,
  Neither Yankee nor Prophet would dare to guess ;
A vision, perhaps, of the King David stamp,
  With a mixture of Cromwell and good Queen Bess.

But we know the result of that glorious day,
  And the victory won ere the night came down,
How Warner charged in the bitter fray,
  With Rossiter and Hobart and old John Brown !

And how in a lull of the three hours' fight
  The Parson harangued the Tory line,
As he stood on a stump, with his musket bright,
  And sprinkled his text with the powder fine :

" The sword of the Lord is our battle-cry !—
  A refuge sure in the hour of need,
And Freedom and Faith can never die,
  Is article first of the Puritan creed !"

" Perhaps the occasion was rather rash,"
  He remarked to his comrades after the rout,
" For behind a bush I saw a flash,
  But I fired that way and put it out."*

And many the sayings, eccentric and queer,
  Repeated and sung through the whole country side,
And quoted in Berkshire for many a year,
  Of the Pittsfield march and the Parson's ride.

General Stark who lived in the house with him, and
who was eighteen years old when the general died.
Another granddaughter explained it in the same way
to Secretary William M. Evarts when he was at Ben-
nington at the centennial of the battle in 1877.
" Oh," said Evarts in reply, " he called her, then, Molly
when he wished to mollify her !"
  * The firelock which Rev. Thomas Allen used

Honor to Stark and his resolute men—
  To the Green Mountain Boys all honor and praise—
While with shout and cheer we welcome again,
  The Parson who came in his one horse chaise.*

HYMN ON THE BATTLE OF BENNING-TON.

By Mrs. Marie Mason.†

(On the occasion of the centennial of the battle of Bennington.)

One hundred years! a nation's joys
  Resound along the prospered way
That Stark and his Green Mountain Boys
  Made ours one hundred years to-day.

God bless the standard of the free!
  God bless this peaceful, happy land!
Our fathers' God! we lift to Thee
  Our praise for gifts on every hand.

---

for this confessed purpose was that of his brother Joseph, who stood near him, he not having taken one into the action. It is still preserved in Pittsfield by the descendants of Joseph.

* Among the re-enforcements from Berkshire came a clergyman with a portion of his flock—the boys marching on foot and the parson driving through the muddy roads in his primitive chaise (" History of Berkshire").

† Mrs. Mason, the wife of the distinguished musical composer of Boston, Mass., was herself a poetess of no mean rank. She is now dead.

And for our country's honored head *
  Our reverent lips ask this alone ;
That Thou wilt guide his feet to tread
  In footprints of our Washington.

Our counsellors with wisdom fill ;
  Let parties die; let factions cease ;
Let all men seek with single will
  Our country's unity and peace.

Then not in vain the patriot blood
  Was poured upon the crimsoned clay,
When side by side our fathers stood
  One hundred years ago to-day.

THE BATTLE OF BENNINGTON, AUGUST 16, 1777.

By Rev. Thomas P. Rodman.

Up through a cloudy sky the sun
  Was buffeting his way
On such a noon as ushers in
  A sultry August day.
Hot was the air—and hotter yet
  Men's thought within them grew ;
They Britons, Hessians, Tories, saw,
  They saw their homesteads too !

They thought of all their country's wrongs ;
  They thought of noble lives
Poured out in battle with their foes ;—
  They thought upon their wives,

---

* President Hayes was present on this occasion.

Their children and their aged sires,
    Their firesides, churches, God !
And these deep thoughts made hallowed ground
    Each foot of soil they trod.

Their leader was a veteran man—
    A man of earnest will ;—
His very presence was a host ;
    He'd fought at Bunker's Hill !
A living monument he stood
    Of stirring deeds of fame ;
Of deeds that shed a fadeless light,
    Of his own deathless name !

Of Charlestown's flames, of Warren's blood,
    His presence told the tale ;
It made each patriot's heart beat quick,
    Though lip and cheek grew pale ;
It spoke of Princeton, Morristown ;—
    Told Trenton's thrilling story ;
It lit futurity with hope,
    And on the past shed glory.

Who were those men ? their leader, who ?
    Where stood they on that morn ?
The men were northern yeomanry,
    Brave men as e'er were born ;
Who, in the reaper's merry row,
    Or warrior's rank could stand ;
Right worthy such a noble troop—
    John Stark led on the band.

Walloomsack* wanders by the spot
    Where *they* that morning, stood ;

* For an able article, by Hon. S. D. Locke, of
Hoosic Falls, N. Y., showing that the battle of Ben-

Then rolled the war cloud o'er the stream,
   The waves were tinged with blood ;
And the near hills that dark cloud girt,
   And fires like lightning flashed ;
And shrieks and groans, like howling blasts,
   Rose as the bayonets clashed.

The night before, the Yankee host
   Came gathering from afar,
And in each belted bosom glowed
   The spirit of the war !
All full of fight, through rainy storm,
   Night cloudy, starless, dark—
They came and gathered as they came,
   Around the valiant Stark !

There was a Berkshire parson*—he
   And all his flock were there,
And like true *churchmen* militant,
   The arm of flesh made bare.
Out spoke the Dominie, and said :—
   " For battle have we come,
These many times : and after this,
   We mean to stay at home,

"If now we come in vain"—Said Stark :
   "What ! would you go to-night,
To battle it with yonder troops ?
   God send us morning light,
And we will give you work enough ;
   Let but the morning come,
And if ye hear no voice of war,
   Go back and stay at home."

---

nington should be called the battle of Walloomsack,
see *National Magazine* for April, 1892.

   * Parson Allen. See poem *ante* by Bruce.

The morning came—there stood the foe;—
  Stark eyed them as they stood ;
Few words he spoke—'twas not a time
  For moralizing mood ;
" See there, the *enemy*, my boys—
  Now, strong in valor's might,
Beat them, or Betty* Stark will sleep
  In widowhood to-night !"

Each soldier there had left at home,
  A sweetheart, wife or mother ;
A blooming sister, or perchance,
  A fair-haired, blue-eyed brother ;
Each from a fireside came, and thoughts
  These simple words awoke,
That nerved up every warrior's arm,
  And guided every stroke.

Fireside and woman—mighty words !
  How wond'rous is the spell
They work upon the manly heart,
  Who knoweth not full well ?
And then the *women* of this land,
  That never land hath known
A truer, nobler hearted race,
  Each Yankee boy must own.

Brief eloquence was Stark's—not vain ;
  Scarce uttered he the words,
When burst the musket's rattling peal ;
  Out leaped the flashing swords.
And when brave Stark in after time
  Told the proud tale of wonder,
He said " the battle din was one
  Continual clap of thunder."

---

* General Stark's wife's name was *Elizabeth Page.*

Two hours they strove, when victory crowned
  The valiant Yankee boys ;
Naught but the memory of the dead
  Bedimmed their glorious joys !
Aye—there's the rub ; the hour of strife
  Though follow years of fame,
Is still in mournful memory linked
  With some death-hallowed name.

The cypress with the laurel twines—
  The Pæan sounds a knell—
The trophied column marks the spot
  Where friends and brothers fell !
Fame's mantle, a funeral pall
  Seems to the grief-dimmed eye ;
For ever where the bravest fall,
  The best beloved die !

REMNANT OF AN OLD CONTEMPORARY.

(Song about Bennington.)

To take the stores and cattle
  That we had gathered then,
Burgoyne sent a detachment
  Of fifteen hundred men.

They came as brave men ever come,
  To stand, to fight, to die ;
No thought of fear was in their heart,
  No quailing in the eye ;
If the lip faltered, 'twas with prayer,
  Amid these gathering bands,
For the sure rifle kept its poise
  In strong, untrembling hands.

POEMS ON THE BATTLES OF SARATOGA.

(SEPTEMBER 19 AND OCTOBER 7, 1777.)

A STORY OF BEHMUS' HEIGHTS.

(OCTOBER 7, 1777.)

(Written by E. W. B. Canning, a trustee of the Saratoga Monument
Association, for the Springfield *Republican*, December 13th, 1885.)

" PLEASE tell us," said the boys who stood,
    With eyes brimful of fun,
Beside their grandsire—" how you fought
    Red-coats at Bennington ;
And Col. Cilley's battle-tug
    Over the twelve-pound gun."

"You've got a little mixed, my boys,
    'Twas not at Bennington,
But Behmus'* Heights, where Cilley took
    And christened that big gun ;
And I was there and helped hurrah,
    When the brave deed was done.

" You see we'd been a fighting hard
    Through all the afternoon ;
And 'mongst the trees a thousand balls
    Still sung their deadly tune ;
And shot and shell knocked bark and boughs
    Over our whole platoon.

---

* See Appendix No. X. for different spellings of
this name.

"We drove the red-coats rods away,
    And then they drove us back;
Briton and Yankee lay in scores
    Along the bloody track;
And neither side would bate a jot—
    'Twas give and take the whack.

"So back and forth the battle swayed,
    As ocean's surges sway;
And round that gun that stood between
    The dead lay piled that day.
Though captured oft, we had no time
    To pull the thing away.

"Four times 'twas ours, and four times, too,
    They drove us from our prize,
Which made the sparks of anger flash
    From Cilley's gleaming eyes.
'The next time, boys, we'll hold it, or
    Beside it die'—he cries.

"A rush, a shout, a volley's crash,
    And it was ours again;
And furious as a horde of wolves,
    We drove them down the glen.
Then on the war-dog Cilley sprang
    And waved his sword amain.

"And cried aloud, 'To Liberty
    I dedicate the gun!'
Then whirled it round and bade its charge
    Help its late owners run.
We shouted it to camp, and thus
    Was the twelve-pounder won."

POEM BY PROFESSOR ROBERT T. S. LOWELL.*

ON THE OCCASION OF THE CENTENNIAL OF THE BATTLE OF BEMUS HEIGHTS, SEPTEMBER 19, 1777.

Prelude.

As while about some restful, wide-shored bay,
All hid in fog, landward and seaward lay,
Came far-heard voices forth, from men unseen,
Or low of herd, or roll of slow-worked oar,
Heard here and there, throughout that floating screen,
Made us no longer lonely, as before ;
Nay, as might chance, the eyes, long-straining, wist
Where shapes walked, great and dim, within the mist.

So, we may think, with former men, that by
This life's wide shore in memory are nigh,
But hidden deep in folding mists of Past ;
Still may the stronger eye, the finer ear,
Find, through the floating clouds about them cast,
The men that did their work and left it here,
The past that lived is but a little far
Within this self-same life wherein we are.

---

* Robert Traill Spence Lowell, clergyman, was born in Boston, Mass., October 8th, 1816. He was at Round Hill School, Northampton, Mass., in 1823–28, under Joseph G. Copwell and George Bancroft, and graduated from Harvard in 1833. In 1873 he became professor of the Latin language and literature in Union College, Schenectady, discharging the duties of that department for six years. He was quite a voluminous author, and was a frequent contributor in both verse and prose to reviews, magazines, and literary journals. He died September 12th, 1891.

BURGOYNE'S MARCH.

To the drums' echoing beat,
And thrilling clarion's cry—
England's red banner as a sheet
Of flame against the sky—
With the strong tread of soldiers' feet
Burgoyne's good host went by,
The gleaming bayonets flashed pride in every eye.

A hundred golden summer suns
Have filled our fields with June
Whose morn and noon and twilight runs
Each to its end too soon,
Since, basking in the wealth of day,
Saint John's broad fort and village lay.
While through the streets, and from the fort,
Company, regiment, brigade,
Were marched as for a last parade,
Crowding the sunny port.

The town all thronged the beach;
No work was then, for far or near:
No work, unless to see or hear,
And little speech, but cheer on cheer;
Or, here and there, beyond the common reach,
Some prayer, some sobbing speech;
But shout and martial strain
Make the banks ring again,
As the men took ship, to sail up Lake Champlain.

The general had stood awhile
Within the maple's shade,
With quickening eye and lofty smile;
Since the dread game of war was played
Were never better soldiers made.
To conquer for the world-conquering Isle;

To win back, for the English Crown,
Before which, fate, the might of France went down,
Fortress and farm and town,
Along the lakes, and rich Mohawk Vale,
To the old solid town that stands
Embosomed in fair lands,
And rich with many a peaceful sail.

Fort William—Beaverwick—the good town, Albany ;
While Howe, or Clinton, from the sea,
Should set the river-country free
From a base rule by countryman and clown.
Then would a loyal wall keep wide
The rebel lands that lay on either side,
Till more calm time and wiser thought
Should bring all mad revolt to naught ;
And the great realm that rounds the world and ever
        fronts the sun,
Once more, from shore to answering shore,
By land, by sea, one realm should be ;
Unbroken, as it was of yore,
Throughout all earth but one.

Strange, one might think, breathing June's happy
        breath,
Hearing glad melodies in all the air,
Seeing the red and gold that brightened everywhere ;
Strange that all these, so merry and so fair,
Should deck the trade of death !
As well the clouds of sunset heaped,
All tinged with red and gold,
The while the nightfall cricket cheeped,
Might into sudden storm have leaped,
And wreck and ruin manifold,
With thunderbolt of fabled Thor,
As this become death-dealing war !

It would but be a month's parade ;
The rebel fort would yield at call,
To earth the rebel flag would fall ;
The king would be obeyed.
To sweep, with summer breeze, the lake,
In the night wind a bivouac make,
Beneath the starry arch ;
To scout, in underwood and brake,
Would be a pleasure-march !

So, to an English eye, our country's cause would fail
(The hurried ending of a tale
Told overnight),
                When brave Burgoyne set sail.

Our countrymen that season lay
As men that wake in night but fear the day,
The leaguer-fires of Bunker Hill
Were yet scarce trodden out ; and still
There were true men, whose steadfast will
Set all it had at stake ;
Would never bow to might or ill ;
Rather their country's soil would fill
With clay of heroes' make.

St. Clair and Schuyler had trod back
The long road of retreat ;
The foe was heard upon their track,
And, foot by foot—as waters roll—
So, following foot by foot, he stole
Their country from beneath their feet,
Crown Point, Ticonderoga, fell ;
Fort George, Fort Edward—need we tell
Stout Warner's gloomy overthrow ?
Or the great loss at Skenesborough ?

Let our hearts honor, as they can,
Schuyler, the gracious gentleman.

His countrymen called back their trust
He waited not till they were just,
Took lower place, and felt no shame;
Still gave a heart and hand, the same
That chose this cause when it began,
And, in his honor, give its share
To the strong patience of St. Clair.
Our tide of strength was running low;
On its swift ebb was borne the foe
And, as men speak, God willed it so.

Not always will the tide turn out:
Not always the strong wind of fate
Shall drive from off the harbor's gate
Those who, fast-anchored, wait and wait
'Till their own time shall come about;
Yield never to the crime of doubt.

So everywhere great hearts were true,
The world looked dark; here—only here—
A hand-breadth of the sky was clear;
But the world's work was here to do!
Manhood in France was in the dust,
The prey of rank, and greed, and lust;
And little despots, otherwheres,
Laid out the trembling world in shares;
And England—England of the free—
Set safe by God amidst the sea,
To keep the light of liberty—
Under a foreign rule
Had learned in that bad school;
Forgotten that, *where law has sway,*
They must make law who law obey.
England was reading all her story back.
To our true-hearted sires all the world's sky
    looked black,

Save one clear hand-breadth in the west;
Darkness and clouds held all the rest.

The time soon comes : men fill our camps;
On fortress-wall the sentry tramps
With *The New Flag* on high,
That in the ages down through time
Should shelter all weak things but crime ;
And all strong wrongs defy.
Now gain comes in where came in loss ;
Great names are made, or take new gloss ;
As fearless Herkimer—so wise
To see beyond the young, rash eyes,
Where needless, useless, labor lies ;
But fatherly and true,
To bear their rashness through ;
So Willett won at Schuyler fort,
And the brave leader Gansevoort :
Then, with Stark's day at Bennington,
The first great prize of war was won,
The conquering of Burgoyne begun.
There was no choosing in the dark,
God made the general, John Stark—
Our tide swelled toward high water mark.

Three months of summer time were past
Since, with a gallant host,
'Mid beat of drum and trumpet-blast,
And with more lofty boast,
Burgoyne his march had forward cast;
Through fort and field his easy play
Would be a conqueror's holiday—
To that proud time his thoughts might stray
When Gates's army barred his further way.

On Bemis Heights our fathers stood,
While all the land looked on ;

Could they not make their footing good,
Then Albany was gone !
Then all the hearts that beat for right
Would draw sad presage from the fight ;
Then a most heavy blow would smite
The heart of Washington !

When the day opened, fair and still
And clarions, with alarum shrill
Drew echoes from each other's hill,
If man his brother's blood must spill,
Let not God's word, " *Thou shalt not kill*,"
Bring judgment on our head !
And let the right stand, come what will,
Though we go to the dead !

They met the foe.—We will not say
All that was done, of deadly fray ;
How forward, now, now back they sway,
'Till the night settled late.
But by the first strong stand here made
Burgoyne's long summer-march was stayed,
And many an anxious one took breath,
Who watched the turn, for life or death,
In the young country's fate.

Here, once for all, his march was crossed ;
He tried again, again he lost ;
And ere the season, growing old,
Knew summer out of date,
And hung the woods with red and gold,
Burgoyne's short story has been told ;
A brave heart, but his cause was cold ;
God willed our free-born state.
And so Burgoyne's last march was made :
Between our line he led his last parade.

AFTER BREATH.

Now, with still years between, when through we gaze
On those dim dead—the strong of earlier days—
Now that all strife is still—the great meed gained
For them that lived or died, with loyal heart,
In alien faith, but to great manhood strained
Unyielding sinews, honor now !　Our part
To lay ourselves, as very sod or stone
Of trench, when called, to keep our land our own.

ALFRED B. STREET'S POEM.*

READ BY COLONEL E. HOWE ON THE OCCASION OF THE
CENTENNIAL OF THE SURRENDER OF BURGOYNE.

WHEN fell Rome's fabric in the chasm it wrought
Dense darkness rushed without one star of thought:

---

* Alfred Billings Street, author and poet, born in
Poughkeepsie, N. Y., December 18th, 1811.　In 1839
he removed to Albany, N. Y., and 1843–44 edited
the *Northern Light*, and from 1848 until his death
he was State Librarian.　Mr. Street began at an early
age to write poetry for the magazines, and, as his
biographer in " Appleton's Cyclopedia " has justly said,
" he attained a respectable rank as a descriptive poet."
Some of his productions were highly praised by critics,
and several of his poems have been translated into
German.　Chief among his poems may be mentioned
" Frontenac : A Metrical Romance " (London, 1849),
" The Burning of Schenectady " (Albany, 1842), and
" Drawings and Tintings " (New York, 1844).　One of
his chief prose works was " Woods and Waters on the
Saranac and the Racket," describing a trip in the Adi-

Scowled the whole midnight heaven, one general tomb,
Where formless monsters moved in Gothic gloom.
What though breathed Music in Provençal bowers,
And architecture wreathed its fadeless flowers :
The loftiest virtues of the soul lay dead.
Right, swordless, crouched to Wrong's crowned con-
        quering head.
And though grand Freedom's essence never dies,
It drooped, despairing, under despot skies.
If aught it asked, Darius-like the throne
At its awed look, in wrathful lightnings shone.
Its food the acorn and its home the cell,
Its only light but showed its manacle :
Until its eye, at throned Oppression's foot,
Saw slavery's towering tree, its heart the root,
Cast Upas shadow o'er one common grave,
With naught but its own soul its life to save.
And then it rose ; up with one bound it sprang ;
Thunder from a clear sky its war-shout rang ;—
Out like a sunburst, flashed its falchion wide,
And gladdened thousands sought its warrior side ;
As the mist streaming from some towering crag,
It spread the blazon of its glittering flag.

In savage gorges which the vulture swept,
In lonely caverns where the serpent crept,

---

rondack Region (New York, 1860). He was present on
the occasion of the dedication of the Saratoga Monu-
ment in 1877, on which occasion, being too feeble
himself, his poem was read by Colonel Howe, and the
writer well remembers riding with him in the same
carriage in the procession on that occasion and having
the felicity of hearing the choice gems which dropped
from his mouth at that time.

Close where the tumbling torrent hurled its spray,
And shadowy cedars twine a twilight day:
Clutching its sword and battling on its knee,
Still Freedom fought; and though the swelling sea
Of cruel Wrong still drove it struggling higher
It could not quench its pure celestial fire;
From peak to peak it rose until the height
Showed it but heaven wherein to take its flight.
Round flew its glance, it saw its myriad foes
Following, still following, rising as it rose;
Following, still following! was no refuge nigh?
Naught on the earth, and only in the sky?
Round flew its glance, it pierced beyond the wave!
Ha! the new world emerges!—shall it save?
Hark, a wild cry! It is the eagle's scream!
See, a broad light, the far league-conquering stream
Linking all climates, where it reaching flows;
Its head the snow-drift and its foot the rose.
Mountains rise there that know no tread of kings;
Blasts that waft liberty on chainless wings:
Lakes that hold skies, the swallow tries to cross;
Prairies, earth-oceans; woods a whirlwind's toss
Would seem a puny streak: and with one tongue
All thundered " Come!" the welkin, echoing, rung
" Come!" and it went; it took its Mayflower flight;
Fierce raged the blast, cold billows hurled their might:
Winter frowned stern, it pierced to Freedom's heart;
White spread the strand and hunger reared its dart;
Round the frail hut the panther prowled, the gloat
Of the wolf's eyeball starred the chimney's throat;
Though winter entered in its heart, it braced
With strength its frame; its feet the forest traced
Despising hardship; by the torrent rocked
Its bark canoe; the wild tornado shocked

Way through prostrate woods, it grazing, sent
No dread, as by its roof it whirling went:
From choice it climbed the dizzy cliff to glance
O'er its realm's magnificent expanse.

Oh, glorious Freedom ! grandest, brightest gift
Kind heaven has given our souls to heavenward lift !
Oh, glorious Freedom ! are there hearts so low
That its live flame finds there no answering glow ?
It soars sublime beyond the patriot's love
Stateliest that sways save thought that dwells above.
Slaves love their homes, a patriot glad will die
For native land, though she in chains may lie ;
Noblest of all the soul that loves to fall
In the red front at Freedom's sacred call ;
His heart right's shield, he braves the despot's ban.
Not for himself to perish, but for man.

So when crowned Wrong made here, his first advance,
Flashed from our fathers wrath's immediate glance ;
Freedom their life, the sceptre but essayed
Attempt, to send their swift hand to their blade.
Their serried front said " stay !" their eyes " beware !
Rouse not the still prone panther from his lair ! "
But vain the mandate, vain the warning spoke,
The king strode onward and the land awoke.

Stately the sight recording History shows
When the red walls of our Republic rose.
Reared in deep woods, beneath a scarce-known sky
In puny strifes that hardly claimed the eye ;
Of lands still trembling with the thundering track
Of Saxe and Marlborough ; where startling back
Russia's black eagle had the Crescent hurled
Threatening so late to dominate the world.

     *   *   *   *   *   *   *   *

Three threatening strands were woven by the Crown—
One stretching up Champlain; one reaching down
The Mohawk Valley, whose green depths retained
Its Tory heart, Fort Stanwix, scarce restrained,
And one up Hudson's flood—the three to link
Where stood Albania's gables by its brink.

Glance at the picture, ere we spread our wing,
Of the grand battle whose famed deeds we sing.
Here spreads Champlain with mountain-skirted shore—
Caniadere Guarentie—open door
Of the fierce Iroquois to seek their foes
In regions stretching from Canadian snows.
West, in a purple dream of misty crag,
The Adirondacks wavy outlines drag:
East the Green Mountains, home of meadowy brooks,
Of cross-road hamlets, sylvan school-house nooks,
Church-covered hills and lion-hearted men,
Taught by the torrent tumbling down the glen,
By the grand tempests sweeping round the cliff,
By the wild waters, tossing by their skiff,
Freedom, till Freedom grew their very life,
And slavery with all earthly curses rife.
Next the dark Horican, that mountain-vein,
Bright islet-spangled tassel to Champlain;
The Highlands, souled with Washington and grand
With his high presence watching o'er the land;
Thy heights, oh Bemis! green with woods, yet white
With flakes of tents, zigzag with works and bright
With flags; while in perspective, we discern
Grouped round grand Washington, with features stern
In patriot care and doubt, the forms of Wayne,
Putnam and Greene and all the shadowy train
Of congress, wrapt spectators from afar
Of where fierce Battle drove his flashing, thunder-
        ing car.

As when some dream tumultuous fills the night
With changeful scenes and plunges past the sight
In hazy shapes looks frowning, till at last
With all its weird, wild phantasm it is past,
So the broad picture as it melts away,
And once more in our hearts peals out our trumpet-lay.

A deep, stern sound ! the startling signal-war !
And up Champlain Burgoyne's great squadron bore.
In front his savage ally's bark canoes
Flashing in all their bravery wild of hues;
Their war songs sounding and their paddles timed ;
Next the bateaux, their rude, square shapes sublimed
With pennon, sword and bayonet, casting glow
In pencilled pictures on the plain below ;
Last the grand ships, by queenly Mary led,
Where shines Burgoyne in pomp of gold and red,
And then in line St. George, Inflexible,
And Radeau, Thunderer, dancing on the swell
The glad wind made ; how stately shone the scene !
June in the forests, each side smiling green !
O'er her dark dome the chestnut's tassels stretched
Like golden fingers ; pearl that seemed as fetched
From Winter's heart the locust mantled o'er,
While its rich, creamy mass the dogwood bore,
Like a white helmet with its plumes atop.
And the sweet basswood higher appeared adrop
With ivory gems : the hemlock showed its edge
Fringed with fresh emerald ; even the sword-like sedge
Sharp 'mid the snowy lily-goblets set
In the nook shallows, like a spangled net
Was jewelled with brown bloom.   By curving point
Where glittering ripples amber sands anoint
With foamy silver ; by deep, crescent bays
Sleeping beneath their veil of drowsy haze.

By watery coverts shimmering faint in film,
Broad, rounded knolls, one white and rosy realm
Of laurel blossom, with the Kalmia-urns
Dotted with red, the fleet, as sentient, turns
The winding channel; in tall towers of white
The stately ships absorb the emerald light
Glossing the lake; like huge, dark claw-urged crabs
Ply the bateaux their poles; the paddle-stabs
Of the canoes make music as they move,
Gliding along unjarred, as in its groove
The car-wheel glides; the panther views the scene
And bears her cubs within the thicket's screen;
The wolf lifts sharpened ear and forward foot;
Waddles the bear away with startled hoot,
As some sail sends a sudden flash of white
In the cove's greenery, slow essaying flight
The loon rears, flapping, its checked, grazing wings,
'Till up it struggling flies and downward flings
Its Indian whoop; the blue bird's sapphire spark
Kindles the shade; the swarming pigeon's dark
Deep blue breaks out; the robin's warble swells
In crumply cadence from the skirting dells:
And restless rings the bobolink's bubbly note
From the clear bell that tinkles in his throat.
Thus stately, cheerily move the thronging fleet!
O'er the lake's steel the blazing sunbeams beat;
But now a blast comes blustering from a gorge,
The whitecaps dance; it bends the tall St. George
And even the Thunderer tosses: the array
Breaks up; canoe, bateau grope doubtful way
Through the dim air; in spectral white each sail
Glances and shivers in the whistling gale;
All the green paintings of point, bank and tree
Vanish in black and white, and all but see

A close horizon where near islands lose
Their shapes and distant ranks of forest fuse
Into a mass ; at last the blast flies off,
Shallows stop rattling, and the hollow cough
Of surges into caves makes gradual cease
'Till on the squadron glides, once more in sunny peace.
So in some blue-gold day white clouds up-float
In shining throng, and then are dashed remote
By a fierce wind, next join in peace again
And smoothly winnow o'er the heavenly plain,
Or some fleet of wild fowl on the lake
Dipping and preening quiet journey take,
Till the sky drops an eagle circling low
For the straight plunge, wild scattering to and fro.

     *   *   *   *   *   *   *   *

When lay Champlain in eve's gold-plated glass,
And rich, black pictures etched the glowing grass,
The crews debarked, their camp-fires round would rear,
And hang their kettles for their nightly cheer ;
Then rose the tents, like mushrooms to the moon,
Swords would be edged and muskets polished ; soon
Slumber would fan its wings, and in the bright,
Soft, delicate peace would croon the summer night.

Then the gray day-dawn through the leaves would look,
Red-coats would gleam in every emerald nook
And weapons glitter ; as the mist would crawl
From the smooth lake and up the forest-wall,
Sails would shine out and spottings of canoe
Moored with bateau would thicken on the view ;
Rings of dead ashes, fallen trees half burned,
Trunks into black Egyptian marble turned,
Where curling fires had scorched the streaky moss,
Roofs of dead leaves where branches stooped across,

And soil burned black and smoking still would show
Where through the night had shone the camp-fire
     glow;
Limbs drooping down and logs with gaping cuts
Where the brigade had reared their bushy huts;
A deer's head on a stump, a bear skin cast
On trampled ferns—the red man's late repast;
The damp drum's beat would sound, and shrilly fife,
Dingle and aisle would flash with martial life;
Once more the fleet would start and up their way
Take as the whole scene brightened into day.

On Lady Mary's deck Burgoyne would stand,
Drinking the sights and sounds at either hand,
Replete with beauty to his poet heart,
Laughing to scorn man's paltry works of art,
The grassy vista with its grazing deer,
The lone loon soaring on its shy career,
The withered pine tree with its fish-hawk nest,
The eagle eyrie on some craggy crest,
The rich white lilies that wild shallow told,
Their yellow sisters with their globes of gold
At the stream's mouth; the ever changeful lake,
Here a green gleaming, there a shadowy rake
Of scudding air-breath; here a dazzling flash
Searing the eyeball; there a sudden dash
Of white from some swift cloud; a streak of white
The wake of some scared duck avoiding sight.

*   *   *   *   *   *   *   *

Changing the scene, Burgoyne his camp would trace
Round the Red House at the Great Carrying Place;
There when the sun is bright the sentry sees
Madame Riedesel dining under trees,

As the chasseur beholds her gliding round
Off flies his bear-skin helmet to the ground.

    *   *   *   *   *   *   *

Meanwhile the tidings of Oriskany
And Bennington careered, and glad and free
Hope spread white pinions; throngs to Schuyler pour
Swelling his ranks, all abject terror o'er.
Poor Jennie's mournful doom has roused an ire
Wrapping the region with consuming fire.
The boy strode downward in his rustic sleeves,
His coarse frock fragrant with the wheaten sheaves;
The old blue swallow-tailed artillery coat
Trod by the hunting shirt from wilds remote.

    *   *   *   *   *   *   *   *

But on! the morning dawns: still on! the height
Of Saratoga hails the pallid light
Of closing eve, and here at last the weighed
And weary step of poor Burgoyne is stayed.
Gates follows after from the jewelled isles
Of Horican, the stately rocky piles
Of blue Luzerne, where the majestic crags
Of " Potash Kettles" change the clouds to flags.
Within a ball-swept tent Burgoyne sits now
In council with despair upon his brow ;
Curtains of scowling blackness fold him round,
Closed is the net and he is firmly bound.
Turns he toward Horican ?* the foe is there !

---

* Horican (Horicon), a name never an Indian name,
but merely, as Cooper himself says, a fiction, and which,
therefore, has not the merit even of historical truth. A
tribe once lived in that vicinity, and therefore he took
the liberty of calling Lake George by that name. This
is all well enough in novels, but so far as historic truth
is concerned it should be mentioned. Cooper should

East, Fellows'* cannon-lightnings scorch the air.
West, the live forest but his coming waits,
And in his rear the frowning front of Gates.

*   *   *   *   *   *   *   *

On the Fort Hardy green,† this dainty day,
The conquered hosts of England march, to lay
Their weapons down.   The hour has struck, and now
With heavy footstep and with sullen brow
They come, but with no patriot eye to see,
For nobly Gates in generous sympathy   ·
Has banished all within their tents.   They come
Yet with no banner spread, no beating drum,
Tramp, tramp, they come ! tramp, tramping rank on
     rank !
Tramp, tramp, they come ! tramp, tramping ; hark,
     that clank !
Those piling arms! clank, clank ! that tolling knell
To bowed Burgoyne ! what bitter, bitter swell

---

never be considered an authority in anything pertaining to historical truth.   In fact, he is greatly overrated.

   * General Fellows having got in the rear of Burgoyne's army, between the latter and Fort Edward—the objective point of Burgoyne's retreat—nothing was left for the British general but to surrender.

   † Fort Hardy.   This fort was erected during the administration of Governor Hardy of the province of New York.   It was built by the colony of New York to ward off the ·incursions of the French and the Indians in their employ.   It never was a great strategic work, though for political purposes it was in the New York Assembly called a "great work."   It was here that Burgoyne's army "stacked" their arms, and the outworks of which are still (1893) to be seen by the curious tourist.

Of his proud heart! ah, sad Burgoyne! what death
To thy high hopes, all vanished like a breath!

*   *   *   *   *   *   *   *

Loudly may laureled Saratoga claim
A marble tribute to her splendid fame!
In the grand chariot which her war-steeds drew
She first placed Freedom, pointed to her view
The glorious goal.   Shall pagan Egypt bid
The heavens be cloven with her pyramid?
Shall Greece shrine Phidias in her Parthenon
To live till fade the stars and dies the sun?
Rome with her mighty Coliseum whelm
The earth with awe?—a peerless, wondrous realm—
And our free nation meanly shrink to write
With marble finger in the whole world's sight
Grand Saratoga's glory?   Sound aloud
Song thy wide trumpet! let the heavens be bowed
With love of country's wrathful thunders, till
A reverent people with united will
Shall bid the monument arise and stand
Freedom's embodied form forever in the land.

GENERAL J. WATTS DE PEYSTER'S ODE.

READ BY REV. D. K. VAN DOREN, ON THE OCCA-
SION OF THE CENTENNIAL CELEBRATION OF BUR-
GOYNE'S SURRENDER.

THE SURRENDER OF BURGOYNE, " SAR-
ATOG," 17TH OCTOBER, 1777.

BROTHERS, this spot is holy!—Look around!
    Before us flows our mem'ry's sacred river,
Whose banks are Freedom's Shrines.   This grassy
    mound,
    The altar, on whose height the Mighty Giver

Gave Independence to our country ; when,
Thanks to its brave, enduring, patient men,
The invading host was brought to bay, and laid
Beneath " Old Glory's" new-born folds, the blade,
The brazen thunder-throats, the pomp of war,
And England's yoke, broken forever more.

Like a destroying angel, Burgoyne's host
  Burst through Ticonderoga's bulwarks, hoary ;
And flaming wrecks, wide ruin 'long its coast,
  Renew'd past awful scenes of Champlain's story,
When France's Lilies dy'd themselves in blood,
Floated to triumph on Algonquin flood—
Made William Henry's siege a tale of horror—
Made Abercrombie's failure land-wide sorrow,
Like many conflicts though right bravely fought—
The only comfort was by Schuyler brought.
Our frontier people shrunk before the scare ; *
The load was left for Schuyler 'lone to bear.

---

* The scare or panic which succeeded the first ap-
pearance of Burgoyne was of the same character with
that which shook the whole country after the Bull Run
First, July 21st, 1861, and was equally causeless. The
people recovered from it much quicker in 1777 than
in 1861, for Oriskany and its rich harvest, due to
Schuyler, which broke the spell, was fought exactly
one month to a day after the fall of Ticonderoga,
whereas the victory won by General Thomas, the
Schuyler of the Slaveholders' Rebellion, at Mill Spring,
which taught the North that, under an honest and
able leader, theirs were the best men, was not achieved
until January 19th, 1862, *six* months after the first
battle of Bull Run.

And how he bore it, now, at length, we know;
  How steadfastly he damm'd the crimson tide;
Baffled and stopp'd the five-fold stronger foe; *
  To timid counsels hero strength supplied.
Burgoyne victorious, ere he left Champlain,
Startled perceiv'd his brilliant prospects wane;
Saw in the Lion's path a Nimrod stand;
Saw all his mighty projects counterplann'd;
Ere Burgoyne reached the Hudson, fast *empoign'd*
In Schuyler's grasp, he felt he was "Burgoyn'd."

O mighty soul!—by envious souls decried,
  New York's great son in giant height now stands;
Argus to watch, Ulysses to decide,
  Gath'ring resources with Briarean hands,
His the victorious field Harkheimer made
St. Leger's † foil, stopp'd Johnson's tiger raid;

---

* Allen says Schuyler did not have over 1000 men
at Fort Edward, and even after he got down to Half-
Moon, it would appear that the majority of his troops
were boys, old men, negroes, and parti-colored.   If
the real truth could be reached, there is very little
question but that proof exists that Burgoyne had over
10,000 men, Regulars, Provincials or Loyalists, Cana-
dians and Indians, when he started on this expedition.
He himself admits 7863 men.   Schuyler at Fort Edward,
when Burgoyne was within twenty-one miles of him,
had only 1500 miserably furnished troops.   Burgoyne
surrendered, valids and invalids, 5763 men to Gates,
who had, besides staff, bateau-men, artificers, etc., a
force numbering 18,624, according to official returns.
Governor and General Clinton, of New York, estimated
the forces of General Gates at between 23,000 and
24,000 armed men.

    † For a sketch and account of General St. Leger

Fort Stanwix sav'd, the Mohawk valley sav'd—
Was all his work, who coward counsels brav'd;
Stak'd honor, fortune, all, upon the throw,
So by the cast he beat his country's foe;
Oriskany is due to New York's son;
Likewise to Schuyler's *brain* is Bennington,
Fought on our own State soil, on Hoosic's hill,
Vict'ries that yet the nation's pulses thrill.
At length Burgoyne, the haughty, brought to bay
  At Saratoga knew our country's might;
At Freeman's Farm saw triumph fade away;
  Saw Hope itself take wings on Bemis Height.
Barr'd, baffled, beaten, crippled, short of food,
In vain his craft, his vet'ran multitude,
Caught in the toils through which he could not break,
Chain'd like a victim to the fatal stake
Just where we stand—thanks to Sabaoth's Lord
Boasting Burgoyne gave up his vet'ran sword.

Here Albion's battle flag, which, round the world,
Following the sun at morning-gun's unfurl'd,
Here, where we stand, the crucial flag of Mars
Stoop'd, in surrender, to our Stripes and Stars,
Where at an army's head was first display'd
Our Starry Flag with triumph's halo ray'd.
A century since Burgoyne surrender'd here!*
British dominion its Centennial year

---

and his dissolute life, see Stone's "Johnson's Orderly
Book," Appendix (Munsell's Sons).
  *The New Netherlands were not definitely ceded
to Great Britain, and did not become permanently
New York until February 9th, 1674, by the peace
signed at Westminster. The city of New Amsterdam
or New York was not finally yielded up, however,
until November 10th, 1674.

Had just completed—which its Lion tore
From Holland's zone, the richest gem it bore,—
And now assembled thus, we celebrate
The triumph sure which seal'd th' invader's fate;
Without this deed, Freedom had not been ours;
Without this fact, unbroken Britain's powers;
Burgoyne defeated, France became our friend,
A source of strength on which we could depend,
For all that War's strong sinews constitute—
To foster Freedom's tree—*'neath us the root.*

All was decided here, and at this hour
Our sun leap'd up, though clouds still veil'd its power.
From Saratoga's hills we date the birth,—
Our Nation's birth among the powers of earth.
Not back to '76 New Yorkers date:
The mighty impulse launched our "Ship of State"
'Twas given here—where shines our rising sun
Excelsior! These hills saw victory won.
This vale the cradle where the colonies
Grew into States—despite all enemies,
Yes, on this spot—Thanks to our Gracious God
Where last in conscious arrogance it trod,
Defil'd as captives Burgoyne's conquered horde;
Below * their general yielded up his sword

---

* "*Below.*" On the alluvial flat, a few feet distant
from the foundation of the contemplated Saratoga
Monument (according to W. L. Stone), Burgoyne
went through the ceremony of resigning his sword to
Gates. The Duke de Rochefoucauld-Liancourt (II.,
302), who visited "Saratog" in 1795, says that the
ceremony took place in the courtyard of Schuyler's
ruined homestead.

There * to our flag bow'd England's, battle-torn.
Where now we stand † th' United States was born !

---

* "*There.*"   About a hundred rods to the front and
eastward, near the site of old Fort Hardy and present
village of Schuylerville, the British forces laid down
their arms.

† "*Here where we stand.*"   The Convention of Sara-
toga traversed all the British plans, lost to the crown
an army which could not be replaced, won for the Col-
onies the French alliance, without whose men, material,
and money, independence was still an impossibility.
And afterward no great general battle was fought, nor
did the English achieve a single success which led, even
comparatively speaking, to important results.   The
sun of October 17th, 1777, witnessed the safe delivery
of the infant United States.

The writer of these verses has endeavored to convey
in a few lines facts worthy of remembrance, which
thus concisely put could be recalled without exertion,
and read or listened to without fatigue.   The facts
thus grouped together in rhyme, and so briefly pre-
sented, were the result, however, of years of the closest
study.   The author's researches had already borne
fruit in a series of publications.   The most prominent
of these was an Annual Address, delivered on Janu-
ary 22d, 1877, before the New York Historical
Society, and entitled " Major-General Schuyler and
the Burgoyne Campaign, in the Summer of 1777,"
June, October, 1777 ; " Justice to Schuyler," published
in the New York *Citizen, Citizen and Round Table*,
in or about January, 1868 ; also " Schuyler and Prac-
tical Strategy," published in the *Army and Navy
Journal*, January 27th, 1865, Vol. III., page 336.
The last two were published in 1876 as a mono-

graph, with notes. In addition to these, the author, Major-General J. Watts de Peyster, prepared a series of nineteen articles, bearing the general title "The Revolutionary Year, 1777," which came out in the New York *Evening Mail* and New York *Mail*. The first appeared on April 5th and the nineteenth on December 13th, 1877. The series treated of all the prominent events of "the real beyond contradiction, Centennial year." They filled nearly thirty columns of this evening daily. Over and above this immense labor, the same exponent of the truth of American history wrote twelve voluminous articles on the Burgoyne campaign for the New York *Daily Times*, treating in detail not only the Burgoyne campaign proper, but all the military operations bearing upon or connected with the same. These occupied at least thirty-six columns brevier and agate type in this prominent daily journal. Some of them were pronounced by experts to be exhaustive of facts and authorities. Nor was this the entirety of his labors. He furnished a monograph and poem on the battle of Oriskany, with notes, to Stone's New York *Military Gazette*, of November 15th, 1860, and a detailed article on the same subject to the New York *Historical Magazine* (new series, Vol. V., No. 1), for January, 1869. The poem which first appeared in the *Military Gazette* was considered of sufficient merit to be translated into German and republished in Hon. Friedrich Kapp's " Geschichte der deutchen Anwanderung in Amerika," Vol. I., " *Geschichte der Deutschen in Staate New York bis zum Anfange des neunzehnten Jahrhundert*," New York, 1867, pages 389-90. It was again reproduced in the *Staats Zeitung* of August 6th, 1877. His second poem on Oriskany, written for the occasion, was read at the Centennial Anniversary of this decisive battle, noteworthy in connection with the battles and capitulation of Saratoga, because it did decide the fate of the Burgoyne campaign. This received the most flattering notice from the press throughout the State, as well as elsewhere.

The motive for all this work was patriotism in the sense in which it was applied in olden times, when a man's sympathies were not expected to embrace a continent: Love of New York, the Empire State, in the truest sense of such an appellation, imperial even in its errors. With gradually developing thought, even New England has attained the majesty of justice to Schuyler. (See Stevens's "Burgoyne Campaign," page 27.)

Alas! this justice comes just one century too late. New England's envy and injustice, in 1777, deprived Schuyler of his glory in the very hour of triumph— New England, for which Washington had so little good and so much bitter both to say and to write.

All the conflicts of the Burgoyne campaign were fought on New York soil, and all the great factors in the triumph, except the mere nominal chief actor, were born within the limits of the original colony of the New Netherlands, afterward New York. Children of its soil fought out the question on the Upper Hudson (underlying Fort Anne), at Oriskany and in the passes of the Highlands. Namesake and kinsman, blood relation and connection, neighbor and dependent, met breast to breast to solve the great problem whether their country should be happier under a constitutional monarchy or a constitution and congress.

They did not decide it then, and it is an enigma which still remains unsolved. Events are tending fast to its solution, but the tangled skein is certainly not yet entirely unravelled.

What scathing words Washington hurls around him at various members of the old original Thirteen! He is unsparing. New England does not escape, nor Pennsylvania, nor even his own native Virginia.

" In 1777" (says Theodore Parker in his " Historic Americans"), "when the British held Philadelphia, and Washington went into winter quarters at Valley Forge, only a day's march off, at a time of the greatest peril, the . . . State of Pennsylvania had but twelve hundred militia in the field to defend their own firesides." " Pennsylvania . . . did little for independence."

These are quotations. If the charges are unfounded, let the author justify them. One fact is patent, just as in 1862 and 1863, Pennsylvania had to call in 1777 upon her sister States to protect her homesteads.

Meanwhile, what is the record of the Rev. William Gordon (III, 399), in regard to New York, which, " though consuming at both ends and bleeding at every pore, had her complement of Continental troops (Congress soldiers Regulars), in the field, beside having raised in the month of May [1780] eight hundred new levies to guard the frontiers?"

In 1780, when New York was devastated (at its heart) by her own offspring, while thus suffering and still exerting itself, several of her sister States were in full and peaceable possession of their territories, seemingly slept in security, and had not a third of their quota in the field. " Yet (at this very period), in 1779-80, General Arnold, the traitor, with less than two thousand men (British Regulars and Loyalists), ravaged the whole State of Virginia for two years. Jefferson did nothing against him." (Parker's " His-

toric Americans," Washington, 144.) Nor was the
Father of his Country less severe on the original co-
lonial Virginia militia or provincial troops. (*Ibid.*,
86–88.)

This theme might be pursued with healthful in-
structiveness through pages for the edification not
merely of the men of the day, but of posterity, to show
that not only were the shores of the noble river
which bears his name " the loveliest country (ac-
cording to Hudson) on which the foot of man was
ever set," but the men who were bred and born along
this majestic stream and its affluents were worthy of
such a partial soil.

The first North American Congress met at New
York in 1690 (Lamb, 1, 379). The second (by many
styled the first) celebrated Congress, consisting of dele-
gates from all the Colonies, convened at Albany in
1754.

The fate of the Thirteen Colonies was decided in the
State of New York one hundred years ago ; and the
first President of the United States was inaugurated
in the city of New York eighty-eight years ago in
Federal Hall.

So much space has been devoted to this illustration,
because if General de Peyster's part in the exercises
on October 17th, 1877, at Schuylerville was com-
paratively small, his "chivalric" labors to place the
State of New York upon the grand elevation its ma-
jesty deserves have not been exceeded by any " son
of the soil" since first it had a literature and records.

THE FIELD OF THE GROUNDED ARMS, SARATOGA.

WRITTEN IN 1831 BY FITZ-GREENE HALLECK.*

(Read by General James Grant Wilson, Halleck's biographer.)

STRANGERS ! your eyes are on that valley fixed
Intently, as we gaze on vacancy,
    When the mind's wings o'erspread
    The spirit world of dreams.

---

* Fitz-Greene Halleck, poet, born in Guilford, Conn., July 8th, 1790; died there November 19th, 1867. In May, 1811, he left his native town to seek after fame and fortune in New York, and in June of the same year he entered the counting-room of Jacob Barker, in whose service he remained for twenty years. He early became a poet, and it was on the occasion of the death of his intimate friend, Joseph Rodman Drake, that he wrote those exquisitely touching lines beginning

    " Green be the turf above thee."

In 1819 these two formed a literary partnership, and afterward produced the humorous series of the " Croaker Papers," published in the New York *Evening Post*, then edited by their friend, Bryant. He was the author of numerous poetical works and short pieces—among them " Fanny" and " Marco Bozzaris"—and was justly held in high regard both as a poet and as a man. Nor can I allow this opportunity to pass without here paying a personal tribute to the subject of this sketch. When a young man and first embarking on the untried sea of authorship, he gave me much encouragement, and it is due to him in a measure that I was emboldened to continue that voyage.

True, 'tis a scene of loveliness—the bright
Green dwelling of the summer's first-born hours,
    Whose wakened leaf and bud
    Are welcoming the morn.

And morn returns the welcome, sun and cloud
Smile on the green earth from their home in heaven,
    Even as a mother smiles
    Above her cradled boy,

And wreathe their light and shade o'er plain and
    mountain,
O'er sleepless seas of grass, whose waves are flowers,
    The river's golden shores,
    The forest of dark pines.

The song of the wild bird is on the wind,
The hum of the wild bee, the music wild,
    Of waves upon the bank,
    Of leaves upon the bough.

But all is song and beauty in the land,
Beneath her skies of June ; then journey on,
    A thousand scenes like this
    Will greet you ere the eve.

Ye linger yet—ye see not, hear not now,
The sunny smile, the music of to-day,
    Your thoughts are wandering up,
    Far up the stream of time.

And boyhood's lore and fireside listened tales
Are rushing on your memories, as ye breathe
    That valley's storied name,
    FIELD OF THE GROUNDED ARMS.

Strangers no more, a kindred " pride of place,"
Pride in the gift of country, and of name,
    Speaks in your eye and step—
    Ye tread your native land.

And your high thoughts are on her glory's day,
The solemn Sabbath of the week of battle,
    Whose tempest bowed to earth
    Her foeman's banner here.

The forest leaves lay scattered cold and dead,
Upon the withered grass that autumn morn,
    When, with as widowed hearts
    And hopes as dead and cold,

A gallant army formed their last array
Upon that field, in silence and deep gloom,
    And at their conqueror's feet
    Laid their war-weapons down.

Sullen and stern, disarmed but not dishonored;
Brave men, but brave in vain, they yielded there:
    The soldier's trial-task
    Is not alone " to die."

Honor to chivalry ! the conqueror's breath
Stains not the ermine of his foeman's fame,
    Nor mocks his captive doom—
    The bitterest cup of war.

But be that bitterest cup the doom of all
Whose swords are lightning-flashes in the cloud
    Of the invader's wrath,
    Threatening a gallant land !

His armies' trumpet-tones wake not alone
Her slumbering echoes; from a thousand hills
    Her answering voices shout,
    And her bells ring to arms !

The danger hovers o'er the invader's march,
On raven wings hushing the song of fame,
    And glory's hues of beauty
    Fade from the cheek of death.

A foe is heard in every rustling leaf,
A fortress seen in every rock and tree,
    The eagle eye of art
    Is dim and powerless then,

And war becomes the people's joy, the drum
Man's merriest music, and the field of death
    His couch of happy dreams,
    After life's harvest-home.

He battles heart and arm, his own blue sky
Above him, and his own green land around,
    Land of his father's grave,
    His blessing and his prayers;

Land where he learned to lisp a mother's name,
The first beloved in life, the last forgot,
    Land of his frolic youth,
    Land of his bridal eve—

Land of his children—vain your columned strength,
Invaders! vain your battles' steel and fire!
    Choose ye the morrow's doom—
    A prison or a grave.

And such were Saratoga's victors—such
The Yeoman-Brave, whose deeds and death have
       given
    A glory to her skies,
    A music to her name.

In honorable life her fields they trod,
In honorable death they sleep below;
    Their souls' proud feelings here
    Their noblest monuments.

SARATOGA.

By Charles H. Crandall.*

(Written for the dedication of the battle monument at Schuylerville, N. Y.)

Historic Hudson! Haste not by to-day!
More gently let thy waters take their way

---

*Crandall, Charles Henry, born June 19th, 1858, in the town of Easton, near the village of Greenwich, Washington County, N. Y. His father was Henry Sargent Crandall, who spent many years in public service as Assistant Assessor of Internal Revenue, and in several positions in the New York Post Office and Custom House. The Crandalls trace back to a follower of Roger Williams, Rev. John Crandall, who founded the town of Westerly, R. I., about 1635. On his maternal side the poet sprang from Mills, Carmichael, Canfield, and Waters families. His great-grandfather, Jeremiah Newbury, fought throughout the whole Revolution, and is buried at Greenwich, N. Y.

Our subject was educated at common schools and the Greenwich Academy until he was fourteen years old, when he had to take up the problem of working for a living, first on the ancestral acres and afterward in mercantile life in New York. Tired of the latter, he went on the staff of the New York *Tribune* in March, 1880, and has written for it since more or less, contributing correspondence, special and editorial matter. His vein of poesy first flowed through the columns of the *Tribune,* opening with a graceful sonnet, and continuing with some scores of poems—grave, gay, patriotic or elegiac. Afterward his verse found acceptance with the *Century, Harper's Monthly*, the *Atlantic, Cosmopolitan, Lippincott's*, etc. Among many magazine articles he has written a full treatment of the Bur-

As on thy banks we dedicate
This shaft unto the dead, the great,
Whose memory, like thy stream, a shining story,
Shall broaden to a boundless sea of glory.

The dwellers in Manhattan's crowded mart
May here see Nature play her silent part.
    The stream that brings them wealth
    Here steps with bashful stealth,
Soft, as in moccasins an Indian maiden,
Its breast with trees, like tresses, overladen.

---

goyne campaign, published with illustrations in the
American Magazine. His interest in the Burgoyne bat-
tle monument may be partially due to the fact that his
birthplace, two miles away, is in view from its top. In
1890 Mr. Crandall published through Houghton,
Mifflin & Co. a collection of "Representative Sonnets"
by American poets, with an exhaustive study and his-
tory of the sonnet in all literatures since its birth in
the thirteenth century. The work was at once cordially
greeted, as a credit to American literature, by such
critics as Stedman, Gilder, Horace E. Scudder, the
Evening Post, Critic, etc.

In 1892 Mr. Crandall was requested to write a poem
for the two hundred and fiftieth anniversary of the
founding of Stamford, Conn., near which city he now
resides, mingling farm life with literary pursuits. He
has been twice married: to Miss Kate V. Ferguson
(deceased) and to Miss Mary V. Davenport, of the
family so closely connected with the history of Con-
necticut. He has three sons—Arthur, Robert and
Roland—and finds even greater pleasure in his sons
than his sonnets.

As now for many a path in life you meet,
The hills in their immortal verdure greet,
   Come with me in my boat of rhyme,
   Come and ascend the stream of time,
Back when the nation was a century newer
And held true heroes, though her sons were fewer.

Quiet for many a year has here been found—
The wild bird feared no martial sight nor sound.
   Under the peaceful fields, well-kept,
   The ashes of the soldier slept,
With summer's guard of tasselled corn around,
And winter's snow-shroud hallowing the ground.

On yonder plain, where England's grenadiers
Laid down the arms they loved, with bitter tears,
   The armies of the grass and grain
   Have struggled o'er and o'er again,
In changing regiments of green and yellow,
Through lusty June, through August ripe and mellow.

Honor the past ! Already has there flown
From Saratoga and from Horicon
   All but their names—whose gentle sounds
   Still linger round the burial mounds—
Of that dark race, which, ever westward flying,
Now, like a sunset's light, is slowly dying.

The modern spirit would itself demean
Did we not flock, to-day, to such a scene ;
   For from the nation's rugged past,
   The rude days when her fate was cast,
Has flowed the stream that makes all men draw near
     her,
The Freedom that has made the world revere her.

Here fell the blow that made Oppression reel,
And set on Freedom's cause its brightest seal.

Honor to Schuyler, Morgan, Gates,
The victors over threatening fates,
And praise for him whose niche has but a name,
Too valiant to forget, to base for fame !

Honor to every nameless, fallen one !
Honor them all, each one the country's son !
   Stonė for their fitting monument
   Nature to Art has kindly lent,
And every block that lifts this tapering spire
Is sacred as if touched with holy fire.

First on the soil the flag we love to name
Flew in the wind, a never-dying flame !
   Giving a heart-beat to the land,
   Binding it with a silken band—
An amulet where'er its name is spoken—
'Gainst which no sword shall ever fall unbroken !

And when this ceremonial pomp shall pass,
And undisturbed shall glow and fade the grass,
   While storm and sun and shadow chase
   Across each bronze, stern-featured face,
Yet shall this place to many a one be dear ;
And Liberty shall love to linger here !

To multitudes who come with pilgrim feet
The sculptured tablets will their tales repeat :
   Again in fancy will be seen
   The red-coats on the meadows green,
And Jane McCrea shall leave her pillow gory,
Or hearts be moved by Lady Acland's story.

For she whose love was greater than her fears,
Who sought our camp and conquered it with tears,
   Was but a type of woman's heart—
   Which ever bravely plays its part—

Which soothes in peace, in war gives cheering word,
Melts lead to ball and reaches down the sword

Long may our tribute to the brave endure,
Here where the winds and waters journey pure,
    And give to all who on it gaze
    The spirit of those olden days,
When love of right and liberty unbound
The strongest clasp that loved ones threw around.

Speak! Sons of Saratoga here to-day,
Shall it not be this valley's boast to say:
    The soil of Saratoga sends
    The kind of man that never bends,
Whether in council hall a vote he wield
Or grasps a gun upon a battle-field?

And you, fair village, with your skyward spires,
Your leisurely canal, your factory fires,
    Keep for yourself as fair a fame
    As his who gave to you a name—
The courtly soldier gentlemen who now,
Kindly in bronze, meets you with open brow.

England! a foe no longer, peace to thee!
A common lineage throbs beneath the sea;
    And though this day brings nearer heart
    The nation's friends who took our part,
We send to her who rules thy fair demesnes
Greeting from sixty million kings and queens.

The nation that forgets its Marathon
Has lost the choicest glory it has won.
    Then let this granite shaft of grace
    Forever be a rallying place
For liberty and honor, till the day
The stone is dust, the river dried away!

And when, a century hence, this column hath
Whirled with the world through space its spiral path,
   And men of grander, later days,
   With faces strange, upon it gaze ;
'Twill draw our thought, like lightning from the skies:
The man who dies for country never dies!

THE STAR-SPANGLED BANNER, PARA-PHRASED FOR THE OCCASION BY COLONEL B. C. BUTLER.*

READ BY WILLIAM L. STONE, SECRETARY OF THE SARATOGA MONUMENT ASSOCIATION.

O SAY, can you see, by the dawn's early light,
   On Saratoga's broad plains what so proudly is
     streaming,
Whose broad stripes and bright stars through the
     perilous fight,
   O'er the ramparts we watched were so gallantly
     streaming?
For our fathers this day to this field made their way
To glory in the conquest of the foe's proud array.
And the star-spangled banner in triumph shall wave
O'er the land of the free and the home of the brave.

In its field stood the plough, the axe ceased in the wood,
   From his log cabin gladly the wild hunter sallied,
From city and glen they came like a flood
   To the ranks where the brave and the valiant
     were rallied.

---

  * Colonel Benjamin C. Butler, a distinguished lawyer for many years of Saratoga Springs, N. Y.   He always took great interest in everything relating to the Revolutionary period.   He died about 1879.

O let Stillwater's Heights and Saratoga's dread fight
Tell how nobly our sires fought and bled for the right
While the star-spangled banner in triumph doth wave
O'er the land of the free and the home of the brave.

This day, when our sires trod on sceptre and chain,
    And the foes of proud Britain were scattered before us,
Then went up to heaven with loudest acclaim
    From the hearts of true freemen, that victory is o'er us.
'Twas Huzzah! Huzzah! from the lake to the shore,
Our cause it has triumphed, we are subjects no more—
The star-spangled banner in triumph doth wave
O'er the land of the free and the home of the brave.

O, thus be it ever, when freemen shall stand
    Between their loved home and the foes' desolation,
Blest with victory and peace, may the heaven-blest land
    Praise the power that hath blest and preserved it a
        nation.
Then conquer we must, for our cause it is just,
And this be our motto, " In God is our trust,"
And the star-spangled banner in triumph shall wave
O'er the land of the free and the home of the brave.

APPENDIX I.

THE RELATIVE FORCES OF THE TWO ARMIES AT THE SURRENDER.

FORCE UNDER GATES.

In Volume IX. of the manuscript papers of General Gates, in the Library of the New York Historical Society, is the official written return of the number of Gates's army present at the surrender of Burgoyne. It is entitled "A General Return of the Army commanded by Major-General Gates at the Convention of Saratoga, October 17th, 1777," and gives the numbers and commands as follows:

Continental Brigades and Corps.

Nixon's....................	1,430	
Poor's....................	1,466	
Glover's...................	1,479	
Patterson's................	1,300	
Learned's.................	1,257	
Morgan's Corps............	712	
Engineers and Artificers......	72	7,716

Militia, Brigades and Corps.

Warner's....................	1,371	
Annexed to Poor's..........	933	
" Glover's.........	610	
" Patterson's.......	468	3,382
		11,098

In his "Narrative," p. 27, Burgoyne says : "I shall close the whole of this by delivering at your table, from the hands of my secretary, an authenticated return of the force of General Gates, signed by himself, and the truth of it will be supported from ocular testimony by every officer of the British Army." It is dated October 16th, 1777, and is printed and apparently carefully tabulated in full in the Appendix to the "State of the Expedition," and states his entire force as 18,624. Why there should be such a great discrepancy from the original manuscript return above given is not easily explained, unless the following extract from Dr. Gordon's " History," Vol. II., p. 268, American edition, does so : " Burgoyne was desirous of a general return of the army commanded by Gates at the time of the convention. The latter understood him, and was careful not to lessen the return a single man. . . . The number of the militia was continually varying, and many of them were at a considerable distance from the camp.'

FORCE UNDER BURGOYNE.

The army which took the field in July, 1777, consisted of seven battalions of British infantry—viz. : 9th, 20th, 21st, 24th, 47th, 53d, and 62d regiments, of each of which (as also of three regiments left in Canada) the flank companies were detached to form a corps of grenadiers and light infantry, under Majors Acland and the Earl of Balcarras. The German troops consisted of a few Hessian rifles (the regiment of Hesse-Hanau), a corps of dismounted dragoons, and a mixed force of Brunswickers. The artillery was composed of 511 rank and file, including 100 Germans, with a large number of guns, the greater part of which, however, were employed only on the lakes. The ordnance which accompanied the force on their line of march consisted of thirty-eight pieces of light artillery attached to columns, and a pair of six twenty-four pounders, six twelve-pounders, and four howitzers.

The Royal Army was divided into three brigades under Major-General Phillips, of the Royal Artillery, and Brigadier-Generals Fraser and Hamilton. The German troops were distributed among the three brigades, with one corps of reserve under Colonel (Brigadier-General) Breymann, and were immediately commanded by Major-General Riedesel. Colonel Kingston, and Captain Money acted as adjutant and quartermaster-general, and Sir James Clerke (killed at Saratoga in the action of October 7th) and Lord Petersham (afterward Earl of Harrington) were aides-de-camp to General Burgoyne.

General Burgoyne's original manuscript (also among the Gates; papers in the New York Historical Society Library), entitled "State of the British Troops at the Convention the 17th October, 1777," and "Liste de la Force du Corps des Troupes Allemands,* le jour de

---

* A great deal of nonsense has been written in condemnation of the English Government employing Germans in the war for the subjugation of her revolted American colonies. But does any soldier work for pure patriotism and not for hire? Besides, at that time, the German soldier belonged body and soul to him to whom he had sold himself: he had no country; he was severed from every tie—in fact, he was, in every sense of the word, the *property* of his military lord, who could do with him as he saw fit. Again, it may well be asked, wherein did this action of the British Government differ from that of the United States, employing in our late Civil War recruiting agents in the different German ports for the express purpose of fill-

la Convention le 17ᵐ d'Octobre, 1777," both on one
sheet, signed by himself separately in his own hand,
and delivered to General Gates, gives all his regiments,
the strength of each, and the total force he surrendered,
as follows :

" *Regiments.*	*Rank and File.*
9	411
20	367
21	412
24	440
47	342
62	277
Canadian Companies of Grenadiers and Light Infantry	345
Lieutenant Nutt, of 33d Detachment, doing duty with Artillery	95
Royal Artillery	212
	2,901
Officers of all grades	478
	3,379

" J. Burgoyne."

" État General	33
Regt. des Dragones	36
Bat. des Grenadiers	270
Regt. de Rhetz	420
" de Riedesel	457
" de Specht	414
Bat. F. L. de Barnes	182

ing up her depleted armies, and also purchasing sub-
stitutes in Canada ?

Regt. de Hes. Hanau............... 525
Artillerie de Hes. Hanau............ 75

2,412
" J. BURGOYNE."

The endorsement on the back of the return is:

" English....................... 3,379
German....................... 2,412

In all........................ 5,791"

Dr. Gordon, whose statements have been proved in most every case unusually accurate, also gives the number 5791.

APPENDIX II.

GENERAL HORATIO GATES.

As a sketch has been given of Burgoyne, it seems well to say something of General Gates, though he really deserves no recognition except as having received the sword of Burgoyne ; for he appears to have been utterly lacking in personal courage, having not only, in anticipation of the defeat of the American army at Saratoga, had his wagoners keep their horses hitched to the wagons, to be in readiness to retreat in case the day went against him,* but in his subsequent duel

---

* While Gates cannot of course be censured for guarding against every emergency, he certainly looked forward to a possible retreat ; and he was, to say the least, not animated by the spirit which led Cortez to burn his ships behind him. At the beginning of the battle Quartermaster General Lewis was directed to

with Wilkinson, and at the unfortunate battle of Camden—in which De Kalb, at the sacrifice of his own life, played the same rôle to Gates, though without the same result, that Arnold did at the battle of Saratoga—he showed the same white feather.

General Gates was born in Malden, England, in 1728. The story told by that unmitigated old woman gossip, Sir Horace Walpole, that he was a natural son of Sir Robert Walpole (the father of Horace) is utterly without foundation.*　　He was born in lawful wedlock,

---

take eight men with him to the field to convey to Gates information from time to time concerning the progress of the action.　　At the same time, the baggage trains were all loaded up ready to move at a moment's notice.　　The first information that arrived represented the British troops to exceed the Americans, and the trains were ordered to move on; but by the time they were under motion, more favorable news was received, and the order was countermanded.　　Thus they continued to move on and halt alternately until the joyful news—"The British have retreated"—rang through the camp, which reaching the attentive guard of the teamsters, they all with one accord swung their hats, and gave three long and loud cheers.　　The glad tidings were transmitted with such rapidity from one to another that by the time the victorious troops had returned to their quarters, the American camp was thronged with inhabitants from the surrounding country and formed a scene of the greatest exultation. (Stone's "Burgoyne's Campaign.")

* Horace Walpole seems to have had a monomania on the subject of natural sons.　See sketch of Burgoyne, *ante*, where he makes that general a natural son of Lord Bingley—a statement also utterly without legal foundation.

his parents having been the butler and the housekeeper
of the Duke of Leeds. He entered the army—doubt-
less under the auspices of that duke—when a mere
youth, and served in the command of the king's New
York Independent Company. He displayed so much
ability that, in 1755, he was stationed at Halifax,
N. S., where, under the patronage of the Honorable
Edward Cornwallis, he rose rapidly to the rank of
major. He was with Braddock in his disastrous
campaign, receiving a shot through the body at the
slaughter of the Monongahela. At the beginning of the
Revolution he offered his sword to Congress ; and in
July, 1775, he received from that body the commission
of adjutant-general. Two years later, through cabals
in Congress, he was appointed to supersede Schuyler;
and having reaped the fruits of what that general had
so carefully sown, and having also, by the merest
accident, received the sword of Burgoyne, he en-
deavored to supplant Washington, and was appointed
to the command of the Southern Department.* His
disastrous defeat at Camden, however, and his
irresolute, not to say cowardly conduct on that

---

* Flushed with his fortuitous success, or rather with
the success attending his fortuitous position, he did not
wear his honors gained at Saratoga with any remarka-
ble meekness. On the contrary, his bearing toward
the commander-in-chief was far from respectful. He
did not even write to Washington on the occasion of
the victory until after a considerable time had elapsed ;
and it was not until November 2d that he deigned
to communicate to the commander-in-chief a word
upon the subject, and then only incidentally, as
though it were a matter of but secondary import-
ance.

occasion* soon pricked the bubble of his reputation ;
and his subsequent life was mostly passed in compara-
tive obscurity.   At the close of the war he retired to his
estate in Virginia, where he lived until 1790, when he
removed to New York City.   In 1800 he was elected
to the New York State Legislature, but for political
reasons resigned soon after taking his seat.   His death
occurred, after a long illness, at his house, now the
corner of Twenty-second Street and Second Avenue,
then the Bloomingdale Pike.   He is buried in Trinity
Churchyard.†

* " I will bring the rascals back with me into line,"
exclaimed Gates, as the militia broke and fled at Camden;
and leaving De Kalb to bear the brunt of the attack,
he spurred after them, not drawing rein till he reached
Charlotte, sixty miles from the field of battle !" (Green's
*German Element in the War of American Indepen-
dence.*)   Perhaps, however, Gates's horse was unman-
ageable and took the bit into his own mouth !

†Through the courtesy of my friend, Rev. Dr. Mor-
gan Dix, I am enabled to set the much-mooted question
as to where Gates is buried, at rest, as will be seen by
the following leaf from the Register of Trinity par-
ish, kindly copied and sent to me by that gentleman :

1805.	Persons Deceased.	Where Buried.	Years.	Months.
April 11.	General Horatio Gates.	Trinity................	78	....

A true copy from the Register of Burials of the par-
ish of Trinity Church in the city of New York.
             Attest : MORGAN DIX, Rector.

Gates was a man of great plausibility and address, of gentlemanly instincts, of a handsome person and fair education, and a great lion in society.   Though having many faults, the chief of which was an overweening confidence in his own ability, combined with arrogance, untruthfulness and apparently a lack of personal courage, he had also some noble traits of character. Before removing to New York from Virginia, he emancipated his slaves, providing for such of them as could not take care of themselves.   In his domestic relations he was an affectionate husband and father,* and during the last years of his life a sincere Christian. He married Mary, only child of James Valence, of Liverpool, who, at her father's death, before the Revolutionary War, emigrated to this country, bringing with her $450,000.   In the struggle for independence Mrs. Gates freely expended nearly all of her fortune in a lavish hospitality upon her husband's companions in arms, especially those who were in indigent circumstances; and many of the Revolutionary heroes were participants in her bounty, particularly Thaddeus Kosciusko,† who, when wounded, lay six months at

---

* For a charming and loving letter to his wife, just after the battles of Saratoga, see my *Burgoyne's Campaign.*

† There are, perhaps, few now living who are aware that Kosciusko left behind him in America a testimonial of his fervent love of liberty, as eminently characteristic of the man as was his famous reply to the Emperor Paul, who on Kosciusko's release from prison wished to restore him his sword.   " I have no need of a sword, since I have no longer a country !"

The will of Kosciusko (on record in the clerk's office of Albemarle Co., Va.), dated " Wills, 1819,"

her house, tenderly nursed by herself and her husband. Mrs. Gates, who survived her husband, left the residue

---

was attested by Thomas Jefferson. The will was written by Kosciusko in 1798, on the occasion of his visit to America during that year, when, having been released from prison, he came to renew his old associations. The will reads as follows: " I, Thaddeus Kosciusko, being just on my departure from America, do hereby declare and direct that should I make no other testamentary disposition of my property in the United States, I hereby authorize my friend, Thomas Jefferson, to employ the whole thereof in purchasing negroes from among his own or any others, and giving them liberty in my name ; in giving them an education in trades or otherwise, and in having them instructed for their new condition in the duties of morality, which may make them good neighbors, good fathers or mothers, and in their duties as citizens, teaching them to be defenders of their liberties and country, and of the good order of society, and in whatsoever may make them happy and useful. And I make the said Thomas Jefferson executor of this, 5th day of May, 1798. 			T. KOSCIUSKO.

It is not known in what the property of Kosciusko consisted (very likely land given him, as to Steuben, John Rose and others, by Congress, in recognition of their services) nor, indeed, what disposition was made of it. But whatever the property may have been, the desire that it should be put to the use indicated by the will is highly characteristic of the philanthropic patriot, whose whole life was one of continual sacrifice to the well-being of others ; who had early emancipated his own Polish serfs ; who had given money and personal service to the cause of American freedom ; and whose

of her fortune ($90,000) to several relatives, whose descendants are still living in New York and Philadelphia.*

To sum up, had not Gates allowed his ambition to overstep the bounds of loyalty to his chief, he would have remained among the first of our Revolutionary heroes. As it is, he is known merely as the chance conqueror at Saratoga, and as one, moreover, who, by base chicanery, endeavored to the utmost of his ability to supplant Washington himself.

APPENDIX III.

BURGOYNE'S PROCLAMATION.

(From the Providence " Gazette" of August 16th, 1777.)

[The following address from General Burgoyne to the *Tories and timid Whigs* was last week received from Rhode Island, and is here inserted (*Connecticut Journal*, August 27th, 1777) lest they should suspect that any Matter is suppressed which they might suppose tended to their political salvation. As this performance is written in the true Rhodomontade and bombastic Stile of a Don Quixote, and absolutely contains almost as many Falsehoods as Assertions, it is judged unnecessary for the present to make any

---

last and most strenuous exertions, that found a sad culmination in his imprisonment for years and exile from his country, were in behalf of that down-trodden fatherland. (See *Scribner's Monthly*, February, 1879.)

* Letter from Thomas Singleton, of Philadelphia, Pa. (a descendant of Mrs. Gates), to the writer.

Remarks thereon. It may, however, not be improper to observe (from authentic Intelligence received) that since this curious address made its appearance, Burgoyne's motley troops (composed of black and white savages) have actually *butchered* and *scalped* a considerable number of *those very Tories* to whom he had promised *Protection,* and whose " Undertakings" he had plighted his Faith to *assist* and *encourage.*]

PROCLAMATION.

By JOHN BURGOYNE, *Esquire, etc., etc., Lieutenant-General of his Majesty's Forces in America, Colonel of the Queen's Regiment of Light Dragoons, Governor of Fort William in North Britain, one of the Representatives of the Commons of Great Britain in Parliament [author of a celebrated* Tragic Comedy, called the *Blockade of Boston]* and *commanding an army and Fleet in an Expeditiou from Canada, etc., etc.*

" The forces entrusted to my command are designed to act in concert, and upon a common principle, with the *numerous* armies and fleets, which already display in every quarter of America the power, the *mercy* of the king; the cause in which the British arms are thus exerted appeals to the most affecting interest of the human heart, and the military servants of the crown, at first called forth for the sole purpose of *restoring* the rights of the constitution, and duty to their sovereign, the other extensive incitements, which spring from a due sense of the general privileges of mankind. To the eyes and ears of the temperate part of the public, and to the breasts of suffering thousands in the provinces be the melancholy appeal. Whether the present unnatural rebellion has not been made the foundation of the completest system of tyranny that

ever God, in His displeasure, suffered for a time to
be exercised over a froward and stubborn generation,
arbitrary imprisonments, confiscation of property, perse-
cution and *torture*, unprecedented in the inquisitions
of the Romish Church, are among the palpable enor-
mities that verify the affirmation. These are inflicted
by assemblies and committees, who dare to profess
themselves friends to liberty, upon the most *quiet*
subject, without distinction of age or sex, for the sole
crime, often from the sole suspicion of having adhered
in principle to the government under which they were
born, and to which *by every tie divine and human* they
owe allegiance. To consummate these shocking
proceedings, the profanation of religion is added to
the most profligate prostitution of common reason!
The consciences of men are set at naught, and multi-
tudes are compelled not only to bear arms, but also
to swear subjection to an usurpation they abhor. Ani-
mated by these considerations, at the head of troops
in the full powers of health, discipline and valor, deter-
mined to strike when necessary, and anxious to save
when possible, I, by these presents, invite and exhort
all persons in all places where the progress of this army
may point, and by the blessing of God I will extend
it far, to maintain such a conduct as may justify me in
protecting their lands, habitations and families. The
intention of this address is to hold forth *security*, not
depredation, to the country; to those whose spirit and
principle may induce them to partake in the *glorious*
task of redeeming their countrymen from dungeons,
and re-establishing the *blessings* of legal government,
I offer encouragement and employment; and upon the
first intelligence of their association, I will find means
to assist their undertakings. The domestic, the indus-
trious, the infirm, I am desirous to protect, provided

they remain quietly at their houses, that they do not
suffer their cattle to be removed, or their corn or forage
to be secreted or destroyed ; that they do not break up
their bridges or roads, or by any other acts, directly or
indirectly, endeavor to obstruct the operations of the
king's troops, or supply or assist those of the enemy.
Every species of provision brought to my camp will
be paid for at an equitable rate, in solid coin.

"In consciousness of *Christianity*, my royal master's
clemency, and the honor of soldiership, I have dwelt
upon this invitation, and wished for more persuasive
terms to give it Expression : and let not people be led
to disregard it by considering the immediate situation
of my camp : I have but to give stretch to the
Indian forces under my direction—and they amount
to thousands—to overtake the hardened enemies of
Great Britain and America : I consider them the
same wherever they lurk.   If notwithstanding these
endeavors and sincere inclination to assist them, the
frenzy of hostility should remain, I trust I shall
stand acquitted in the eyes of God and of men in
denouncing and executing the vengeance of the State
against the wilful outcast.   The messengers of justice
and of wrath await them in the field, and devastation,
famine, and every concomitant horror that a reluctant
but indispensable prosecution of military duty must
occasion will bar the way to their return.

"J. BURGOYNE.

"*Camp at the River Bouquett* [*sic* Bouquet] *June* 23*d*,
1777. By order of his Excellency, the Lieutenant
General.

"ROBERT KINGSTON,
"*Secretary*."

COMMENTS ON THE ABOVE.

Now, while Burgoyne was greatly ridiculed by the
patriots of the day for this proclamation, yet from the
standpoint of those who most conscientiously believed
it was wrong to rebel against the king and his legiti-
mate government, it seems to me that he only did
what his duty required. Seen now from a distance, it
must be admitted that there were many good men—
men of established integrity—who believed the colonists
were wrong in the stand they took. I know it is the
habit to ridicule all such ; but while myself believing
that the colonists were right in throwing off the yoke
of the mother-country—which had become most in-
tolerable—yet it seems to me that some charity should
be exercised toward those who conscientiously at the
time believed the contrary. Hence this practice of
sneering at those who were not willing at once to re-
nounce their allegiance to their king is not to be com-
mended. Take, for example, our late Civil War. We
of the North believed that the South had no right to
rebel ; yet the right to rebel is an inherent right. We
of the North put the rebellion down, and rightly ; still,
had the South been *successful* they would have
been considered deserving of praise and would have
been patriots among their *own section.* They did not ;
hence they were rebels. In the same way, had the
colonists in our Revolutionary contest been un-
successful, they would have been rebels. Success,
after all, makes the great difference. Of course, it must
be taken into account that the South were fighting, so
to speak, for *slavery,* which in itself damned their cause,
and *justly.* Still, I think that the inherent right to
rebel is universally admitted. As I say, had the
American colonists not been successful they would

have been rebels, and Washington an arch conspirator. They were successful—hence it was all right; in other words, *success* is the great arbiter of future opinion.

Burgoyne, therefore, in his proclamation, as a loyal subject of his *king*, *did right* and does not deserve the sneers which have been thrown at him. Had the cause of the crown succeeded, Arnold, even, would have been considered only a man who went back to his allegiance, in the same way, that, had the South succeeded, Lee and Davis would now be looked upon as saviours instead of rebels. Still, this does not justify Arnold in *betraying* the cause of the colonists, which he had espoused. Had he come out frankly and above board and said to Washington, " I am convinced that I have been wrong, and I herewith renounce my position as general," no sensible man could have blamed him. His treachery, however, puts him beyond the pale of any sympathy. Burgoyne, however, as a loyal subject of his king does not merit sarcasm.

APPENDIX IV.

TIMOTHY MURPHY, THE SHARP-SHOOTER.

THE soldier who shot General Fraser was Timothy Murphy, a native of Pennsylvania. He enlisted in Northumberland County in July, 1775, in Captain John Loudon's company, First Pennsylvania Continental Line. He was detached with Captain James Parr, who succeeded Loudon, under Morgan, when that officer was ordered by Washington to the assistance of

General Gates, on August 16th, 1777, and arrived in Gates's camp on the 22d of that month.*

The first we hear of Murphy was his being one of the best shots among Morgan's sharpshooters. At the second battle of Saratoga the latter noticed repeatedly during that conflict a noble-looking British officer, who, mounted upon a magnificent black charger, dashed from one end of the line to the other, appearing wherever the danger was greatest, and by his judgment, courage and activity, frequently retrieving the fortunes of the day when all seemed on the point of being lost. He recollected having seen this officer in the battle of September 19th, having on that occasion admired him for the skill and bravery which he displayed. While this officer lived, Morgan considered the issue of the contest a doubtful one. He therefore, as stated in the text, selected twelve of his best marksmen, and leading them to a suitable position, whence he pointed out the doomed officer, he told them to kill him when next he came within reach of their rifles.† Several of the sharp-shooters discharged their pieces without effect, but when Murphy fired Fraser fell.

Nor, while in Gates's camp, was he distinguished solely as a "crack shot." His coolness and daring also made him a man of mark. It is related that "just before the first battle of Saratoga he went out of the American camp, and having ascertained the British countersign, he went into one of their tents, and seeing an officer writing alone, he whispered to him (pointing to his hunting-knife) that if he spoke a word

* Letter to the author from Hon. James B. Linn, of Harrisburg, Pa.
† Graham's "Life of Morgan."

he would make daylight shine through him.   The offi-
cer, not having a sword or pistols near him, reluctantly
marched before him to the American camp.   At the
last battle of Saratoga, in which both armies were
engaged, Murphy was, as he states, within five feet of
Arnold when he passed over the fortifications, sword in
hand.   Murphy to the day of his death ascribed the
chief honor of Burgoyne's defeat to General Arnold,
and believed the latter never would have betrayed
his country had he received the honors he so richly
merited."

After the capture of Burgoyne, Murphy returned
with Morgan's corps to the Southern department, and
was also present at the battle of Monmouth in June,
1778.*   A short time after that action, Lieutenant-

---

* The effective usefulness of this famous body of
experienced riflemen in checking the aggressive and
savage bands of Indians which formed a portion of
Burgoyne's army was soon apparent to General
Gates, to whom Washington had sent it in August.
The corps, as soon as it reached the Northern army,
not only worsted the Indians in the various encoun-
ters in which they became confronted, but it also
created such a panic among the red men that they at
once lost all interest in fighting and scouting for Bur-
goyne, and hastily departed for their homes.   Gates
then employed the corps as sharp-shooters and skir-
mishers, in which line of duty it did splendid service.
After Washington's army had been compelled, as the
result of the battle of Brandywine, to retire before the
larger force of Sir William Howe, the commanding
general's situation was such as to ask for its return to
him.   His letter to General Gates embodying the re-
quest is as follows :

Colonel William Butler, with the Fourth Pennsylvania Regiment and three companies of riflemen from Morgan's corps, under Major Posey, commanded by Captains Long of Maryland, and Parr and Simpson of the First Pennylvania, were ordered up to Albany and thence to Schoharie. Thus, Lieutenants Thomas Boyd and Timothy Murphy again went to New York to defend the frontier from the savage enemy; and upon the disbanding of those troops—their term of enlistment having expired—Murphy and some others remained and served in the militia until the end of the war. His skill in the desultory war which the Indians carried on gave him so high a reputation, that though not nominally the commander, he usually directed all

---

"Camp near Pottsgrove, September 24, 1777.

Sir: This army has not been able to oppose General Howe with the success that was wished, and needs a re-enforcement. I therefore request, if you have been so fortunate as to oblige General Burgoyne to retreat to Ticonderoga, or if you have not, and circumstances will admit, that you will order Colonel Morgan to join me again with his corps. I sent him up when I thought you materially wanted him, and if his services can be dispensed with now, you will direct him to return immediately. You will perceive I do not mention this by way of command, but leave you to determine upon it according to your situation; if they come, they should proceed by way of water from Albany as low down as Peekskill; in such case you will give Colonel Morgan the necessary orders to join me with dispatch. I am, sir, your most obedient servant,

"Go. Washington.
"Major-General Gates."

the movements of the scouts that were sent out, and on many important occasions the commanding officers found it dangerous to neglect his advice ; his *double rifle*, his skill as a marksman, and his fleetness, either in retreat or pursuit, made him an object both of dread and of vengeance to the Indians ; they formed many plans to destroy him, but he always eluded them, and sometimes made them suffer for their temerity.

He fought the Indians with their own weapons. When circumstances permitted, he tomahawked and scalped his fallen enemy ; and he boasted after the war that he had slain forty of the enemy with his own hand, more than half of whom he had scalped : he took delight in perilous adventures, and seemed to love danger for its own sake.

The Indians were unable to conjecture how he could discharge his rifle twice without having time to reload ; and his singular good fortune in escaping unhurt led them to suppose that he was attended by some invisible being, who warded off *their* bullets and sped *his* with unerring certainty to the mark. When they had learned the mystery of his doubled-barrelled rifle, they were careful not to expose themselves too much until he had fired twice, knowing that he must have time to reload his piece before he could do them further injury.

One day having separated from his party, he was pursued by a number of Indians, all of whom he outran, excepting one ; Murphy turned round, fired upon this Indian, and killed him. Supposing that the others had given up the pursuit, he stopped to strip the dead, when the rest of his pursuers came in sight. He snatched the rifle of his fallen foe, and with it killed one of his pursuers ; the rest, now sure of their

prey, with a yell of joy heedlessly rushed on, hoping
to make him their prisoner. He was ready to drop
down with fatigue, and was likely to be overtaken,
when, turning round, he discharged the remaining bar-
rel of his rifle, and killed the foremost of the Indians.
The rest, astonished at his firing three times in succes-
sion, fled, crying out that he had " a great medicine of a
gun that would shoot all day without loading." In-
deed, so dangerous was Murphy regarded, that it was
not long before the Tories set an extra price on his
scalp—a price that was never paid, although many
Indians lost *their* scalp in trying to win the reward.
One of the attempts to capture him which is still
handed down in Schoharie tradition, as having occurred
toward the close of the Revolution, was as follows:
Murphy had a cow, on the neck of which he had placed
a bell, that he might the better find her in the woods.
A shrewd Indian took the bell off the cow's neck, and
having placed it on his own, went jingling it about in
the woods, hoping by this means to entice the cow's
owner within killing or capturing distance. The scout,
however, knew too well the different music produced
by a cow and an Indian; and so driving the animal
home from another part of the woods, he left the
" ding-dong" warrior to the enjoyment of his own wit.
On another occasion, while on Sullivan's expedition,
he and twenty-five others were surrounded by five hun-
dred Tories and Indians, under Butler and Brant. Two
attempts to cut their way out had resulted in failure,
with the loss of seventeen of their number. The third
attempt was more successful; for Murphy, having
tumbled a huge warrior into the dust (which caused
his dusky brethren to laugh even in the heat of battle),
effected an opening in the circle, through which his
comrades fled—*sauve qui peut*—the Indians giving

chase. After a little Murphy observed that he had distanced all his pursuers except two—one a tall and the other a short Indian. Several times as they neared him he would raise his rifle (which was unloaded) as if to shoot, whereupon they would fall back. Finding as he ran that, owing to the swelling of his feet, his moccasins began to pain him, he opened a clasp-knife, and while running slit the tops of the moccasins (at the risk of cutting the tendons of his feet) and so got relief. Shortly after, entering a swale and getting his feet caught in the long grass, he fell at full length. It was to this at first seemingly untoward accident that he owed his temporary safety and final escape; for the long grass affording a favorable place for concealment, he lay still until his pursuers had passed on. Loading his rifle, he went on his way rejoicing at his fortunate escape, and with reason; for had he been captured he knew that any hope for mercy would have been in vain, since at that very time he had an Indian's scalp in his pocket and the same hairless redskin's moccasins on his feet. He had not gone far, however, before he saw an Indian approaching him. The discovery was mutual, and they simultaneously took trees. After dodging each other for some time, Murphy resorted to a very old and, one would think, a worn-out ruse. He drew his ramrod, and placing his hat upon it, gently moved it on one side of the tree. The Indian at once put a ball through it, and it dropped. Whereupon, running up to obtain the scalp, he received Murphy's bullet in his breast; and as he fell he exclaimed, " O-nah !" Lieutenant Boyd, the commander of the party, and who attempted to escape with Murphy, was less fortunate. Less fleet of foot, he was captured and subjected to horrible torture. The Seneca Indians, under Little Beard and instigated by Butler, made an incision in his abdomen, fastened his intestines to a tree, and compelled him to walk around it until they were all drawn out. They then enlarged his mouth, dug his nails out, cut his tongue out and his ears off, cut his nose off and put it in his mouth, dug his eyes out, and as he was dying cut off his head, which was their most humane act. "After this," says a writer personally cognizant of the affair, "there began to be mysterious disappearances of Tories and Indians; and it was noticed that, coincident with each disappearance, there would be a brush-heap fire in the vicinity, in which the missing person was last seen. It is to be supposed that calcined bones might have been found by those who cared to look in the ashes of these brush fires. The remaining Tories and Indians took the hint, and left that part of the country, so that the inhabitants at length breathed freer."

At the close of the war, Murphy, who had meantime married, instead of returning to his native State, Pennsylvania, settled in Schoharie as a farmer. But, if tradition is to be believed, his old habits still clung to him. When peace was declared many of the Schoharie Indians had the temerity to return and settle again among a people whose houses and barns they had burned and whose friends and relatives had fallen beneath their tomahawks. Among them was one Indian, named Seth Henry, who had killed more Schoharie people than any other man. His nature, even for an Indian, seemed an unusually cruel one; and he would sometimes leave a war-club upon the dead body of his victim, with a horrid row of notches cut on it, each notch indicating a scalp taken. An energetic savage, he once led a party from Fort Niagara in the winter to capture certain Schoharie patriots; and he succeeded, travelling six hundred miles, though, to do so. He, too, had the audacity to come back, but he was much upon his guard. One day he started to go from one house to another. Murphy was also observed to go in the same direction shortly afterward; and it is a curious coincidence that, as far as can be ascertained, Seth Henry never reached his destination, nor was he ever afterward seen either alive or dead.

Murphy's passions were easily aroused, and as is the case with such natures, as easily subdued. The following anecdote is an instance in point.* Some time in the latter part of the Revolution Murphy had charge of a small scout which went to reconnoitre in the vicinity of Oquago. While there they took three prisoners, one of whom was a Scotch lad, and soon after started on their return to Schoharie. In the night the boy escaped, taking along Murphy's rifle, an act not very pleasing to the fearless ranger. Some months afterward the boy was retaken by another scout, and with him the stolen firelock. When its owner learned that the boy was taken, and was approaching as a prisoner, his passions took fire, and he declared his intention of killing him, arming himself with a tomahawk for that purpose. Elerson, a fellow-scout, and who told this anecdote to Mr. Simms, reasoned the matter with him. He told him to put himself in the boy's place, and asked if *he*, similarly situated, would not have acted in the same manner as the boy had done. Murphy's better nature soon yielded to this reasoning; his anger was appeased, and the boy was brought into his presence without receiving any injury. The boy was afterward taken to Albany and sold, according to the custom of those times, into servitude for a short period. Murphy, speaking of this affair after the war,

---

* Related by Jeptha R. Simms.

expressed his gratitude that he was prevented by his friend from injuring the lad who had stolen his gun.

He had also a good heart. On one occasion, on March 15th, 1784, the ice lodged in the river near Middleburg and overflowed the flats near his residence. Many cattle and sheep were swept off in the freshet and killed. In an attempt to save the family of John Adam Brown, a near neighbor, he waded into the water among the floating pieces of ice, and succeeded in bearing to a place of safety his two sons; but Brown himself and Lana, his only daughter, then about twelve years old, were, unfortunately, in the lower part of the house and were drowned.

Many anecdotes are also told of Murphy's great skill as a marksman. The two following seem well authenticated, and are taken from Simms's "Frontiersmen of New York:"

During the winter of 1781–82 Murphy killed quite a number of deer on the Schoharie mountains, and dressed their pelts very handsomely. In the spring, to break the monotony of a camp life, he got up a shooting match at the Upper Fort, by way of testing the skill of his comrades in arms in the sale of his deerskins. He occasionally took a shot himself, and usually won back his property; but as some objected to his firing, he desisted, as he had been well paid for it, and whoever could bore off the beautiful buff leather. After the skins were all disposed of, " Now," says Murphy, "let us shoot for a gallon of rum." A large white oak tree was " blazed" near the ground, a line drawn round in the exposed wood, and in the circle a small piece of white paper was fastened by a brass nail. The distance fired was one hundred yards. Several close shots had been made, and it became Murphy's turn to fire. He laid down on the ground at full length, resting his rifle on his hat, as others of his competitors had done, and after glancing over the barrel, he was heard to say, " Sure, and I believe I can see that nail." Again he sighted his piece ; it exploded and the paper fell. An examination showed a centre shot ; the ball had driven the nail exactly in.

Again, in the fall of 1799, four Schoharie riflemen of Revolutionary days and deeds met at the residence of Captain Jacob Hager, in Blenheim, on their return from either a hunt or a shooting match. Before separating, it was proposed to shoot at a mark. A target was made by pinning a small piece of white paper to a board some two feet long, and the parties repaired to a field a few rods south of the house. They paced off one hundred yards from their standing point, to which the target was taken by one of the four, who held it between his knees to receive the bullet of a comrade, who in turn held it for another, it being thus alternately held until all had fired. Each of the first three shots cut the edge of the paper—that of William Leek on the right, that of David Elerson on the left, that of a third, whose name is now forgotten, on the bottom. Murphy made the last shot, and the paper fell. On examination it was found that his ball had driven the pin through the board.*

---

* David Elerson, mentioned in the text, and who was a private in Captain Long's company of Morgan's rifle corps, and a companion of Murphy in many hazardous enterprises, related the following anecdote to Mr. Simms in 1837 : " Morgan's riflemen had acquired much celebrity as marksmen while under Gates. When in the vicinity of Albany, on their return from the Northern army a gentleman near whose residence they halted expressed a wish to

In person Murphy was stout and well made, with dark complexion, rather a large body and small limbs, handsome in face, with jet black hair, and an eye that would kindle and flash like the lightning when excited. He was exceedingly quick in all his motions, and possessed an iron frame that nothing apparently could affect. What, moreover, is very remarkable, his body was never wounded or even scarred during the whole war.*

" It was Murphy's misfortune," says Simms, " like many other master spirits of the Revolution, not to have the advantages of an early education, even such as our common schools now afford. In fact, he possessed not those elements of an education—the art of reading and writing. For this reason he

---

witness their skill. The captain signified his willingness to gratify his curiosity, and a piece of paper was fastened upon a small poplar tree. Elerson handed his rifle—one of the best in the company—to John Gassaway, who took a surer aim than himself. The rifle was levelled one hundred yards distant from the mark and fired. The leaden messenger passed through the paper and the tree, splitting the latter several inches and ruining it. Said the gentleman, looking at his crippled tree, which had been converted into a weeping willow (it will be remembered that fashion had made the poplar a very desirable shade tree), 'I do not wonder the Indians are afraid of Morgan's riflemen, if that is the way they shoot.' He then treated the company to liquor, as was the custom of the times, expressed his satisfaction at their skill, and the troops resumed their march."

* Communicated to the writer by one who knows a friend of Murphy.

declined accepting a proffered commission, know-
ing that he would be subjected to much inconven-
ience and be liable to be imposed upon by design-
ing men.   Had he been an educated man, he might
have made another Wayne or Morgan ; but the want
of the rudiments of an education compelled him to
see others less fitted in other respects than himself
occupying stations of profit and honor." At the
termination of the Revolutionary war he took charge
of his father-in-law's farm.   He appears to have been
a citizen much respected in his county, and as a
father he was indulgent to a fault, having, says Simms,
been known to bring home from Albany for a
daughter some five or six dresses at one time.

Although Murphy could neither read nor write, yet
he was a powerful stump speaker, and for many years
wielded powerful political influence in Schoharie
County.   He was largely instrumental in bringing his
young friend and neighbor, the Honorable William C.
Bouck, into public life, was zealous in obtaining for
him the appointment of sheriff, and indirectly contrib-
uted to his subsequent election as Governor.   Murphy
died of a cancer upon his neck, June 27th, 1818, which
was said by some to have been caused by his exposure
while attempting to rescue the Brown family in 1784,
and by others, by the recoil of his rifle on his cheek.*

---

* The late General Epaphras Hoyt, of Deerfield,
Mass., a most accomplished writer and reliable historian,
left at his death a work for publication, with maps, en-
titled " Burgoyne's Campaign."   He served under
Gates, and his published letter on a visit to the Saratoga
battlefields not only corroborates the above incidents
in Murphy's life, but is a most valuable military criti-
cism of those battles.   We intend to give this letter

APPENDIX V.

LADY HARRIET ACLAND.

Two shining examples of female conjugal devotion stand out prominently in our Revolutionary annals— the Baroness Riedesel and Lady Harriet Acland. The life of the former has been given with accuracy in her "Letters and Journals:" that of the latter has never been narrated either with fulness or correctness. To supply this defect is the object of the present paper.

Lady Harriet, as she was commonly called, was the fifth daughter of Stephen, first Earl of Ilchester, and a cousin of the celebrated Charles James Fox. She was born on January 3d, 1750. Her full name was Christian Henrietta Caroline Fox Strangways, and she was married in September, 1770, to John Dyke Acland, of Columb-John, Devonshire. Her elder sister was the Lady Susan O'Brien—mentioned in "Graydon's Memoirs" and in the writer's " Life of Sir William Johnson"—who in June, 1765, was, with her husband, a recipient of the courtly hospitality of the baronet at Johnson Hall. By her marriage with William O'Brien, an actor, in the spring of the previous year, she had alienated her family, and had consequently sailed with her husband for America, arriving in New York in April. Sir William Johnson was advised of their arrival by her uncle, the first Lord Holland, who in April wrote to him detailing the

in our forthcoming work on "The Visits to the Saratoga Battlefield," shortly to be issued by Munsell's Sons.

circumstances of the marriage, and requesting his friendly offices for his niece, who had "just emigrated to the wild woods of America." From letters of Lady Susan in the writer's possession it appears that her host and his Indian wife did everything in their power to render their visit agreeable, and that the baronet was equally at home whether entertaining the rude savage or the scion of a noble house. Molly Brant is spoken of particularly as a "well-bred and pleasant lady," who in many a ramble with her ladyship proved a "delightful companion." Nor was this kindly feeling entirely one-sided. So much did his high-born guest interest Sir William in her favor that shortly after Lady Susan and her husband returned to New York he wrote a letter to Lord Holland begging that the young couple might be again received into the good graces of his family—urging, among other things, that O'Brien seemed to be a "very worthy young man, possessing in the highest degree the affections of his wife."

Lady Harriet appears to have been full as warm-hearted and romantic as her sister, and, although her affections did not lead her into defying the opinions of her family and making a runaway match, yet her conjugal love was equally shown by her braving the perils of a long ocean-voyage and enduring the trials and hardships of a camp-life in an enemy's country rather than be separated from the husband of her choice.

When Burgoyne made up his staff for his contemplated campaign in America, he selected to command the grenadiers Major Acland, an officer greatly in his confidence and possessing high professional attainments and brilliant courage. Lady Harriet, like the Baroness Riedesel refusing to allow her husband to brave the perils of war alone, insisted upon accompanying him to Canada, where they arrived on the last day of June, 1776. Late in the fall of that year the Major, leaving his wife in Montreal, occupied Chambly with the Twentieth Regiment of foot. Soon after taking up his quarters in that fort he fell dangerously ill; and it was here, while languishing in a miserable log hut and destitute of the commonest comforts of life, that he was nursed back to health by his faithful wife, who upon hearing of his condition, in the face of the rigors of an unusually severe Canadian winter and of her own precarious state of health, had hurried on in an open sled to attend him.

On the opening of the campaign the following year the army left its winter quarters, which it was destined never again to occupy, and pushed on to Ticonderoga. Lady Harriet, however, remained behind in Montreal, her husband, in view of the certain hazards of the approaching campaign, positively refusing her permission to be his companion. But chance soon afforded this indomitable woman an opportunity of disregarding his commands. In the action of July 7th, at Hubbardtown, Major Acland was badly wounded. No sooner was this known by his wife when she left Montreal, and having, by the courtesy of General Carleton, been afforded every facility for passing up Lake Champlain, she rejoined her husband at Skenesborough (Whitehall), whither he had been conveyed after the action of the 7th. After his recovery, which he owed in all probability to the careful nursing of his wife, he had no longer the heart to separate her from him ; and as soon as the army arrived at Fort Edward he obtained for her use a two-wheeled tumbrel which had been constructed by the artificers of the artillery —a vehicle somewhat similar to the carriages used a

century since for the mails upon the great roads of
England. During the day she travelled with the bag-
gage-train in the rear of the army, and at night she
shared her husband's tent, which, as Major Acland
commanded the grenadiers, was always the most
advanced post. Indeed, it was this latter circum-
stance that just before the army crossed the Hudson
led to an accident which had nearly proved fatal to
both husband and wife. Major Acland being with
the advanced guard, and therefore compelled to be
constantly on the alert, kept a lighted candle in his
tent throughout the night. It chanced, while the
major and his wife were asleep, that a favorite New-
foundland dog in moving round upset the candle,
which, rolling to the side of the tent, set it on fire.
Fortunately, an orderly sergeant who was on guard
close by rushed in at great risk to himself and dragged
out the first person he caught hold of. This proved
to be the major himself, who in turn, fearing for his
wife's safety, ran back in search of her. The latter,
however, had already made her escape by creeping
under the walls of the tent into the open air; and the
faithful sergeant, dashing in once more, again rescued
his officer, though not before the latter had been
severely burned about the face and arms. All their
camp-equipage—everything, in fact, except the clothes
in which they had slept—was destroyed, but, as Bur-
goyne remarks, "it altered neither the resolution nor
cheerfulness of Lady Harriet, and she continued her
progress, a partaker of the fatigues of the advanced
corps." Nor was it in her wifely devotion alone that
her humanity was shown. She was not only the idol of
her husband, but, together with the Baroness Riedesel,
elicited the admiration of the whole army. She was
continually making little presents to the officers and

privates of her husband's corps whenever she had any-
thing among her stores that she thought would gratify
them.   In return, she received from them every atten-
tion which could mitigate the hardships she daily en-
countered.

The next call upon her fortitude was of a different
nature, and more distressing because of longer sus-
pense. "On the march of September 19th," writes
General Burgoyne, "the grenadiers being liable to
action at every step, she had been directed by the
major to follow the route of the artillery and baggage,
which was not exposed.   At the time the action at
Freeman's Farm began she found herself near a small,
uninhabited hut, where she alighted.   When it was
found the action was becoming general and bloody,
the surgeons of the hospital took possession of the
same place as the most convenient for the first care of
the wounded.   Thus was this lady within hearing of
one continued fire of cannon and musketry for four hours
together, with the presumption, from the post of her
husband at the head of the grenadiers, that he was in
the most exposed part of the action.   She had three
female companions—the Baroness Riedesel and the
wives of two British officers, Major Harnage and
Lieutenant Reynell—but in the event their presence
served but little for comfort.   Major Harnage was
soon brought to the surgeons very badly wounded, and
a little time after came intelligence that Lieutenant
Reynell was shot dead.   Imagination will want no
helps to figure the state of the whole group."

In the second battle of Saratoga (October 7th)
Major Acland commanded the grenadiers, who, after
maintaining their ground with the greatest and
most persistent valor, were finally forced to retreat,
leaving the eminence on which they had been

stationed " a scene," in the language of Wilkinson,
" of complicated horror and exultation." In the
square space of twelve yards of ground eighteen grena-
diers lay in the agonies of death, while three officers
were propped up against stumps of trees, two of them
mortally wounded and almost speechless. While pur-
suing the flying grenadiers Wilkinson heard a feeble
voice exclaim, " Protect me, sir, against that boy."
Turning his eyes, he saw a lad taking deliberate aim
at a wounded British officer, whom he at once knew to
be Major Acland. Wilkinson dismounted, and, taking
him by the hand, expressed the hope that he was not
badly wounded. " Not badly," replied the gallant
officer, " but very inconveniently, as I am shot through
both legs. Will you, sir, have the goodness to have
me conveyed to your camp?" Wilkinson at once
directed his orderly to alight, and, lifting the wounded
man into the vacant seat, had him conveyed to head-
quarters.

During the battle Lady Harriet was stationed in a
tent on the river bank about a mile to the left of the
scene of action, in full hearing of the roar of the artil-
lery and surrounded by the wounded that from time
to time were brought in, and whose dying groans were
not calculated to diminish the agony of her suspense.
" My Lady Acland," writes the Baroness Riedesel in
alluding to events at this particular time, " occupied a
tent not far from our house. In this she slept, but
during the day was in the camp. Suddenly one came
to tell her that her husband was mortally wounded
and had been taken prisoner. We comforted her by
saying that it was only a slight wcund ; but as no one
could nurse him as well as herself, we counselled her
to go at once to him, to do which she certainly could
obtain permission. She loved him very much, although

he was a plain, rough man. He was an excellent offi-
cer, and she the most lovely (*allerliebste*) of all
women. I spent the night in this manner, at one
time comforting her, and at another looking after my
children, whom I had put to bed." "You can natu-
rally conceive," writes Lieutenant Aubrey at this time,
"what were the feelings of Lady Harriet—having
every apprehension not only for her husband, but for
her brother*—who, after hearing the whole of the
action, at last received the shock of her individual
misfortune, mixed with the general calamity of the de-
feat."

The day after the battle was passed by Lady Harriet
and her companions, the Baroness Riedesel and the
wives of the other officers, among the wounded and
dying, since not a tent or a shed was standing except
what belonged to the hospital. Her suspense, more-
over, was rendered the greater from the fact that no
tidings had been received from her husband since the
first announcement of his capture. Her unhappiness
would have been increased had she known that the
British had that very day refused a flag under cover of
which General Wilkinson, with his usual gallantry tow-
ard the fair sex, attempted at every part of the line to
convey a letter to her from her husband, then in Gates's
camp.

Meanwhile, Burgoyne, having scrupulously fulfilled
the dying wish of his loved companion-in-arms, the

---

* Hon. Stephen Digby Strangways—the brother of
Lady Acland mentioned in the text—was a captain in
the Twenty-fourth Regiment of foot, and upon the
promotion of Captain William Agnew to the majority
of the regiment (July 14th, 1777) became its senior
captain.

chivalric Fraser, began his retreat on the evening of the 8th in the midst of a pouring rain, and two hours before daybreak of the 9th arrived at Dovegat, where he halted.

During the halt at Dovegat* there occurred one of those incidents which relieve with fairer lights and softer tints the gloomy picture of war. The circumstances which led to this incident are thus given by the Baroness Riedesel: " During this halt it rained in torrents. My Lady Acland had her tent set up. I advised her once more to betake herself to her husband, as she could be so useful to him in his present situation. Finally, she yielded to my solicitations, and sent a message to General Burgoyne, through his adjutant, my Lord Patterson [Petersham], begging permission to leave the camp; I told her she should insist on it; which she did, and finally obtained his consent. . . . I saw her again afterward in Albany, at which time her husband was almost entirely recovered, and both thanked me heartily for my advice." This case of private distress, if we may believe Aubrey, greatly increased the cares and anxieties with which Burgoyne was at this time surrounded. Regarding, however, the manner in which that general received Lady Acland's request no doubt can be entertained. "When the army," he writes, " was on the point of moving after

---

* Within the last year (1893), this " Dovegat House " has been torn down; almost the last existing landmark of " Burgoyne's Campaign." It is very sad to think that then is not enough patriotism among the American people to prevent such an act of vandalism; but so it goes! Indeed it is *shameful* that New York State should not have prevented this by buying it, even if the State should have had to surround it with a wall of glass!

the halt described, I received a message from Lady Harriet submitting to my decision a proposal (and expressing an earnest solicitude to execute it if not interfering with my designs) of passing to the camp of the enemy and requesting General Gates's 'permission to attend her husband. Though I was ready to believe (for I had experienced) that patience and fortitude in a supreme degree were to be found, as well as every other virtue, under the most tender forms, I was astonished at this proposal. After so long an agitation of spirits, exhausted not only by want of rest, but absolutely by want of food, drenched in rains for twelve hours together, that a woman should be capable of such an undertaking as delivering herself to the enemy, probably in the night and uncertain of what hands she might first fall into, appeared an effort above human nature. The assistance I was enabled to give was small indeed. I had not even a cup of wine to offer her, but I was told she had found from some kind and fortunate hand a little rum and dirty water. All I could furnish to her was an open boat and a few lines, written upon dirty wet paper, to General Gates, recommending her to his protection.

" Let such," continues Burgoyne, " as are affected by these circumstances of alarm, hardship, and danger recollect that the subject of them was a woman—of the most tender and delicate form, of the gentlest manners, habituated to all the soft elegancies and refined enjoyments that attend high birth and fortune, and far advanced in a state in which the tender cares always due to the sex become indispensably necessary. Her mind alone was formed for such trials."

The letter given her by Burgoyne, and now among the " Gates Papers" in the New York Historical Society, reads as follows :

"SIR : Lady Harriet Acland, a lady of the first distinction of family rank and personal virtues, is under such concern on account of Major Acland, her husband, wounded and a prisoner in your hands, that I cannot refuse her request to commit her to your protection. Whatever general impropriety there may be in persons of my situation and yours to solicit favors, I cannot see the uncommon perseverance in every female grace and exaltation of character of this lady, and her very hard fortune, without testifying that your attentions to her will lay me under obligation.

"I am, sir, your obedient servant,

"J. BURGOYNE."

As an additional protection, another letter was also furnished by Burgoyne's deputy adjutant-general, Robert Kingston. This letter—likewise preserved among the "Gates Papers"—was written in the open air, in the midst of a pouring rain, as is evident from the stains of the water-splashes with which the paper is thickly sprinkled, and is as follows:

"October 9th, 1777.

"The Rev⁴ Mr. Brudenel, chaplain to the staff, accompanies Lady Harriet Acland as a protection till she arrives at Mʳ Genˡ Gates's quarters.

"His Excellency, Lieut.-Genˡ Burgoyne, makes no doubt he will be treated with every regard due to his character, and allowed to return the first convenient opportunity.

"Rᵀ KINGSTON, *D. Adjᵗ-Genᵗ.*

"*To* MR GENL GATES."

In the midst of a driving autumnal storm, and with nothing but a little spirits and water, obtained from the wife of a soldier, to sustain her, Lady Harriet set out at dusk in an open boat for the American camp. She was accompanied by Rev. Edward Brudenel, by Hannah Degraw, her waiting-maid, and by her husband's valet, who had been wounded in the shoulder while searching for his master upon the battlefield. Another of her companions was Mr. George Williams, a young gentleman from Newfoundland, who in after years became a colonel in the army and the first member of Parliament for Ashton-under-Lyne. He survived until December, 1850—the very last, in all probability, of Burgoyne's army. At ten o'clock they reached the American advanced guard, under the command of Major Henry Dearborn. Lady Harriet herself hailed the sentinel, and as soon as the guard, apprehensive of treachery, had very properly communicated with Major Dearborn, the bateau was allowed to land. This delay was only momentary, and not "seven or eight dark and cold hours," as stated by Burgoyne in his " State of the Expedition." Upon landing, the party, carrying with them their bedding and other necessaries, were immediately guided to the log cabin of Dearborn, who had been ordered to detain the flag until morning, the night being exceedingly dark and the quality of the lady unknown. Major Dearborn gallantly gave up his room to his fair guest, a fire was kindled, a cup of hot tea provided, and as soon as Lady Harriet had made herself known her mind was relieved of its anxiety by the assurance of her husband's safety. " I visited," says Adjutant-General Wilkinson, " the guard before sunrise. Lady Acland's boat had put off, and was floating down the stream to our camp, where General Gates, whose gallantry will not be denied, stood ready to receive her with all the tenderness and respect to which her rank and condition gave her a claim. Indeed, the feminine figure, the benign aspect, and polished manners of this charming woman were alone sufficient to attract the sympathy of the most obdurate; but if another motive could have been wanting to inspire respect, it was furnished by the peculiar circumstances of Lady Harriet, then in that most delicate situation which cannot fail to interest the solicitude of every being possessing the form and feelings of a man. It was therefore the foulest injustice to brand an American officer [Major Dearborn] with the failure of courtesy where it was so highly merited."

But while General Gates was disposed to, and did, accord to Lady Harriet a most courteous and hearty welcome, both for her own sake and the amenities of military etiquette, he was not willing that, as between himself and the British commander, these courtesies should be all on one side. Justly indignant at the inexcusable conduct of Burgoyne during his retreat, he sent him the following polite yet caustic reply to the letter brought by Lady Harriet:

" SARATOGA, October 12th, 1777.

" SIR : I had the honor to receive Your Excellency's letter by Lady Acland. The respect due to her ladyship's rank, the tenderness due to her person and sex, were alone sufficient recommendations to entitle her to my protection ; and, considering my preceding conduct with respect to those of your army whom the fortune of war has placed in my hands, I am surprised Your Excellency should think that I could consider the greatest attention to Lady Acland in the light of an obligation.

" The cruelties which marked the retreat of your army in burning the gentlemen's and farmers' houses as it passed along is almost, among civilized nations, without precedent : they should not endeavor to ruin those they could not conquer ; their conduct betrays more of the vindictive malice of the monk than the generosity of the soldier.

"Your friend, Sir Francis Clerke, by the imformation of Dr. Potts, the director-general of my hospital, languishes under a very dangerous wound ; every sort of tenderness and attention is paid to him, as well as to all the wounded who have fallen into my hands, and the hospital which you were necessitated to leave to my mercy. . . .

"I am, sir, etc.,

"HORATIO GATES.

"GENERAL BURGOYNE."

Lady Harriet tarried a few days in the American camp, during which time "she was treated by General Gates," writes Dr. Thacher, "with the tenderness of a parent ;" and then, under the escort of that general, she rejoined her husband in Albany, whither he had been conveyed the day after the action of the 7th. In a letter written at this time to his wife General Gates thus speaks of his distinguished prisoners and guests : "I hope Lady Acland will be here when you arrive. She is the most amiable, delicate piece of quality you ever beheld. Her husband is one of the prettiest fellows I have seen—learned, sensible and an Englishman to all intents and purposes ; has been a most confounded Tory, but I hope to make him as good a Whig as myself before we separate."

After remaining in Albany until her husband's wounds were healed, Lady Harriet accompanied him to New York ; and while in that city on his parole, before returning to England, the major reciprocated the kindness shown to his wife by doing all in his power to mitigate the sufferings of the American prisoners.

Hitherto, Lady Harriet's life, after her return to England, has been little known, and that little very incorrectly stated. It has been published as veracious history that shortly after the arrival of her husband and herself in England the former became involved in an altercation with a Lieutenant Lloyd, a brother-officer, in which he defended the Americans against the aspersion of cowardice; that a duel followed, which resulted in the death of Major Acland, who fell at the first fire; and that Lady Harriet thereupon became insane, remained so for two years, and finally married Chaplain Brudenel. Wilkinson appears to have first given currency to this story, and he has since been followed by Mrs. Ellet, Mr. Lossing, Fonblanque in his " Life of Burgoyne," myself in the " Campaign of Burgoyne," and, in fact, by all who have written on this subject. Even Miss Warburton, in a letter to her nephew, the late Sir John Burgoyne (Fonblanque, p. 301), relates substantially the same story, varying the narrative, however, by stating that the duel was fought with swords and that Acland, in "making a pass at his adversary, slipped on a pebble, struck his temple upon it in falling, and instantly expired."

Being desirous of ascertaining what the truth really was, I recently wrote to Sir Thomas Dyke Acland, of Exeter, England,, whose father was an own nephew of Major Acland, asking what were the real facts of the case. He with great courtesy replied at once, stating that all the generally received statements regarding his aunt's and uncle's last days were without the least foundation ; that Major Acland died in his bed of a cold shortly after his return to England; and, further, that Lady Harriet remained a widow until her death, at Tetton, on July 21st, 1815. In corroboration of this latter statement, Sir Thomas Acland enclosed me a copy of the burial-register of the parish where Lady Harriet lies, in which she is called " The Right Hon. Lady Harriet Acland, widow."

In person Lady Harriet was highly graceful and delicate ; her manners were elegantly feminine, her outward personal charms being in harmony with those of her mind.* While wrapped up in the care of her children, hers was not a selfish devotion which would shut out all sympathy for others and forbid appreciation of those with whom she had been united in ties of interest and affection, whether in high or low station. There is yet standing in a quaint little churchyard in Beckenham, Kent, with a solitary yew tree watching over it like a faithful sentinel, a moss-grown slab bearing this inscription: "To the memory of Hannah Degraw, born at New York 18th May, 1742. Erected by Lady Acland in grateful remembrance of thirty-six years' services."

On Lady Harriet's return to England she was, for a time, the cynosure of all eyes. Mrs. Perez Newton commemorated her sufferings in a touching poem; and before she left New York a portrait of her lady-ship, standing in a boat with a white handkerchief in her hand, as a flag of truce, was exhibited at the Royal Academy, London. An engraving from this picture was extensively circulated in Europe and America ; and long after the incident to which it gave rise had faded from public remembrance, she herself continued

---

* The picture of Lady Acland, one of the *alto rilievos* in the Saratoga monument, is a correct likeness of that lady, having been taken from a photograph of a painting of her by Sir Joshua Reynolds. This photograph was taken and very kindly sent me by the late Lord Carnarvon, a grandnephew of Lady Acland.

to be regarded with a respect and tenderness rarely
accorded even to one of her sex.   But to her the
scenes through which she had passed were ever vivid ;
and, as the widow of General Montgomery—who for
forty years had remained faithful to the memory of
her "soldier," as she always called him—swooned away
as the steamboat passed her mansion on the North
River bearing the body of her husband to its final
resting-place beneath St. Paul's, so Lady Harriet
Acland, though surviving *her* "soldier" thirty-seven
years, could never hear an allusion to him without
tears.   "Attached to her husband as she was," writes
Miss Warburton, " having suffered so much for his sake,
and having, as she supposed, brought him home to
safety, and a life of future happiness, to have all this
cheering prospect dashed by his death was, one would
have thought, more than human nature could support
or sustain.   But she had a mind superior to every trial,
and even this, her severest affliction, she bore up
under with resignation and fortitude.   I saw her again
many years afterward, when her sorrows had been
somewhat tempered by time.   She was still handsome,
but her bloom and vivacity were gone.   I placed
myself where I could unobserved contemplate the
change she had undergone since I had first seen
her.   Her countenance was mild and placid, but there
was a look of tender melancholy mingled with resig-
nation that made her the most interesting object I had
ever beheld."

APPENDIX VI.

LAST DAYS OF JONES, THE LOVER OF JANE McCREA.

A Scrap of Unwritten History.

[This story is told by Julia C. Smalley in the *Catholic World* for December, 1882.]

In the course of an evening conversation with the cheerful circle in which our easy-chair is permitted for the present to fill the privileged place accorded to its invalid occupant, we fell to relating incidents connected with the early history of our republic. An aged member of that circle sat diligently plying her knitting needles, a silent listener to our chat, instead of supplying the share which we knew full well she could have drawn from her own knowledge of many interesting events of that period, at the time of their occurrence or soon after. She was, therefore, very warmly urged by the younger part of the company to "tell us a story," even though it might prove, as she hinted, but a "twice-told tale" to some of her listeners.

It so happened that she had on that day taken up a stray number of Lossing's "Pictorial Field-Book of the Revolution," and while glancing drowsily over its pages her eye was attracted by his account of the tragical death of Jane McCrea, near Fort Edward, on the Hudson River, in July, 1777. Having frequently in former years visited an aged relative who lived in Bennington, Vt., through the war of the Revolution, and who was well acquainted with the unfortunate girl, and with the Mrs. McNeil whom Miss

McCrea was visiting at the time of the sad event, she had heard the painful story in all its mournful details from the lips of that relative, with the shuddering horror and tearful sympathy which it would naturally awaken in a sensitive young heart.

At the close of his narration Lossing remarks that there were various accounts in the vicinity of Fort Edward as to the subsequent fate of Lieutenant Jones of the British army, to whom Jane McCrea was engaged; and that he heard, from a lady at Glens Falls who was related to the Jones family, that he lived with his friends in Canada many years after the terrible event—a melancholy and lonely man.

It is curious to note how some such trivial cause as this renewal of her acquaintance with that sad story will often impel an old person to rake up the dying embers of the past and draw from them living sparks which had long been smouldering beneath their dust. It was thus with our serene old friend as she closed the book that afternoon and settled back in her " old arm-chair," musing upon the narrative and recalling scenes of her early life which she had not thought upon for years. Hence it followed, of course, when our evening chat dipped into history, and she was urged to bear her part in it, that she should recur to the subject of her late reading and revery, and to the fact that she knew more of the later life of Lieutenant David Jones than was recorded by Lossing. " For," said she, " all the early years of my life, with the exception of occasional visits to friends in Vermont, were passed on the American shore of the St. Lawrence. It was then a wilderness from Sackett's Harbor to the ' Rapids,' only broken by the little village of Ogdensburg, just starting into existence, and by small openings made here and there by

such hardy pioneers as dared encroach within its for-
bidding boundaries.

" Schools there were none up or down the river
from Ogdensburg, and the children of the ' settlers'
had no means for instruction, unless taught at home
or sent across the river to attend schools already estab-
lished in the older settlements on the Canadian shore.

" No sooner had my father taken up a large tract of
land and planted our pleasant home in this wilderness
—indeed, before we had been there long enough
to get it reduced to a tolerable state of order we were
visited by the residents of that shore up and down the
river, and afterward formed many permanent friend-
ships with them, among the most highly valued of
which were members of the Jones family. So it
befel that when I was old enough to be sent away to
school I was admitted into one of those families
more as a household pet than a boarder, and was
cordially invited to range freely through the whole
circle. As every separate family was blessed with
daughters near my own age, I was decidedly ' in
clover' among them—clover the luxury of which for
me, who had no sister or young companions at home,
save the little squaws from a neighboring Indian
encampment, cannot possibly be conceived by any
small lassie who lives amid abounding youthful com-
panionship. I revelled in it. Such parties as were
given weekly at one and another house ! Such multi-
tudes of dolls as went with us in every variety of cos-
tume ; among which my own, large and small, figured,
copper-colored and in full Indian dress, with hair
banged according to the most approved aboriginal
style—which has been adopted by our modern fine
ladies—and was necessary to the completion of the
Indian toilet that I took pride in arranging for them

in honor of my special pets, the *papooses* of the wig-
wams.

"Among the young girls of the Jones connection
was one to whom I was particularly attracted, as she
was to me, by the similarity of our positions. Her
father lived in a remote district, and her home was
almost as isolated as my own, while she was with their
relatives for the same purpose as myself. At the close
of each term of our school she was, as well as myself,
carried home to pass the short interval between the
terms. On one of these occasions she was so urgent in
her entreaties that I might be permitted to go with
her for the vacation that my father consented, much to
my satisfaction, and we set forth in great glee. Our
journey was very delightful, through a wild and roman-
tic region, and I received a most cordial welcome from
her family at its close.

"The house was more elaborate in style and furni-
ture than our home so recently founded in the woods.
A portion of it was built by her grandfather many years
before, and extensive modern additions had been made
by her father. Her grandfather died the previous
year, and his brother, a very venerable old gentleman
with hair as white as snow, lived in the family. I was
deeply impressed by the countenance and manner of
this granduncle of my friend. An expression of un-
utterable sadness was stamped upon his noble features,
and a gentle dignity—benign to the verge of pity—
marked his whole bearing, even to the softened tones
of his manly voice, especially when addressing the
young in the few slowly uttered but impressive words
which he seldom exceeded when speaking to them.
He was very fond of his grandniece, and, silent and
reserved as he was with others, he never tired of listen-
ing to her sprightly prattle.

" As soon as I found a proper occasion I plied her with questions as to this interesting relative, whom she had never mentioned when telling me about her family. She seemed slightly constrained when speaking of him, but told me he was a bachelor, and that he met with a crushing affliction in his youth, from which he never recovered. With all the eager pertinacity natural to small daughters of Eve I drew from this reluctant witness that her grandfather, Captain Jonathan Jones, and this gentleman, his brother—Lieutenant David Jones—were officers in Burgoyne's army during the first years of the Revolution ; that the lieutenant was engaged to a beautiful young lady, whose brother was a stanch supporter of the American cause and opposed to her union with the Tory officer, and that she was killed and scalped by the Indians while going with a friend and escort to meet that officer in the British camp at Sandy Hill, not long before the surrender of Burgoyne. He was so crushed by the terrible blow, and disgusted with the apathy of Burgoyne in refusing to punish the miscreant who brought her scalp to the camp as a trophy, claiming the bounty offered for such prizes by the British commanders, that he and his brother asked for a discharge and were refused, when they deserted—he having first rescued the precious relic of his beloved from the savages—and retired to this Canadian wilderness, which he had never been known to leave except upon one mysterious occasion many years before.

" She did not know the name of the lady so long and faithfully mourned, but when I asked her if this tragedy did not occur near Fort Edward, on the Hudson, she remembered to have heard that place mentioned in connection with it. She said they were all forbidden to speak in his presence of American affairs or history, but she had once persuaded him to let her see the mournful relic so precious to him. She described the hair as the most beautiful she had ever seen, light auburn in color, soft and glossy as silk, perfectly even, and a yard and a quarter in length.

" ' Well, my dear A——,' said I, ' it so happens that I know more about this sad affair than even yourself, who have always lived in the house with him. When my father and mother used to visit his oldest sister in Bennington, Vt., they took me with them at her special request ; for, being the only daughter of her favorite brother, she always treated me with more tender affection than she showed toward her other nieces. Her house, which she had long known and occupied, was one where the officers quartered at the time of the battle of Bennington, and I remember the speechless awe with which I was wont to con over and spell out the names of those officers, recorded by themselves, on the eve of the battle, upon a pane of glass in the window with the diamond in a ring belonging to one of their number, who was killed in the conflict of the next day.

" ' My aunt's memory was a storehouse of tales of those times, and I never tired of listening to them. No sooner was one finished than I teased for another, until I am sure the patience of the good dame must have been sorely tried. She knew this young lady, whose name was Jane McCrea, and also Mrs. McNeil, the Tory friend whom Miss McCrea was visiting at the time of their capture by the Indians. I little thought when I cried over the doleful story that the lover was still living, much less that I should ever see him !'

" A——did not dare repeat to her venerable relative what I had told her, but she ventured to beg that I might be allowed to see the beautiful hair of his lost love.   He was deaf to her entreaties, assuring her that she was the only one who had or would see it while he lived, and that he wished to have it buried with him when he died.

"After our return to school I drew from her some facts in relation to the mysterious journey she had mentioned his having once taken. 'I do not know much about it,' she said. 'I heard it from an old servant-woman of the family, who told me that many years before I was born a stranger came there one evening, who appeared to be a gentleman's valet. He brought a fine-looking, intelligent young boy with him, and inquired for my grandfather, Captain Jonathan Jones.'

"The substance of my friend's account was that, after an interview of some length with her grandfather, his brother, the lieutenant, was called in, and the three were together in the library during most of the night, discussing some very interesting matter connected with the boy.   The butler had been ordered to prepare refreshments in the dining-room, and Robert, one of the waiter-boys—an urchin gifted with a larger amount of mischief and curiosity than his small frame could possibly enclose, insomuch that they were continually overflowing, to the annoyance of the whole household—was directed to remain within call to serve them when required.   It was not in the nature of this valet that he should remain idle at his post during the long hours of the night, and his faculties were too much on the alert as to the subject engaging his superiors to yield to drowsiness ; so, in perfect submission to his ruling instincts, he plied the keyhole diligently for such information as it might convey to his ear when the parties became so excited as to raise their voices above the low tone to which most of their conversation was confined.   He gathered from these snatches that Captain

Jones was urgently entreated to perform some service for the boy which he was reluctant to undertake. He heard him exclaim vehemently : ' I will not be persuaded to receive under my roof the son of that detestable traitor, whose treason, although to an unrighteous cause, caused my dearest friend, one of the bravest and most noble officers in his Majesty's service, to be hung like a dog by the vile rebels. I should be constantly haunted with the thought that I was nurturing a viper to sting me when occasion offered.' His brother David said something in reply, of which Robert heard only enough to infer that there was a retired officer of the American army across the river who might be persuaded to do what was desired. ' Very well,' said the captain ; ' you can undertake the task, if you see fit, but I have no belief that you will gain the consent of one who loathes the father so bitterly to take charge of the son. Still, as he is a bachelor, he would escape the risk of exposing a family to injurious consequences, and as sufficient provision will be made for the support and education of the boy, there will be no pecuniary risk ; it will also, no doubt, be easier, as you say, to keep the secret of his birth in the States than there in the vicinity of his father's retreat. You may perhaps succeed, and I wish no harm may come of it if you do.'

" Robert heard no more, and soon after these remarks the confab broke up, and he was called to serve the refreshments in the library.

" The lieutenant departed with the boy and his attendant the next day. He was absent some days, and nothing further was known as to his journey, its object and result, than was gathered from Robert's story, which was soon circulated through the neighborhood. It formed the basis of many conjectures and discussions among the country people and servants. These

were renewed with increased excitement when, after
some months, it was discovered that a stone cottage in
the English style had been built in the midst of a
dense wilderness some miles back from a Canadian
village situated on the bank of the St. Lawrence, and
was occupied by an old man, whose sole attendant was
a servant, who visited that village occasionally for sup-
plies, but utterly refused to answer the questions of the
villagers or give any information as to his master's
name or history.

" I afterward learned from other sources the further
particulars that at the period to which this account of
my young friend referred a settlement was rapidly
forming on the American shore opposite to this Ca-
nadian village, and that the fact that a leading man in
the newly rising community, a bachelor and retired
officer of the American Revolution, had adopted a boy
whose origin was unknown, but who bore the name of
a traitor—most odious to all American people—who was
evidently not dependent upon his patron for anything
but care and direction, set rumor 'with its hundred
tongues' busy connecting the youth with the mysteri-
ous recluse of the 'forest lodge'—as the place was
named by the country people—and set all eyes to
watching him and his movements for any circumstance
that might confirm these suspicions. Hence when it
became known that the boy sometimes crossed the river
and disappeared with an Indian hunter in the woods,
under pretence of hunting the game which abounded
there, remaining upon each occasion for some days, it
was taken as 'confirmation strong as Holy Writ' of the
prevailing conjectures, and he was generally regarded
with increased aversion. Despite these unfavorable
influences, however, he lived and flourished, became
an enterprising, respectable citizen, and a distinguished

officer in the volunteer service during the War of 1812,
his zeal and valor in the cause winning for him the
public respect and esteem so long unjustly withheld.
He married a niece of his benefactor, and they were
united in their devotion to the interests and comfort
of her uncle in his old age, inheriting a large portion
of his estate at his death.

" The mystery surrounding the recluse, the problem
of his suspected identity with the notorious American
traitor, and his possible relationship with the boy in
question were never solved.

"It continued for many years to be the subject of
evening gossip by rural firesides in that region, and
strange stories were told by Indian and white hunters
and trappers of the startling things they had seen and
heard in the vicinity of the lonely cottage—long since
fallen into decay—both during the occupancy of its
owner and after his disappearance. Whether he died
there, or left for some far-off country before his death,
was never known."

APPENDIX VII.

SKETCH OF GENERAL JOHN WATTS DE PEYSTER.

GENERAL J. WATTS DE PEYSTER, the author of the
poems on Oriskany and Saratoga, was born at No. 3
Broadway, in the city of New York, March 9th, 1821.
He is the descendant, in direct line, in the *seventh*
generation, of de Peysters who resided in, and in the
sixth of those born in, the First Ward of that city ;
and through connections by blood and by marriage, his

people filled the highest and most important offices under the Dutch and English or British rule. His mother's father, John Watts (2d), was the last Royal Recorder of the City and the Founder and Endower of the Leake and Watts Orphan House, to whom the general erected, in 1892, a bronze statue in Trinity Churchyard, which has been pronounced one of the finest in the country and was considered such an admirable specimen of art, that a duplicate was selected and sent to the Centennial Exposition at Chicago. His father, Frederic de Peyster, stood in the highest rank in literature, philanthropy, and usefulness in New York, and it was said of him in published obituaries: " He has probably been connected as an active officer with more social, literary and benevolent societies than any other New Yorker who ever lived." His historical and biographical publications were numerous and valuable, and to sum up, " to him might justly be applied the expressive lines of Tennyson as to what constitutes a gentleman.

His son, the subject of this sketch, inherited the literary tastes and industry of his family. He commenced to write for the public press at eleven, and since that time he has continued to publish works in every literary branch, year by year, ever since he came of age.

To a very great extent a firm believer in absolute predestination, he claims that, as St. Paul remarks, " what hast thou that thou didst not receive," and as any talent and the power of applying it came from God, from Him came the reward in whatever form conferred. Nevertheless, the general's labors have not been without recognition.

Although only an officer of Militia, or, as they were afterward styled, " Military Forces of the State

of New York," now National Guard, his every pro-
motion was made especially for "meritorious conduct"
or " important services," and after the rebellion he was
brevetted Major-General State of New York for
" meritorious services" by " Special Act," or Concurrent
Resolution, New York State Legislature, April, 1866
[first and only general officer receiving such an honor
(the highest) from State of New York, and the only
officer thus brevetted (Major-General) in the United
States]. He represented the State as Military Agent
for observation abroad, endorsed in the highest terms
by the United States Executive, President Fillmore,
and Government Secretaries of State and of War. His
Reports on Tactics, Uniform, Organization, Arms,
and Armament—Arms and Ordnance—were acknowl-
edged to contain " most valuable suggestions" by
Jefferson Davis, then Secretary of War, and his collec-
tion of Foreign Arms was commended at Washing-
ton, whither they were sent, by request, for inspection.
His suggestion for the adoption of the twelve-pounder
Napoleon-gun several years before its approval by the
United States Army Board, his ideas of Uniform and
designation of rank were adopted or imitated by the
rebel military authorities, and he was one of the first
to promote the institution of the Municipal Police,
and the substitution for the then existing Volunteer
Fire Department of a Paid Organization, with steam fire
engines and a fire escape both economical and effec-
tive. In recognition of his services as Military Agent
of the State of New York in Europe he received an
elegant gold medal from Hon. Washington Hunt,
Governor of the State of New York, and, by a Special
Order, another gold medal was conferred under the
same Executive "for zeal, devotion, and meritorious
service," and his appointment as Brigadier-General

was the first made by any governor independently and, as stated therein, " for important services."

His works on Military History and Criticism have received the highest endorsement even to the extent of the opinion that his judgment in Strategy and Grand Tactics was almost infallible, and his views or ideas on practical strategy elicited from General Sir Edward Cust, B.A., author of " The Annals of the Wars, 1700 to 1715," in eleven volumes, and "Lives of the Warriors, XVIIth Century," a "Letter Dedicatory," dated March, 1869, of 29 pages. He was also the first to demonstrate to the American people the vast influence, in a series of works, volumes, and articles, upon human progress exercised by the Seven United States of Holland, a subject which has latterly been presented in a more popular and digested form by the late Mr. Campbell in his book "The Puritan in Holland, England, and America;" and in a series of centennial articles in the New York *Times*, New York *Mail*, and other prominent papers he presented the operations of the Revolutionary War from a point of view based on original authorities, seldom if never consulted, demonstrating errors that should never have occurred and which have become strengthened by repetition.

For a life of the Swedish Field Marshal Torstenson, who may be justly claimed to have decided the result of the Thirty Years' War, and was pronounced by Gustavus Adolphus as his pupil fittest to command his army, or any army, he received three beautiful silver medals from Oscar I., King of Sweden, besides being honored with other badges and insignia for similar work subsequently done in military, historical, and biographical essays.

Many years ago he was invested with the degree of

LL.D., subsequently with that of Master of Arts, Columbia College, and recently with that of Litt.D., Doctor of Letters or Literature (the last a degree conveying highest collegiate distinction, superior to LL.D.), Franklin and Marshall College, corner-stone laid by Benjamin Franklin, 1787 ; reorganized 1853), Lancaster, Pa., 1892. He is also an honorary member of historical societies too numerous to mention; and, indeed, since this sketch is in type he has received notice of his having been elected Honorary Fellow of the Society of Science, Letters, and Art, of London.

Invidious remarks having been made in regard to General De Peyster not going into the field in 1861–65, the all-sufficient answer is that a soldier to be of any value in active service requires sound health and certainly strong digestion. The famous General Wolfe wrote that he chiefly valued his promotion as general because that rank enabled him to command comforts without which it was impossible in his state of health to perform his duties efficiently. This remark was made at a time when even field officers enjoyed advantages now beyond the conceded rights in the field of any but the highest in command.

Doctors of the highest ability advised him that if he did take the field there was only one chance out of ten of his being able to remain there or of surviving the necessary acclimatization to perform any effectual service. Nevertheless, he did offer to go more than once, and to furnish admirable troops, or serve in any capacity in which his health would justify the appointment " due to acknowledged ability." He was at one time considered for chief of the personal staff which President Lincoln talked of organizing, until persuaded not to do so for reasons best known to those who combated the idea.

At the age of eighteen he was seized suddenly with such a peculiar and severe affection of the heart that it was deemed worthy of record in permanent medical reports. The effects of this continued for years. When it ceased to trouble him persistently it was followed by hemorrhages, which drained his life. At one period this continued for six years continuously, and returned from time to time without notice. It did not preclude at times extraordinary temporary activity, if rest, relief, and remedies were possible upon the first symptoms of exhaustion or of the return of heart trouble. It is said that "whoever excuses himself accuses himself," but that man is the worst of fools who is aware of any insuperable obstacle and then undertakes to act against knowledge, when failure will be attributed by meanness or injustice to the worst motives or to any but the true cause.

His works on military subjects—on the Militia and on the Fire Departments of Europe—are masses of information, whose only fault is concentration. They would make a dozen books, and for this reason have perhaps been more profitable to the fame of those who have subsequently turned them over than to that of the original compiler and author, who, at much personal expense of time and money, collected them during a visit to Europe. They still offer abundant resources for the improvement of our institutions.

Nor, have General de Peyster's writings been confined solely to works of a military character. Besides biographies of our leading generals, representatives abroad, and other celebrities, he has written and published a number of others of a high literary character, which have met the approbation of the severest critics and the praise of one of the best judges, the lamented Bryant; likewise an historical drama, " Bothwell," the successful lover and third husband of Mary Queen of Scots, partly in blank verse and partly in prose, which received the following stamp of excellence from *Le Livre*, the highest literary tribunal : " Magnificent to read although impossible to act"—impossible to act because, as remarked by an experienced stage manager, it required too many first-class actors to fill the leading rôles and too expensive or perhaps too difficult scenery to produce and manage. In fact, the list of the general's publications, books, pamphlets, and contributions to periodicals fill eleven pages of one volume of the " Bibliography of the American Historical Association" besides a supplementary list in the succeeding volume, and the enumeration is by no means complete.

It only remains, in order to fill out and complete this picture, to speak of its subject as a man. In person, General de Peyster is erect in carriage, and bears so much the stamp of a military personage, that a stranger, observing him, would put him down at once as belonging to that profession. In character, notwithstanding his ill-health and his being almost continuously racked with pain, he is eminently genial and possessed of so much *bonhommie* as to make him a most charming companion, and the writer recalls many delightful hours spent with him at his classic country-seat at Tivoli, N. Y., which overlooks, so to speak, the scene of Sir Henry Clinton's expedition against Æsopus during the Revolution. He possesses, moreover, most endearing and affectionate traits, and no one is more charitable to the faults of others than himself. Nor are these characteristics confined solely to the *human* family. His considerate treatment of all dumb animals is remarkable, and a tombstone in his grounds, which commemorates an affectionate dog, serves also both to mark the grave and the kindness of heart which prompted its erection.*

In fine, to apply to him the tribute which dear old Horace gave to his friend Fuscus :

> " Integer vitæ scelerisque purus
> Non eget mauvis jaculis, neque arcu."

APPENDIX VIII.

Rev. Thomas Allen, the " Parson" who forms the subject of the ballad on the " Catamount Tavern," was born at Northampton, Mass., January 7th, 1743, and graduated from Harvard College in 1762, being ranked among the first classical scholars of his time. It will thus occur to the reader that the " Parson," as he is called in tradition, in a jocular manner, is hardly in keeping with his real character. Rev. Mr. Allen studied theology under Rev. Mr. Hooker, of Northampton, and was ordained April 18th, 1764, as the first minister of Pittsfield, Berkshire County, Mass., which was named in honor of William Pitt, and which was then a frontier town, in which a garrison had been kept during the French War. The Indian name was Pontoosuc. At the time of Mr. Allen's settlement Pitts-

---

* The writer likewise appreciates fully this particular trait in General de Peyster's character, since he, also, has placed a marble slab over the remains of a dog which during life was more faithful to him than many of his so-called "friends."

field contained but six houses not built of logs.   He
lived to see it a wealthy and beautiful town, with six
thousand inhabitants.

In the Revolutionary struggle he was an ardent sup-
porter of the colonies, and twice went out as a volun-
teer chaplain.   From October 3d until January 23d,
1776, he was with the army at White Plains, and in
June and July, 1777, at Ticonderoga.   After the retreat
of the army from that post he returned home.   Upon
the approach of the British, under Colonel Baum, to
the vicinity of Bennington he marched with the Pitts-
field volunteers to repel the invasion.   Prior to the
assault of the intrenchments occupied by the refugees,
he advanced, and in a voice which they distinctly heard
called upon them to surrender, promising good treat-
ment ; but being fired upon, he rejoined the militia,
and was among the foremost of those who entered the
breastworks ; and there is no question but that his ex-
ertions and example contributed materially to the
triumph of August 16th, which so greatly checked
Burgoyne's progress and led to the capture of that
general.   Undoubtedly, also, his experiences in the
service before this, at the battle of White Plains, etc.,
gave him valuable experience as a soldier of the church
militant, and thus aided him in his directions to the
raw levies in the battle.   After the action he secured
the horse of a Brunswick surgeon, which carried a pair
of panniers filled with bottles of wine.   The wine he
administered to the wounded and weary ; but two
large, square, glass-case bottles he carried home as
trophies of his campaign of four days.   Of his after
life there are many valuable accounts, as it was filled
with stirring adventures, especially one, when he crossed
the sea to London to bring home to his family an in-
fant child of his daughter, who died in that city in

1799. While in London he saw the king, as he passed from St. James to the Parliament House, in a coach drawn by six cream-colored horses, and on this sight recorded the following reflections: "This is he who desolated my country, who ravaged the American coasts, annihilated our trade, burned our towns, plundered our cities, sent forth his Indian allies to scalp our wives and children, starved our youth in his prison-ships, and caused the expenditure of a hundred millions of money and a hundred thousand of precious lives. Instead of being the father of his people, he has been their destroyer. May God forgive him so great guilt. And yet he is the idol of the people, who think they cannot live without him." Rev. Mr. Allen died Sabbath morning, February 11th, 1810, in the forty-seventh year of his ministry. (See Allen's "Biographical Dictionary"—from which this sketch has been taken—for a fuller account.)

APPENDIX IX.

THE CATAMOUNT TAVERN.*

By Charles M. Bliss.

THE "Green Mountain Tavern," the resort of the "Green Mountain Boys," is here referred to. In what is now the village of Bennington Center—the Bennington of Revolutionary fame—it had stood until March 30th, 1871, for more than one hundred years, a most noted relic of Revolutionary and even of ante-Revolutionary days. In fact, events which occurred before the Revolution gave it its name and its chief

---

* See Frontispiece.

title to fame. The land controversy between the set-
tlers on the New Hampshire Grants and the provincial
government, but not the people, of New York—a con-
troversy but for which Vermont would not have
been, first brought "Landlord Fay's" tavern into
prominence. Stephen Fay, its proprietor, was himself
one of the prominent actors in this controversy, as he
also was in the preparations for the battle of Benning-
ton. He had five sons in the battle, one of whom
was killed. It was during the long and bitter land
controversy that the settlers placed a large stuffed
catamount, *felis concolor*, over the swinging sign of the
inn, with its face set toward New York, in token of their
defiance of New York authority. Hence the name
"Catamount Tavern."

The early settlers of Vermont held title to their
lands by virtue of grants from New Hampshire, and
the territory so held was called the New Hampshire
Grants. By a right perhaps equally good New York
granted the same lands to others. The crown decided
in favor of the New Hampshire title, but the contro-
versy did not stop. The owners of the New York
grants, having paid for them, demanded of the settlers
under the New Hampshire grants departure or repay-
ment. The settlers refused both. They were not
averse to the jurisdiction of New York; they were to
the demands of the New York claimants. The New
York courts sustained the New York claimants, and
attempted to eject the settlers from their lands by legal
process. This was successfully resisted by force. After
many ineffectual efforts of the court of Albany County
to enforce its decrees a determined attempt was
made, July 19th, 1771, to secure the farm of
James Breakenridge in the town of Bennington, and
this also failed. The sheriff of the county and the

mayor of Albany, with an armed posse of over three
hundred men, were the aggressive party, but the oppos-
ing force, with headquarters at the Catamount Tavern,
and under the lead of Ethan Allen, was too strong for
them. No shots were fired, however, and in the
bloodless victory on this farm, to use the words of the
late Governor Hiland Hall, in his " Early History of
Vermont," "was born the future State of Vermont."

The same year James Duane, of New York City, a
land speculator, and John Kempe, the Attorney-Gen-
eral of the province, made themselves very obnoxious
to the settlers. Their agents were roughly handled by
Robert Cochran, the real owner of some of these lands,
assisted by Ethan Allen, Remember Baker and a few
others. Governor Tryon, considering this a serious
outrage, offered a reward of twenty pounds each for the
arrest of these men. Allen and Baker and Cochran
at once issued a counter proclamation, promising a
reward of fifteen and ten pounds for the arrest of "those
common disturbers," Duane and Kempe respectively,
and their delivery "at Landlord Fay's."

Immediately after the Breakenridge affair, inhabitants
of the towns west of the Green Mountains organized a
military body called the "Green Mountain Boys."
Ethan Allen was their colonel and Seth Warner a
captain. They were "Minute Men," ready and willing
to serve literally at a moment's notice in defence of
their rights. New Hampshire was too far away to aid
them; on themselves they must depend. They did
little actual fighting, however. They had other methods
of defence. In various ways they harassed the New
York officials, and also the New York sympathizers
among the settlers, whom they stigmatized as "York-
ers." These Green Mountain Boys were always on
the watch for them, and they were sure to make

examples of the officers if they caught them. They "chastised them with the twigs of the wilderness," sent them beyond their borders, and commanded them never to return. One contumacious person, a "York-er," they brought to the Catamount Tavern and swung up in an arm-chair under Landlord Fay's sign, where they kept him for two hours, an object of derision to the crowd gathered to see the sport.

These were the men, an organized body, who captured Ticonderoga, May 10th, 1775. It was in the Catamount Tavern that their leader, Ethan Allen, on May 3d, arranged with the Connecticut and Massachusetts men for its capture, the former having brought the funds to pay the expenses of the expedition and the latter a small force to join it. From here went out orders to summon every man to muster for the capture. One of the messengers sent from Castleton travelled sixty miles on foot in one day through the wilderness, from clearing to clearing, on this duty.

The Catamount Tavern was the headquarters of General Stark at the time of the battle of Bennington, and the captured British officers were kept here after the battle as prisoners of war. Contrary to the popular belief of to-day and to the general record of history, Stark was on the march from Manchester *via* Bennington to join General Schuyler on the Hudson, in obedience to the latter's orders. He finally disobeyed those orders, not because of the slight put upon him by Congress, but on the representation of the Vermont Council of Safety, in session in the Council Room at Landlord Fay's.

This Council of twelve members, one of whom, and its secretary, was a son of Landlord Fay, was the provisional but legitimate government of the new State of Vermont, just sprung into being and not yet a twelvemonth old. This civil authority, composed of Vermont men on the ground, was better informed of the plans and movements of Burgoyne than the New Hampshire general just arrived. To them he wisely listened. His own words, written to the *Courant* at Hartford, Conn., two days after the battle, and printed therein October 7th, 1777, make this point clear. He says : "After my arrival at that place [Manchester, Vt.], I received orders from Major-General Lincoln, pursuant to orders from General Schuyler, to march my whole brigade to Stillwater and join the main army under his command. . . . In obedience thereto, I marched with my brigade to Bennington, on my way to join him, leaving that part of the country almost wholly naked to the ravage of the enemy. The Honorable the Council then sitting at Bennington were much against my marching with my brigade, as it was raised on their request, they apprehending great danger of the enemy's approaching to that place, which afterward we found truly to be the case."

To the failure of Burgoyne to cut off New England, then one third of the country, from the rest of the Colonies, is ascribed the willingness of France to aid the American cause openly, and thus to secure the independence of the United States. In achieving this independence, the aid of France is now freely acknowledged throughout our country. That of the State of Vermont is also entitled to mention in history ; and in the making of the nation, the work of the patriots of the Catamount Tavern, founders of a State, coming up, as it does, to the measure of Lafayette's love of liberty, ranks higher in the moral scale than that of the enemies of England at Versailles.

Ethan Allen lived at Landlord Fay's upon occasion, and his name appears in one of Captain Fay's account books, still extant in Bennington. The first legislature of Vermont sat here. Here, in 1778, David Redding was tried as a traitor " for enemical conduct" and was hanged. A peculiarity of the trial was that only six jurors sat. The Governor and Council thereupon ordered a new trial, and thus disappointed the excited patriots who had assembled to witness the execution. Whereupon Ethan Allen assured them that the proceeding was strictly lawful, and that after the new trial if Redding were not hung he would "be hung himself."

To designate the spot where the famous tavern stood, the pedestal of a monument has been placed in position, to be surmounted by a bronze catamount, though with his wrinkled visage smoothed, for after more than a century the war between the Green Mountain Boys and the Yorkers is over. Vermont is a result of that war; the combatants compromised their differences; the fourteen-year-old State was admitted to the Union; the Catamount Tavern, for over twenty years a "lively" inn, subsided to the humdrum occupation of furnishing entertainment for man and beast, coming in large numbers from the less favored parts of New England to this no longer turbulent land of promise; peace reigned, and as of old out of the strong came forth sweetness.

APPENDIX X.

THE CORRECT SPELLING OF BEMUS.

PROBABLY no question in connection with Burgoyne's campaign has given rise to so much discussion as that concerning the spelling of the name of that old settler who kept a tavern on the river-road from Schuylerville to Albany, and from whom the Heights near him took their name. By Burgoyne's chief engineer, in his maps of the two actions (September 19th and October 7th, 1777), and by different historians the name has been spelled in as many ways as there have been writers on our Revolutionary history—Bemis, Bremis, Braemus, Behmus, Behmis, Bemese and Beemis being the most common.

By a letter, however, which I received some years since from that distinguished antiquarian and local historian, Mr. B. B. Burt, of Oswego, N. Y., I am finally enabled to settle this much-mooted point.

Mr. Burt's Letter.

"Oswego, April 22, 1881.

" *Mr. W. L. Stone.*

"Dear Sir: Rev. Samuel H. Adams, a gentleman and a scholar, spent a few days with me the last week, and I learned from him that he was a descendant of the Bemus from whom the Heights of Revolutionary fame were named ; and inasmuch as I knew that the name had been used and spelled in different ways, I asked him to note what he knew about it on the next page. I send you his statement. Truly yours,

"B. B. Burt."

Rev. Samuel H. Adams's Statement.

" My grandmother and her brothers, who were the children of the Mr. *Bemus* from whom the Heights were named, always spelled their name *Bemus*, and she was quite disturbed that the error of *Bemis* should so commonly appear.

" She married Daniel Crawford, Saratoga Springs,

and was for many years the oldest person in Saratoga County. [Was this Crawford the one mentioned in Mr. Huling's 'Reminiscences of Saratoga Fifty Years Ago?'—W.L.S.] Her brother moved to Chautauqua County, and Bemus Point, on Chautauqua Lake, was named from him.

" All his descendants in that county spell the name *Bemus*, and will on no account spell it otherwise. Another, Matthew Pendergrass *Bemus*, was a member of the New York Assembly from 1868 to 1872 inclusive.   SAMUEL H. ADAMS.
'April 18, 1881."

To give, however, all the data on this much-mooted point, the Saratoga *Sentinel*, in reply to the foregoing, printed the following :

" In our investigations we have found that Mr. Adam Snyder, of this village, now over seventy years old, lived with John *Bemis*, who died in this town in 1829. Mr. Snyder spells the name just as we have given it, and says that is the proper way. He does not know the exact relationship of John Bemis of this town to the Stillwater family, but says that he thinks he was a nephew of the owner of the famous Heights. He knows he was a brother of Mrs. Daniel Crawford. whose name is mentioned above, and tells us that he remembers distinctly that Mr. Bemis 'purchased fifty acres of land on the south bounds of the village (being the Crawford Tavern, alluded to by Mr. Stone), about the year 1826, paying $1000 therefor. Mr. Crawford had become somewhat embarrassed by reason of giving surety for a man, and his brother-in-law, John Bemis, bought the place for him on that account. John Bemis died childless in 1829, as above noted. The different branches of the same family vary in spelling their name sometimes, and it may be the parties referred to by Messrs. Burt and Hall have done so, and now claim it to be the original.

" Since writing the foregoing we have conversed with C. E. Durkee, Esq., on the subject. Mr. Durkee has a taste for genealogical studies and has many books on the subject, among them a history of Watertown, Mass., wherein it is stated that the Bemis who settled in this county emigrated from Watertown, and while the members of the family are said to have spelled their name variously, Bemis is given as the prevailing and most usually adopted way."

In answer to this last, from the Saratoga *Sentinel*, I append the following, which, I think, conclusively settles the question. However, I give all the *data* on this much-vexed question, and our readers must judge for themselves :

SOME MORE LIGHT ON THE OLD SETTLER BEMUS.

To the Editor of the " Saratogian."

SIR : Since sending you the communication in regard to the spelling of the name of Bemus, Rev. Mr. Adams—the grandson of Bemus—has written the following note to Mr. B. B. Burt, of Oswego, called forth by the publication of his letter to Mr. Burt, in the *Saratogian* of the 5th inst. I give herewith his letter. W. L. STONE.

JERSEY CITY HEIGHTS, May 12.

CLIFTON SPRINGS, N. Y., May 9.

B. B. Burt, Oswego, N. Y.

DEAR FRIEND : . . . I regret that so little information of the old settler, Jotham Bemus, is in my possession. Beyond the facts that he was born about

1738, married Tryphena Moore, was a farmer occupying the Heights (called after him), and kept for many years a tavern (the most popular for many years between Fort Edward and Albany) near the Heights; that he was in easy financial circumstances and was engaged extensively in buying cattle; that he was stoutly built and energetic in all he did; that he died in 1786, leaving four children, viz.: William, Jotham, John and Sally; aside from this outline I know but little.

I may be able to gather something more from my aunt, Mrs. Martha B. Hall, whose husband (formerly of Saratoga Springs), Ezra Hall, is the proprietor of Bemus Hotel, Evansville, Ind. Mr. Crawford was fifty years ago owner and proprietor of what was then known as " Highland Hall," which was a little out from Saratoga village, on the Dunning Street road south.

William, the oldest son of this old settler, Jotham Bemus, was born at Bemus Heights in 1762; married Mary Pendergast, 1782; settled in Pittston, Rensselaer County, and removed thence in 1802.

My grandmother, Sally Bemus Crawford, was born at Bemus Heights in May, 1768, and removed from Saratoga Springs with Mr. and Mrs. Hall to Indiana in 1864. She has spent hours telling me of " Burgine" and his army, which she saw; of the burning of her father's house by the British, and of the sufferings of the family for a time while they were wintering in a barn—Burgoyne having destroyed all their buildings and crops.   Sincerely yours,

S. H. ADAMS.*

---

* In this letter of Mr. S. H. Adams he is hardly correct in one statement—at least, such is the infer-

THE CORRECT ORTHOGRAPHY OF THE GREAT BATTLE GROUND.

In addition to the letters in the last *Democrat* upon this subject, we publish the following obituary notice in the Saratoga *Sentinel* of September 15th, 1829 :

" Died, in this town, on the eighth instant. Mr. John Bemus, in the sixty-sixth year of his age. Mr. B. was born on the farm comprising the celebrated Bemus' Heights, which was owned by his father, and from whose name it received its local designation. Though young, he was in the American service at the capture of Burgoyne, as a teamster, and continued to reside on the consecrated soil of his father until his removal to this place several years since." (The Ballston *Democrat*, Friday, May 13, 1881.)

BEMUS OR BEMIS.

Last week we spoke of various discussions which we had read in the past forty years regarding the

---

ence drawn from a letter to me under date of May 19th, 1893, from Mr. Daniel H. Post, of Jamestown, N. Y., a great-great-great-grandson of Jotham Bemus. Mr. Post writes as follows : " Jotham Bemus had more than five children, viz.: Jotham, Tryphena, William, John, Sally, James and Nancy. Jotham, the son of Jotham first, was a soldier in the Revolution, as was also his brother William, who served as a private in Colonel Van Vecton's Regiment, Woodworth's Company. William removed from Pittston, N. Y., in 1805, to Chautauqua County, N. Y., and, in 1806, settled at what is now known as Bemus Point."

methods of spelling the name of the man from whom one of the great revolutionary battlefields took its principal name, and gave evidence why we considered *Bemis* the more authentic orthography than *Bemus*. Our authorities then were verbal. Now we have the following extract from an obituary notice published in the Saratoga *Sentinel* of September 15th, 1829, as evidence to the contrary spelling:

"Died, in this town, on the eighth instant, Mr. John Bemus, in the sixty-sixth year of his age. Mr. B. was born on the farm comprising the celebrated Bemus' Heights, which was owned by his father, and from whose name it received its local designation. Though young, he was in the American service at the capture of Burgoyne, as a teamster, and continued to reside on the consecrated soil of his father until his removal to this place several years since."

This would seem to be a settler against any bare recollection, such as we gave last week, but we have still further evidence on the same side. In the surrogate's office we find the record of the will of this John Bemus, drawn probably by Judiah Ellsworth, who, together with Samuel Chapman and John H. Steel (all of them leading citizens of this town), sign the same as witnesses, and the name is spelled Bemus in the body of the will and also in what purports to be the signature. But to show how officials vary, we will say that we found the name spelled *Bemis* in the index of the will, apparently made a few years since.

Our conclusion is then that *Bemus* was the orthography preferred by those of the name who resided hereabouts, and we shall use it hereafter, while we have no doubt that the spelling preferred by the old settlers of Watertown, Mass., from whence the family emigrated, was *Bemis*, as given in the history of Watertown referred to last week.

We may add that from the will of John *Bemus* he would appear to have been quite a well-to-do citizen. He gave one half his property to his sister, Sally Crawford, dividing the balance between Nancy Beckwith, Nabby Clements, and Lucratia Wilcox; Benjamin Crawford, Peter Fort, and Joshua Finch were the executors of the will.

Since the foregoing was in type we have been studying the almanacs. We find by the Albany *Evening Journal Almanac* that Solomon K. Bem*us* represents Chenango County in the Assembly. The Albany *Argus Almanac* says that Solomon K. Bem*iss* is the representative of that county, also that he has been postmaster of the town of Pitcher. The *Tribune Almanac* gives the name as Solomon K. Bem*is*. The red book, giving the list of postmasters, spells the name Bem*iss*, as does the *Argus Almanac*, and the official postal guide spells it Bem*is*. If variety is the spice of life, certainly Solomon K. Bem*is-us-iss-is* gives us plenty in the spelling of his name. (The Saratoga *Sentinel*, Thursday, May 19th, 1881.)

APPENDIX XI.

AUSTIN W. HOLDEN, M.D.

By James H. Holden.

Austin Wells Holden, A.M., M.D., historian, patriot and littérateur, was born in the town of White Creek, Washington County, N. Y., May 16th, 1819. His early education was acquired at the St. Lawrence

Academy, Potsdam, N. Y. In 1836 his father removed to Glens Fall, N. Y., where the subject of this sketch began the study of law with the Honorable William Hay, a noted lawyer and writer of that day. Obliged, for pecuniary reasons, to relinquish this profession, he entered his father's cabinet-shop, where he remained until his twenty-second year. During this time he studied diligently the works of ancient and modern writers, and about 1841 began the study of medicine. A little later he entered the Albany Medical College, from which he graduated with distinction in 1848, and opened his office at Warrensburg, the central town of Warren County, N. Y. In 1851, he was married to Elizabeth Buell, of Glens Falls, daughter of the Honorable Horatio Buell, at one time judge of Warren County; sister of the late James Buell, President of the Importers and Traders Bank of New York City, and niece of the late Sarah Josepha (Buell) Hale, for many years editor of *Godey's Lady's Book.* Three children resulted from this union, only one of whom, James A. Holden, of Glens Falls, now survives. In 1852 Dr. Holden removed with his family to Glens Falls, where he located in practice. Five years later, after thorough investigation, he adopted the Homœopathic system of medicine, and became one of the most noted and successful practitioners of that school in Northern New York. In 1861, on the fall of Fort Sumter, Dr. Holden was the first to offer his services to the State, and raised the first company of men in Warren County. This company, with him as its captain, was attached to the famous Twenty-second Regiment, part of the noted " Iron Brigade." After serving as an officer a short time, Dr. Holden, at the request of officers and men, was transferred, as first assistant surgeon, to the medical staff of the regiment, where his services were most needed, and where he did brave and excellent work. After he was mustered out in 1863, he returned as an acting assistant surgeon to the United States Army, serving in various prominent hospitals till Lee's surrender. For meritorious service he received a commission as brevet major from Governor Fenton. Returning home, he resumed the practice of his profession, in which he was most successful. He was one of the most prominent members of the State Homœopathic Medical Society, holding during the course of his membership the offices of censor, vice-president, president and necrologist. In 1879 he was recommended for and received the honorary degree of M.D. from the Regents of the University. During the years 1877–78 he was chief of staff of the Ward's Island Homœopathic Hospital at New York, serving acceptably till failing health compelled him to resign. He was a life-long Democrat, and in 1874 was elected to the Assembly from Warren County, which is strongly Republican in sentiment. He was one of the first members of Queensbury's board of education, formed in 1882, and served for six years. Up to January, 1891, he was a member and president of the local board of United States Pension Examiners. In 1877 he received as an honorarium the degree of A.M. from Union College. Both he and his wife were noted for their liberality and benevolence, their zeal and efficiency in the service of their Lord and Master. For forty years much of Dr. Holden's time was devoted to literary pursuits. He was a voluminous contributor to the public press, a poet of no small degree of excellence, while his researches and labors in the domain of local history have been fruitful in rescuing from oblivion many detached facts and incidents of the past, that in another generation would have been irremediably lost. His chief and lasting monument, which will bear his name down to posterity, is a work entitled " A History of Queensbury, N. Y.," which covers an important era and section of country in relation to American history. In recognition of his literary abilities, he received, in addition to the honorary degree of Master of Arts already mentioned, appointments as corresponding member of the Oneida County, the New York, Wisconsin and Rhode Island Historical societies, and the New York and New England Genealogical and Biographical societies. His most recent historical work was the " History of Jane McCrea," which appeared in the local press, and which he was getting in readiness to publish in book-form. He left a valuable collection of MSS. and historical miscellany, which will prove treasure-trove to some future historian. In January, 1891, Dr. Holden's wife died suddenly. For some months the doctor had been in feeble health. He sank under the additional blow, till death relieved him of the cares and troubles of this life. He fell asleep on July 19th, 1891, and his funeral was largely attended by the various societies to which he belonged, the services being under Masonic auspices. A local paper writes his epitaph as follows : " A patriot and philanthropist was laid at rest yesterday, when the remains of Dr. A. W. Holden were consigned to mother earth. He was an extensive writer and the author of valuable local histories. He was a kind-hearted, genial gentleman and a practical Christian always. Peace to his ashes."

BURGOYNE INDEX.

Balcarras, Lord, Sketch of, 37.

Bancroft, George, 236.

Barlow, Joel, Sketch of, 203.

Barton, William, 26.

Battenkill, 63.

Bauman, Col. Sebastian, 101.

Bedlow, Hon. Henry, 134.

Belden, B. L., 6; Sketch of, 101.

Bemus Heights, Battle of, 3, 241.

Bemus, The Correct Spelling, 342.

Bennington, 29, 56, 215, 216, 224, 230, 234.

Bess, Queen, 227.

Bliss, Charles M., 226.

Boies, Lura A., Sketch of, 119, 176.

Booth Bros., 12.

Botta, Anna C., 224.

Bouquet River, 44.

Boyd, Lieut. Thos., 293.

Brown, Col. John, 36.

Brunswickers, 57.

Bruce, Wallace, Sketch of, 225.

Brooks, Col., Sketch of, 89.

Brudenell, Parson, 112.

Bryant, William C., Sketch of, 218.

Bull Run, 255.

Bunker Hill, 2, 23, 92, 206.

Burgoyne, Gen., Sketch of, 1, 16, 21.

Burgoyne, Sir John, 7.

Butler, B. C., 273.

Butler, Col. Wm., 293.

Butler, Prof. J. D., 66.

Canning, E. W. B., 75, 234.

Carey, Henry, 4.

Carlton, Gen., 2, 37, 68, 69.

Carnarvon, Earl of, 186.

Case, Rev. W., 41.

Catamount Tavern, 225.

Caulfield, Miss Susan, 6.

Champlain, Lake, 2, 34, 59.

Chapin, Rev. E. H., 215.

Cilley, Col., 234.

Clinton, Sir Henry, 2, 22, 256.

Cobble Hill, 23.

Cochran, Deacon Isaac, 67.

Coldstream Guards, 1.

Collins, Isaac, 67.

Columbiad, a Poem, 204.

Commercial Advertiser, 118.

Copwell, Rev., 236.

Cook, Col. Thaddeus, 84.

Cook, Mrs. Rachel A., 190.

Cook, Ransom, 190.

Cooper, James Fenimore, 252.

Council of Safety, 220, 252.

Herkimer, Gen., 36, 256.
Hilmer, Chas. D., 264.
Holden, Dr., Sketch of, 349.
Holden, James H., 349.
Hoosic Falls, 230.
Horicon (Lake George), 252.
Hoyt, Gen. E., 302.

Jefferson, Thos., 39.
Jennings, Rev., 216.
Johnson, Sir William, 28, 89, 108.
Jones, David, 128, 190.
Jordan, J. W., 75.

King, Rev. Jos. E., 195.
Knox, Gen., 18.
Kosciusko, Gen., 132.

Lamb, Col. Anthony, 101.
Lebanon, 74.
Lee, Gen. Chas., 8, 186.
Le Loup, a Wyandotte Chief, 130, 190.
Lexington, Battle of, 67.
Liancourt, Duke de, 258.
Liberty Boys, 67.
Lincoln, Gen., 93.
Lincoln, Pres., 206.
Livingston, Gen., 8.
Locke, Hon. S. D., 230.
Lossing, B. J., 26, 56.

Maccaroni Club, 20.
Markham, J. C., 51, 71.
Marvin, James M., 57.
McCrea, Jane 128, 204, 206.
McCrea, John, 128.
McCrea, Rev., M., 202.
McNeil, Mrs., 130.
Meal Market, 67.
Mohawk River, 2.
Montgomery, Gen., 25, 128.
Montreal, 25.
Morgan, Gen., 2, 18, 112, 293.
Moses Kill, 132.
Mount Defiance, 87.
Munsell, Joel, 220.
Murphy, " Tim," 19, 290.

Newbury, Jeremiah, 268.
New Amsterdam, 257.
Nowell, Garrett, 67.

Oriskany, Battle of, 255, 261.

Page, Elizabeth, 232.
Paterson, 77.
Peck, Rev. J. T., 195.
Phillips, Gen., 34.
Pittsfield, 220.
Poor, Gen., 77.
Posey, Maj., 293.
Post, Daniel H., 347.

Van Vecton, Col., 347.

Washington, Gen., 16, 29, 39.
Walloomsack, 231.
Waldenburg, J. F., 219.
Walworth, Mrs. E. H., 57.
Walpole, Horace, 68, 69.
Walpole, Robert, 68.
Warren, Gen., 219.

Wayne, Gen., 88.
Williams, Roger, 268.
Williams, Col. E., 75.
Williams, Rev. S., 65.
Wilkes, John, 23.
Wilson, Gen. Jas. G., 264.

Yankee Doodle, Origin of, 20, 60.

ERRATA.

Page 37, 5th line from bottom, for " Thompson," read Thomas.

Page 96, 3d line from bottom, for "mind," read wind.

Page 102, last line, for " is" read are.

Page 113, 2d line from bottom, for " Ropes," read Rogers.

Page 114, 3d line from top, for "Lilliman," read Silliman.

Page 188, last line, for " Appendix No. III.," read Appendix No. X.

Page 258, 7th line from bottom, for " contemplated," read present.

Page 335, 7th line from top, for " mauvis," read Mauris.

Page 349, 7th line from top, for " Lucratia," read Lucretia.